A Story of Transformation

MARK JOHNSON

with KRISTEN E. VINCENT

WESTBOW PRESS
A DIVISION OF THOMAS NELSON & ZONDERVAN

WestBow Press books may be ordered through booksellers or by contacting:

WestBow Press
A Division of Thomas Nelson & Zondervan
1663 Liberty Drive
Bloomington, IN 47403
www.westbowpress.com
1 (866) 928-1240

ISBN: 978-1-4908-7571-2 (sc)
ISBN: 978-1-4908-7572-9 (hc)
ISBN: 978-1-4908-7570-5 (e)

Library of Congress Control Number: 2015905449

Print information available on the last page.

WestBow Press rev. date: 5/27/2015

To Bill and Betty, my parents

Jody, Mom, me, Oogie, and Dad at the lake

THANKS

I want to thank Kristen for sharing my six-plus-year journey to tell this story of transformation.

I also want to thank my friends who took the time to be interviewed.

Thanks, too, to Bonnie, Carol, Christine, Courtnay, Eleanor, Gillian and her daughter, Justina, Janine, Joni, Marsha, Susan (my wife), and Rachel, for feedback during the editing process.

I especially want to thank my family, friends, ADAPT, Shepherd Center, and my colleagues in the disability rights movement.

CONTENTS

Section 5: Love

Introduction

I first heard about Mark Johnson in July 2002 when I was doing research to prepare for a job interview. I had applied to be the executive director of the Brain & Spinal Injury Trust Fund Commission and wanted to know as much as possible about the agency and its history. What I learned was that in 1988, the Georgia General Assembly had passed the enabling legislation to establish the Trust Fund, and Georgia voters had overwhelmingly approved it. Still, the funds had not yet begun to flow. As a result, people with traumatic brain and spinal injuries were missing out on money that could have helped them pay for things they needed to live independently but weren't covered by public or private insurance. And Mark Johnson was upset about that. I knew this because of a 2001 *Creative Loafing* article that popped up in my Google search. Reading the article, I understood the challenges for the position—both in terms of administering the funds and handling what was clearly a public relations nightmare. I also understood that, if hired, I was going to have to connect with this Mark Johnson guy. Clearly, he had some influence in the disability community.

After I accepted the job, Rocky Rothrock, one of the founders of the Commission, immediately set out to introduce me to people he thought I should know. I had a lot of experience in nonprofit management, particularly in social justice issues, but I had no experience in the disability rights movement. I needed to start meeting people right away. We went to a gathering at the state's capitol, and there he introduced me to a variety of folks. Sure enough, one of them was Mark Johnson. It was July 26, 2002, the twelfth anniversary of the signing of the Americans with Disabilities Act.

From the very beginning, it was clear that Mark was willing to offer me as much support as possible as I settled into my new position. He always took my phone calls, answered a million questions, gently corrected my attempts to use the accepted language of the disability community, and pushed me on tough issues. He also made sure I met certain people, connected with the right groups, and, most importantly, understood the agency's place in the bigger picture of the disability community, whether locally or nationally. Over time, he became one of my most trusted advisors, in spite of his stream-of-consciousness conversations and cryptic e-mails. Meanwhile, his wife, Susan, who is the director of the brain injury unit of the Shepherd Center, served on the Commission and became another one of my closest advisors. And my husband, Max, a Methodist minister, served as the chaplain on Susan's unit. While it may have all appeared a bit incestuous, we worked well together and, over time, became great friends.

In February 2009, I got an early morning call from Susan. Mark had had emergency surgery the past Saturday—Valentine's Day—and was in the hospital. In the midst of my shock and concern, I heard her say that Mark had experienced a very powerful religious vision the previous two nights and was asking to speak to Max. I called my husband, who turned his car around and headed straight to the hospital to see Mark. Since I had meetings that day and wasn't able to go see him, we decided that I'd come visit him at home a few days later.

I arrived at Mark's house with a basket full of cookies (which, it turned out, he couldn't eat because of his post-surgery diet), prepared to spend the day catching up with him and helping in whatever way I could. I anticipated fetching the pain meds, helping transfer him to the bed, eating delicious cookies on his behalf, or watching reality TV— the man is addicted to the Food Network's "Diners, Drive-ins, and Dives" —with him. Instead, he wanted me to listen as he detailed the religious experience he'd had in the hospital. He explained that the overall message of the experience was about God's love and that he had come away from it feeling that God was calling him to write a book.

He then handed me a box containing letters and cards he'd received since his illness. The box also contained the February 23, 2009 issue of *Time* magazine titled "Mind and Body Special Issue: How Faith Can Heal;" the Spring 2009 issue of *Spinal Column* (a publication of the Shepherd Center), in which James Shepherd wrote, "Your faith can become the ultimate source of hope and strength;" and a copy of *The Daily Word* (a devotional booklet). I tried hard to keep up with his familiar stream-of-consciousness speech pattern, which was now imbued with the energy and focus of someone coming off of a mountaintop experience. He rapidly explained that each memento had come within days of his vision and had all contained the same message: love. Amazed by the timing and synergy with which this was all coming together, he felt compelled to write this book about love, life, and service. He described its outline, its message, and even its title. As he talked, I realized he wanted me to do something with this information and with the box of stuff that sat in my lap. Confused, I asked, "What do you want me to do?"

"Help me write this book," he said.

Now it was my turn to be amazed by God's timing, since I'd recently declared that I wanted to become a writer. Up until that time, I'd written newsletter articles, public policy reports, and other career-related stuff, with a little blogging on the side. The more I wrote, the more I found I liked it. I was curious to see where it might lead. But Mark didn't know any of this. Sure, he'd read reports I'd written and knew I could form complete sentences, but he didn't know I'd just professed this desire for a career change. I knew I wanted to write a book one day but had never thought I'd be doing one so soon. Here I was—being given the opportunity to write a book about Mark, a man who was not only a close friend and someone I admired, but also someone who was making a difference in the world. That was an opportunity I could not pass up.

The day I met with Mark, I'd also brought him a copy of *The Shack*, a book I'd recently read and was promoting with abandon. Mark politely took it and said, "Thanks, but I'm not much of a reader."

"Great," I thought. "You don't read books, and I've never written one. We'll make the perfect team."

It's hard to write someone else's memoir, especially if the subject is fifty-eight years old, and you've known him for only twelve of those years. I wasn't around for all the experiences he wanted to describe. More importantly, I'm not in his head to know how he perceived and interpreted those experiences. Plus, the way I might describe and tell those stories may be very different from the way he would. However, after spending more than four years on this book, including one full year of interviews with friends/ family/colleagues, regular "Mondays with Mark," a field trip through the rural eastern North Carolina countryside to locate the sand quarry where Mark was injured, and an ADAPT action, I think it's safe to say I have a pretty good handle on Mark's life history. As a result, I've made every attempt to tell Mark's story the way he remembers it and to include exact quotes from the people I interviewed. In the case of Mark's participation in Billy Graham's 1972 Crusade in Charlotte, I used archival information to develop the story.

I've also tried to capture and convey Mark's thoughts, inflections, and speech patterns as well as I could. At times, this was difficult. There is one scene where he and his then-girlfriend, Susan, were arguing, and it is clear that Susan was getting frustrated with Mark's stubbornness. I quoted Mark as saying, "And I'm sure my stubbornness isn't helping." After reading this, Mark replaced "stubbornness" with "lack of flexibility."

"Who talks that way?" I said after reviewing his edits.

"I do," he said, rather inflexibly. And so it stayed. And be prepared for all the references to poop. "That's such a juvenile term," wrote one of our early readers. I know, but it's how Mark talks. Just be glad you have the book title you do now. His original vision was "Praying for Poop."

Aside from the wording issue, Mark and I faced three challenges in writing this book. First, Mark doesn't have much of a memory prior to his high-school years, and he is a little fuzzy on college (for example, he couldn't remember the names of his classmates), which makes the writing of a memoir a bit tricky. Indeed, poor memory seemed to be a trait marking the Johnson boys, since neither of Mark's brothers, Oogie and Jody, could do much to fill in the blanks. Thank God, then, for his parents, Bill and Betty, who had great memories, spanning back to their own childhoods as well as armfuls of scrapbooks. Betty is very much the dedicated family historian.

Second, like his mother, Mark is a passionate historian, though his penchant for maintaining history borders on packrat status. He is also an accomplished man. This means he has a basement full of newspaper clippings, magazine articles, books, videos, photos, buttons, banners, and other memorabilia chronicling his involvement in the movement. It would have provided sufficient material for a multi-volume work. With all this, Mark and I originally thought his book would not only be a memoir but also a history of the disability rights movement from his own involvement and perspective. However, we quickly realized that this book was becoming the size of *War and Peace*, as his colleague, Bob Kafka, often joked, and decided to narrow it down. Plus, it wasn't necessary to cover the whole history since there are books that have already been written about the disability rights movement. In the end, we decided to focus on some of the history of ADAPT and its campaign for accessible public transportation; Mark played a critical role in the early development of the group and its history (you can find more on ADAPT's thirty-year history at www.adapt.org). As a result, while we offered a few other events, you don't get much about Mark and his life after 2000 and the tenth anniversary of the Americans with Disabilities Act (ADA). That's why we've created a Facebook page (www.facebook.com/markleejohnson) that contains noteworthy events, stories, and photos that didn't make it into the book. You can also access Mark's extensive collection, which is now housed at the Richard B. Russell Library for Political Research and Studies at the University of Georgia.

The third challenge centered around the fact that, from the very beginning, Mark was clear he wanted this book to be, in part, about his spiritual journey. He wanted to explore and describe his faith story in a way that would be helpful to readers. That was right up my alley, given that I have a Masters in Theological Studies. Plus, I've always known Mark to be very spiritual. Whenever I'd hear him give a speech, he always took the time to acknowledge "faith, family, and friends," as he put it. I was impressed by that; there aren't many people who can work references to their faith into a professional context without coming across as heavy-handed and self-righteous. But then again, Mark has a way of living his faith in a way that is effortless and nonthreatening. His practice is a great example for others. That may be why Mark I. Pinsky chose to feature an excerpt of Mark's story in his book, *Amazing Gifts: Stories of Faith, Disability, and Inclusion*. I relished the opportunity to help Mark use the book to explore the evolution of his faith.

Despite these challenges, we pressed on in a journey that would span more than four years of our lives and encompass several major changes in Mark's life, both personally and professionally. His dad, Bill, passed away in March 2012. Thankfully, he was able to read a draft of the book and see how it honored his own contributions to the world and to Mark's life. Fittingly, Bill's memorial service was filled with laughter, pistachios, Pepsi, and his favorite "isms" —quotes he'd use over and over. And in July 2013, Mark walked his daughter down the aisle and celebrated her marriage to a young man named Taylor. These milestones have given a new sense of urgency to completing this book, both in terms of Mark's time and bank account. Time is passing, and it is time to tell this story of love, life, and service.

As if writing a book wasn't enough, during this period, Mark and I began another project. This project was the result of both his religious vision and days spent wading through the piles in Mark's basement, trying to find content for the book. Amid the stacks of history, we began to discuss the need for archiving; he clearly had the makings of an entire museum exhibit on disability rights history (indeed, the Richard B. Russell Special Collections Library of the University of Georgia has agreed to preserve Mark's collection). From there, we wondered how to encourage others who, like Mark, had historical materials in their basements and attics and needed to preserve them. That led to discussions about legacy: both Mark's and others'. A grant led to an Atlanta gathering of experts in disability rights history from around the country, and The ADA Legacy

Project was born. The Project's focus is to *preserve* the history of the disability rights movement; *celebrate* its milestones, including the twenty-fifth anniversary of passage of the Americans with Disabilities Act (ADA) in 2015; and *educate* the public and future generations of disability rights advocates (www.adalegacy.com and www.ada25.com). Before this book is even published, it is leading to more works of love.

ADA25
AMERICANS WITH DISABILITIES ACT
1990-2015
DISABILITY RIGHTS ARE CIVIL RIGHTS

Mark is an optimist but not in a Pollyanna-ish way. He has the capacity to see the possibilities in people and in situations while still being able to acknowledge and account for potential limitations. Granted, this isn't revolutionary; there are many people who come equipped with a glass-half-full perspective. But what is particular about Mark's way of navigating the world is that he is able to accept people for who they are, including their differences. Where others get stuck on the things that separate us—race, disability, sexual orientation, faith, or fashion preference—Mark is able to embrace those qualities and gifts that make us unique and see what each has to contribute to the conversation at hand. As a result, the man is constantly meeting people and trying to figure out where they—with their abilities and life experiences—fit into the bigger picture. That's one reason Mark's story isn't the only one we've told in this book. There's a significant amount of space devoted to other people's stories, including his parents and some of his colleagues in the disability community. This was intentional. It was a way of illustrating Mark's penchant—nay, obsession—for meeting people, learning their stories, and connecting them with others.

It is this ability to see people for who they are, to embrace their differences and see their potential, that I want to learn. More importantly, I want to be able to pass this onto my son. I'm still very much a work in progress in that area, but luckily for all of us, my son, Matthew, is ahead of the game.

When he was in first grade, I stood at the bus stop one Wednesday afternoon waiting to pick him up. As soon as his feet hit the ground, Matthew came running toward me with a big smile on his face. I could tell something was up. Sure enough, he excitedly announced that he had a disability.

"Really? What is your disability?" I was worried I'd missed something critical during the first six years of his life.

"I'm blind."

"Huh." I paused. "But you can see," I said, pointing out the obvious as carefully as I could. I didn't want to dampen his enthusiasm, still curious to see where this was going.

"But, Mom, my patch," he said, pointing with great indignation to the eye patch he wears over his glasses.

"True enough," I thought. When he was three he was diagnosed with "lazy eye," a condition that is grossly misnamed, given the eye itself is perfectly healthy. The real problem is his brain is just playing favorites, deciding to use only one eye instead of both. It should really be called "lazy brain" or "choosing-favorites brain." This requires Matthew to wear a patch over his "good" eye for up to six hours a day or risk the "lazy" eye going blind. To his tremendous credit, Matthew has worn his patch with very little protest—even at school, on play dates, and to tae kwon do classes—for three straight years. As a result, his eyesight has gone from 20/400 to 20/20, making all of us big fans of the patch.

"Yep," I said, still not getting it.

"This means I have a seeing impairment," he explained.

"Oh, you mean a visual impairment?"

"Yeah," he nodded. "So I have a disability!"

For a moment, I gave thanks that Matthew's school was talking openly about disability issues and trying to create a culture of acceptance and pride. Clearly, it was working, at least on this particular first grader. But I also felt such love and infinite gratitude for Matthew's refreshing innocence and vulnerability; I knew it may, at some point, be replaced by the angst and self-loathing that often comes with adolescence. It's this artlessness that enables Matthew to revel in his difference and still walk confidently through the world, knowing he will be welcomed and loved. It's this self-acceptance that enables him, in turn, to accept his friends and all of their peculiarities. If I could do that—if we could all do that—I can only imagine how much richer our lives would be, how much more peaceful our world would be, and how much more we could appreciate and love today.

Kristen Vincent
September 11, 2014

Kristen with Max, Matthew, and their dog, Gracie

PROLOGUE

Although we met each other in church, neither I nor my friend Tommy Lippard were very religious. He was six and I was seven when our families met at Sharon Presbyterian Church in Charlotte, North Carolina. Charlotte was a town that loved Jesus and fit comfortably within the loops of the Bible Belt, so the worship options were many and varied. This was, after all, the town that had born and bred Billy Graham, who had grown up a few miles from our new house and was now traveling the globe in an endless crusade to win souls and spread the gospel. But we had chosen Sharon, in large part, because it was within walking distance of our house, ensuring that my parents could be as involved as possible.

My family was new, having relocated from Tampa, Florida. Everyone in Tommy's family was a long-time member, so much so that there was a pew commonly known as the "Lippard Pew." Both families had three kids who were roughly the same age, and our moms shared a love of gardening and volunteering in the church. We all started hanging out. Soon it was tradition to spend holidays and summers together, with Tommy and I hunting, fishing, and riding horses.

Like every other kid our age, Tommy and I went to church because our parents did. We sat through the services, always an endurance test for boys with energy to spare. For us, it was like watching the grass grow, one lone, green blade at a time. The one highlight was Mrs. Esther Brown's Sunday school class. She was tolerant of our youthful energy and did her best to teach us while we wiggled and jiggled in our seats. She held "sword drills" to see who could find a particular Bible passage the fastest or who could memorize certain verses. The winners were always rewarded with candy bars, a prize that seemed daring in the midst of such restrained tradition.

It was in Mrs. Brown's class that we began to form our first images of who God is and what he expects from his children. God was good and liked kids who were good. For our little minds, which operated only in concrete terms, that meant no running in the hallways, pulling pigtails, or sticking gum under our desks. And it meant respecting our parents, doing our chores, and working hard in school. That all made sense because these were the same rules handed down to us by our parents, our teachers, our coaches, and probably any other adult we happened upon, only now they were coated with theological meaning and injected with an extra powerful shot of motivation since God, like Santa, could see everything.

I should emphasize, however, that fear was not an ingredient in this spiritual recipe. We weren't raised to believe that God would strike us down in a bolt of lightning or otherwise punish us if we were bad. It was just that we didn't want to disappoint God. Somehow, we knew God loved us and wanted the best for us. And much like the relationship we had with our parents, the thing we feared most was letting him down, or not being deserving enough of God's love. As a result, we did our best to earn the love of our God and our parents, even if it meant sitting quietly through those long church services.

That all changed for Tommy after he left home for college. Tommy took to college life like a duck to water. He wasted no time pledging to a fraternity and was soon enjoying a life of road trips, girls, and frat parties. This left little time for going to class or studying. By his sophomore year, he had been elected president of that fraternity, which meant more fun and even less class time. His lifestyle eventually caught up with him, however, when he attracted the attention of the school administrators, both for hosting a wildly successful party on campus as well as earning failing grades. The school placed him on academic probation and suggested he find better uses for his time.

His parents agreed, and when Tommy came home in April, 1972, they were ready for him. With his girlfriend in cahoots, they persuaded a very unwilling Tommy to go with them to see Billy Graham, who was hosting a hometown crusade. Growing up, Tommy's dad had actually milked cows for Billy's father, and as far as Tommy was concerned, that was as close a connection as he needed with the popular evangelist. But it was Friday night—youth night at the Crusade—and his parents wouldn't entertain any other options. Tommy went.

It so happened that I was there as well, though Tommy didn't know this. But while I had come as a willing participant, Tommy went prepared to sit through it and then be on his way, hopefully, to a night of fun with his girlfriend. Instead, walking into the packed arena, seeing the thousands of people and feeling the anticipation of the crowd, Tommy felt the prickle of goose bumps on his skin and sensed that he was exactly where he was meant to be. He settled into the seat, open for whatever was to come.

When Billy Graham took the stage and began preaching, Tommy was convinced that Billy was speaking directly to him.

"God loves you just the way you are, Tommy," Billy seemed to say. "And it's not about being good. That's not enough to get into heaven. What matters most, Tommy, is do you love the Lord? Do you believe in him? Tommy, do you have faith?"

At the point of the altar call, when Billy invited everyone down to the stage, Tommy shot out of his seat with a mixture of fear and excitement. He ran down and was greeted by a counselor, who prayed with him. That night, Tommy committed his life to the Lord, and from then on, he was never the same. Not long after, Tommy recognized that, once again, his energy was no match for Sharon's restrained worship style, though now it was not so much about the impulsive energy of a child but the electrifying intensity of the newly converted. He soon left the Lippard Pew for the comfort of a more charismatic church in town.

One Wednesday night in the summer of 1972, a preacher with a gift of healing visited Tommy's church. He went about the business of praying over people with illnesses and injuries and, seemingly, healing them. Instantly, Tommy thought of me. About a year earlier, I had been paralyzed in a diving accident, and after spending almost five months in various hospitals, I was now living with my parents in their Charlotte home, adjusting to a life with quadriplegia.

As the healing service ended, Tommy walked confidently toward the front of the church and asked the healing preacher if he could come see me that very night. The preacher couldn't, and for a second, Tommy was disappointed. But only for a second. Still running off the power of his new-found faith, Tommy reasoned that he believed in the same God and had the same amount of faith as the preacher. Surely that meant God could work through him too. Instantly, Tommy was in his car and on the way to my house.

Oblivious to the fact that my long-time friend was on his way to pray over me, I was busy going about my usual evening routine. An hour earlier, I'd finished eating dinner while sitting in bed. The accident had rendered the upper level of my family's split-level house off limits to me, except in the rare occasion when someone carried me upstairs. My parents had gotten used to bringing meals down to my lower-level bedroom. I'd park my wheelchair by the bed, grab the sling on the trapeze bar installed over my bed, and, with their help, swing my body into the bed. From there, they'd help me undress and transfer my catheter from the urine bag that was attached to my leg to the urine bag hanging from my bed—one of those old iron hospital beds with a crank. After I got in, Mom would crank it up and push my bedside table over me. I'd strap on my universal cuff—an elastic, Velcro thing that had a slit for a dial rod, toothbrush, or eating utensil. Then I was ready to dig into whatever yummy dish Mom had cooked up that evening. After eating, I'd brush my teeth using a cup and basin for me to spit in, since my bathroom hadn't been modified yet to allow me independent access from my wheelchair. It wasn't very glamorous, but I was quickly learning that I had to be open and creative if I was going to get through the day with a disability. Finally, Mom would hand me the TV remote, give me a minute to make sure there wasn't something else I needed, and leave me to my channel surfing.

I had just settled on a movie when Tommy knocked on the front door. It was around nine o'clock at night. Dad answered the door.

"Hi, Tommy! Good to see you."

"Hi, Bill."

"What can I do for ya?"

"Well, sir, I was at my church tonight, and there was this preacher who was praying over people so that God would heal them. And I asked him if he would come over and see Mark and pray with him, you know, but he couldn't," Tommy gushed. "But I believe that God can heal Mark, so I wanted to pray with him and lay hands on him, you know? I wondered if I could come in and do that."

He seemed to hold his breath, waiting for my dad to respond.

Dad sized him up quickly, making sure he wasn't kidding, then quickly said, "Sure, Tommy, c'mon in. Mark's downstairs in the bed."

I could hear the rush of someone's footsteps coming down the stairs, and suddenly, there was Tommy, standing in my room. I, too, was surprised to see him. Surprised because it was late, and it wasn't Tommy's style to drop by, especially at this hour. And more to the point, I hadn't seen a lot of him in the year since my accident.

Like most of my friends, Tommy was having a hard time dealing with my injury. What do you say to the guy with whom you've grown up, played sports, chased girls, and run along the beach when he can't walk anymore?

My friends were good about coming to see me when I was first in the hospital. They wanted to see for themselves if I was as bad off as they had heard. They brought cards and flowers, told jokes, and spoke self-consciously about their plans for the summer. They looked anxiously around the room, inevitably settling on the wheelchair that loomed, large and imposing, in the corner. And then they would speak, weakly, of their hopes for me to be healed, even making plans for when I "got better." It was clear that they found it difficult, and excruciatingly painful, to accept the new Mark.

And so it was that as time went on and I was transferred from the hospital to the rehab center, and ultimately, home to my parents' house, the reality of my situation settled in for everyone. Gradually, most of my friends came by less and less.

But there was Tommy, standing at my door. As soon as he entered, I could tell he was not here to shoot the breeze. He was clearly pumped up, shifting nervously from one foot to the other, looking both excited and purposeful.

"Hey, Mark."

"Hey, Tommy. What's up?"

"Can I talk with you?"

"Sure, come on in."

I watched as he paced nervously around the room. We made small talk, but that lasted only a few seconds before Tommy got down to business.

"Tonight I saw this preacher heal people at my church, and it made me think that, you know, that God can heal you too," he said. "I know the doctors said that you were going to be like this for the rest of your life and all, but I don't think it has to be like that."

He paused and took a breath, watching me.

"I mean, I believe that God can heal you if you, I mean, we believe enough. And I asked the preacher if he'd come with me to see you tonight, but he couldn't. But I watched him pretty closely while he was praying over people, and I think I can do what he was doing. I'd like to pray with you and lay hands on you," he said. "I mean, if that's okay with you," he added.

I knew instinctively that this was not a joke. I could tell from Tommy's earnestness that he was doing this out of a real sense of love and concern for me. Not wanting to dampen his spirit, which was by then threatening to consume him, I said, "Sure, no problem."

I caught a quick sigh of relief from him. I was sure this was as awkward for him as it was for me.

Tentatively, he picked up his Bible and started thumbing through it until he found the passage he wanted. He began to read, his voice rising as his confidence grew. After covering several passages of Scripture, he laid his hands on my arms, closed his eyes, and began praying fervently. I closed my eyes too, listening to my friend as he beseeched God to heal me. He prayed for a long time. Then, suddenly, he opened his eyes.

"Mark, give me your hands and let's get on outta here!" he cried.

Quickly, he grabbed my hands and pulled up, lifting my arms high above my head as he shouted, "In the name of Jesus, get up and walk!" My upper body lifted up with the force of his pull, but otherwise I remained still. I certainly wasn't standing up, much less walking. I lay back against the pillow, not really knowing what to think or say.

Tommy realized immediately that his attempt to lay hands on me hadn't worked. He looked stunned and deeply disappointed. I felt the air rushing out of him. He looked at me without speaking. He, too, didn't know what to say. We both started to cry. Tears rolled down Tommy's cheeks as he leaned over to hug me.

"I don't know why…" He shook his head. "But I love you, man, and I'm going to keep praying for you," he said.

"Thanks," I said.

Then, awkwardly, he grabbed his Bible, turned, and headed to the door. "See ya later," he said.

"Okay, see you, Tommy," I called out. But by then, he was taking the stairs two at a time. Within seconds, I heard the door closing above me.

Tommy never came around again.

SECTION 1

REALITY CHECK

"Action springs not from thought but
from a readiness for responsibility."

Dietrich Bonhoeffer,
Letters and Papers from Prison, 1944

Chapter 1

Breaking My Neck

If you're headed out of Greenville, North Carolina west on highway 264/MLK Jr. Drive, eventually you'll come to the intersection with Old Pactolus Road. Turn right there, go down a mile or so, past the trailer parks and small mill houses, and eventually you'll spot a tiny family cemetery on the left side of the road. It's easy to miss if you're not careful. Set off the road a bit and partially hidden by trees, there's a chain-link fence that surrounds eleven gray headstones, all of which are small and blend easily into the sand surrounding the graves. It's an understated plot, quiet and forlorn, that belies the tragedy of the Tingen family.

Marvin Tingen, the family patriarch, was born in 1922. A lifelong resident of Pitt County, he spent most of his life working for the Fred Webb Grain Elevators on the north side of Greenville. But while he seemed to find success in the workplace, Marvin's family life could not have been as happy. Of the eleven headstones in the family cemetery, all but four of them are for children from Marvin's immediate family. Marvin and his wife, Tillie, lost two daughters at birth. Their two boys lived to ages thirteen and fifteen before drowning in a boating accident in 1959. This left the Tingens with only one surviving child, a daughter named Thelma. She made it to adulthood and married Otis Everette, but the family's misfortune continued when Thelma lost a daughter and a son, both stillborn.

You would hope there would be some way for the people traveling by to know the extent of this family's grief and pain. It doesn't seem right that the symbols of one family's deepest pain sit idly along the side of the road, forgotten and unnoticed. Yet hundreds of people drove by this nondescript plot every day, most without realizing it was there, and certainly no one understanding the depth of the trauma it represented.

My friends and I often drove past the Tingen family cemetery, oblivious to the stories it represented. For us, it was simply the landmark that helped us find our swimming hole. Just beyond the graveyard was a narrow, partially hidden trail where there was barely enough room for you to turn your car off of the road. You could then drive about one hundred feet before the hard soil gave way to sand that was too soft to drive in, and park. From there, we would continue by foot along the trail that had been worn into the grass, past the clump of trees and an old green shed now covered in kudzu, to a pond that had been formed by a sand quarry. It was one of many such sand-quarry ponds that dotted this area along highway 264. Many of them turned out to be popular local hangouts where high school and college kids would go to skinny-dip, have a few beers, and make out. We'd tried several spots, but this was our favorite. It was one of the larger ponds. Even though other people hung out there, it was big enough that everyone had their own space, and no one made a big deal when you showed up to skinny-dip. Plus, the fact that it was accessible only by trail and couldn't be seen from the road afforded us a little added privacy and security.

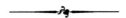

On this particular day, my friends Tom, Luke, Sam, and I were celebrating the end of our sophomore year at East Carolina University. My green Ford Fairlane, Dad's hand-me-down company car, was already packed and ready to take me home to Charlotte the next day. I had my usual summer lifeguard job lined up at the local neighborhood pool, and I was ready to see my old high-school friends and chill out. Tomorrow I'd take my last exam—English, never my best subject—and then jump in the car and head out. But before I left, I wanted to take one last swim. It was May 20, 1971, a Thursday.

Pulling off the road, I felt the same mixture of excitement and anxiety that accompanied each of these trips to the swimming hole. I loved going. I had always loved being in water. Growing up, my family and I had spent as many vacations as possible at Windy Hill, South Carolina beach. And in between, my friends and I spent as much time as we could fishing in local ponds, playing in the neighborhood pool, or messing around at the swimming hole we'd discovered on an afternoon adventure in our hometown of Charlotte, North Carolina. I'd even spent the past three years working as a lifeguard at two neighborhood pools. When I'd gotten to college and learned about the plethora of swimming holes that lay hidden amid the sand quarries on the outskirts of Pitt County, I immediately grabbed several of my buddies and went to check them out.

Still, I dreaded the time when I had to shed my clothes and make that long trip down the trail and to the pond naked. Although I had gone through a growth spurt in college and was now over six feet tall, my emotional self hadn't caught up with my physical self. In my head, I was still the runt of the family. Growing up, both my older brother, Oogie (whose real name is Ogden, but no one has ever called him that), and my younger brother, Jody, were both built like football players, easily towering over me. They'd often gang up on me and tease me about my size.

"Where'd you come from?" they'd say. It didn't help that my mom, too, insisted on calling me her "little lost waif." While she always said it lovingly and with a smile, it made my brothers snicker. They laughed out loud when Mom jokingly compared me to "Speedy," the high-pitched, elfin-like animated character who regularly appeared in the Alka-Seltzer commercials of the time, singing, "Relief is just a swallow away!" Apparently, we were both small in stature and giant in ears.

Oogie, me, and Jody at the beach. Although Jody was two years younger than me, he was already catching up to—and would soon surpass—me in height

By the time I entered Charlotte's South Mecklenberg High School, it wasn't any better. As a freshman, I was 5'7" and weighed a mere ninety-five pounds. What made it worse was that there was another Mark Johnson in my freshman class who was taller and bigger than me. To distinguish us, our friends decided early on to call him "Big Mark," which meant, of course, that I was "Little Mark," a nickname that stuck with me throughout high school.

Though I tried not to show it, I was self-conscious about my size. I would critique myself, always finding fault with my weight, my height, my lack of facial hair, and other features of my body that seemed inadequate, especially in certain places, if you know what I mean. As soon as I put the car into park and turned off the engine, I leaped out of the car and yelled, "Race ya!" to avoid suspicion. I dashed behind the car, threw off my clothes, stashed 'em under the wheel, and took off in a mad dash to be the first one in the water—the first one covered up.

It turned out that the benefit of a small frame was that it made me a natural runner. I'd run track in junior high and cross-country in high school.

Over time, I shed my spikes, declaring them a liability, and developed my signature style of running barefoot. Now, as I ran down the trail, I felt again the sensations and freedom that come with running barefoot across the loose, soft sand. It reminded me of past cross-country meets. I felt the warm May air passing over my body and watched amusedly as a squirrel scurried quickly across the path, trying to get out of my way. At one point in my hurry, I got too close to the brush that lined the trail and felt the privet branches scrape against my calf. I didn't care. I could hear my friends laughing and yelling behind me as they struggled to catch up, but by that point, I had entered the clearing and knew I was going to be the first one in.

As I neared the pond, I noticed a few other groups on the other side, but, luckily, no one was close enough to make me feel even more self-conscious. I picked up speed and fixed on an entry point to the left of my usual spot. I planned to jump in feet first and swim to the area where the land jutted out above the water, creating a tiny island and a place for us to lie in the sun. Instead, I dove in head first, the cool water rushing over me, surrounding me as I descended to the bottom. But it turned out that the bottom wasn't far enough away. In fact, it was really shallow, and within a split second, I felt an enormous thud as my head hit the earth. I opened my eyes and could see only the murky swarm of silt swirling through the water. I knew I was badly hurt, but it wasn't until I tried to turn and swim up that I realized that I couldn't move. I began to panic. I was still underwater and feared I was going to drown.

My buddies hadn't yet figured out that anything was wrong and were busy racing to the island. But Tom, turning to call out to me, saw me floating face-down and realized I wasn't moving. He sprinted over to me and turned me over as I sputtered and gasped for breath.

"C'mon," he half yelled, trying to pretend that everything was alright, though I saw the panic in his eyes.

"I can't," I said. "Something's wrong. I can't move." His eyes grew even wider. "You've got to get me out of the water and cover me up, but be careful moving me. You've got to keep me still," I said. Privately, I was noting the irony of the situation. In my four years as a lifeguard, the only time I'd ever had to do anything remotely lifeguard-like was when a kid dove off the diving board and panicked in the deep end of the pool. I had to dive in, grab him, and swim with him to the side, where I delivered him safely to his slightly amused mom. Never, ever did I have to use my life-saving skills. That is, until now, on myself.

Tom yelled to the others, who raced over to us. He quickly explained the situation, and Luke yelled, "I'll go get help!" He swam to the shore and began sprinting down the trail. Tom and Sam started to drag me, slowly and carefully, through the water before laying me on the edge of the shore. I couldn't tell if my body was still partially in the water or not. My legs felt like they were floating. Tom sat down with me, never leaving my side. Luke paced around nervously, not wanting to look at me and not knowing what to do.

"Tom, I need ya to do something," I whispered. "I need ya to go get my shorts and put 'em on me." The irony was not lost on me; because of my desperation to hide my nakedness and shame, I was now splayed on the ground for all to see. But the need to cover myself up was still strong. Really strong. In fact, it was my primary concern at that moment, if only because it was the easiest thing to focus on. Plus, I knew that people would start to gather as they noticed the unfolding drama. Tom shouted to Luke to run back to the car and grab my shorts, which he did, grateful to have something to do. As soon as he returned, he chucked the shorts at Tom, who caught them and gently put them on me. It was the first time that someone would need to help dress me, the beginning of a life that required assistance.

We ended up waiting for almost an hour for the ambulance to arrive. This was the time before cell phones, so Luke had to run down the street and knock on doors until he was able to find someone who would let him use their phone. In that time, a crowd had indeed gathered. At first, it was a couple of people, then a few more. Eventually, there were probably twenty or more people standing in an arc around us, keeping a respectful distance while they whispered among themselves.

"What happened?" "Is he paralyzed?" "Maybe he just pinched a nerve." Each had his or her own theory. All wanted the situation to be okay.

After I had had some time to calm down a bit, I noticed an arm lying across my face.

"Tom, can you move your arm? It's blocking my view," I asked. I heard sharp gasps from my friends and from the crowd. Tom paused, not sure what to say.

"Mark, um, that's your arm," he said, his voice rising in fear. He took my arm and laid it along my side. The mood of the crowd shifted. Now there was a collective sense of panic. "He's definitely paralyzed," someone whispered, loud enough for me to hear.

The ambulance arrived but was unable to drive across the smooth sand covering the trail. We waited again as the emergency workers carried their equipment down the trail and over to where we were. Immediately, they began to check my vital signs and prepare me for the trip to the hospital. All the while, one EMTs sole job was to hold my chin so that my head didn't move. When two of the EMTs lifted me onto the stretcher, this same guy continued to hold my chin, never letting go until we reached the hospital. Picking up the stretcher, the two EMTs slowly, ploddingly, carried me back along the same trail I had been racing down only an hour before. They raised me up into the ambulance and closed the doors. As the ambulance sped away, I stared up at the ceiling, unable to see the Tingen family cemetery as we turned and headed for the hospital.

THE CLOSET

The phone rang at the house around 9:00 p.m. Mom answered, but the doctor wouldn't talk to her.

"I need to speak to your husband, Mrs. Johnson," he insisted. Dad reluctantly picked up the phone. He had just gotten home from a business trip to Greenville, South Carolina, where he'd also been dealing with a kidney stone attack that had flattened him for a bit. He was tired and not feeling well.

"Can I help you?" said Dad.

"Mr. Johnson, your son has been in an accident and is paralyzed. He's here at Pitt County Memorial Hospital."

"What kind of accident?" my dad asked. "What happened?"

"Mark was in a diving accident," said the doctor.

"A driving accident? Is anyone else hurt?" My dad pictured a grim scene involving several of my friends in mangled cars.

"No, sir, a diving accident. Mark dove into some shallow water and broke his neck," he said.

My father paused, trying to process this. It didn't make sense. All those years as a lifeguard. All that water safety training. It had been my job to save other people from getting hurt in the water. How in the world could I be the one injured?

"Mr. Johnson, it's very late. Why don't you and your family get a good night's sleep and come up in the morning," the doctor suggested.

"To heck with that," my dad thought. "We'll see you in five hours," he said, and hung up the phone.

In the back of his closet—next to a heap of shoes, the overflowing hamper, and a basketball, underneath the hangers that held coats, a couple of suits, and some shirts that Mom had finished ironing—sat Jody. He sat pressed against the smooth sheetrock, huddled deep within the darkness, and sobbed.

Minutes earlier, he'd heard the phone ring. It had come while he was laying on his bed watching *The Outer Limits* and *Twilight Zone*, enjoying the freedom and anticipation that comes from being days away from your high school graduation. No more homework. No more exams. Only summer and freedom, he thought. It was Mom's crying that had alerted Jody to the fact that this had not been a routine telephone call. Bad news, he thought, beginning to worry. Real bad news, he realized, when Dad came into his room, his eyes wet with tears of his own. As Dad delivered the news of my accident, Jody listened but could not hear what he was saying. He felt time stop as his mind tried to process the information. Soon, however, his body accepted the news with a gut-wrenching wave of sobs, and it was then that Jody ran into his closet and shut the door.

In our house, the closet was the place where you took your grief and fear. At least, it was for Jody and me. Ever since we were young boys, we had crawled into it, letting the darkness swallow us up whenever something wasn't right. My grades were never great, but there was a time in elementary school when my report card held particularly grim news, and I was afraid to let my parents see it. I retreated to the back of the closet in the room that Jody and I shared, sitting hidden from view with my fear and anxiety, trying to figure out the best way—the best timing—to break the news to my parents. There was also a day when we came home from school to find a large mound on our driveway covered by a tarp. It turned out that the mound was actually our Great Dane, Jell-O, who'd been hit by a car and died earlier that day. We were devastated. As soon as Mom broke the news, Jody and I raced up to our room, ducked into the closet, and closed its doors. We hunched down, each in a separate corner, and cried.

That's where Mom found Jody when she came up to talk with him. Dad had been overwhelmed by Jody's reaction to the news and asked Mom to go check on him. Once she was able to get him to calm down a bit, they worked together to throw some stuff into an overnight bag. Dad, meanwhile, was making a few phone calls to let people know what was happening. One of the calls was to our minister, who agreed to come over, wait for Oogie, and break the news to him.

Oogie was out with his friends, having recently returned from Vietnam. On the day he came home, our family had picked him up from the airport, thrilled to be reunited. Oogie was dressed in a brand-new army uniform decorated with various medals recognizing his bravery and service to our country. He looked impressive. But underneath the clothes, we could tell he was not the same Oogie who had headed to Vietnam thirteen months ago. He looked older, sadder, more intense. As soon as we got home, he headed straight to his room, where he took off his uniform and threw it into a trash can. He never spoke of Vietnam again. Instead, he did his best to reconnect with his friends and get back to work, hoping to put the pain and guilt of Vietnam behind him. I worried what this news of my injury would do to him and hoped our minister could help him. Hopefully, he could provide the same comfort or release that Jody had found in the depths of his closet and which Oogie so desperately needed.

My parents and Jody jumped in the car and began the long journey to Greenville, North Carolina. For most of the five-hour ride they were silent, each lost in their own fear and despair. They didn't know whether I was going to survive; the doctor had said it was too soon to tell. They were left to fixate on their own worst-case scenarios. Periodically, Jody would break the silence with hushed cries. Several times he said, "It should've been me," which haunted my mother and echoed the very thing my dad had been thinking about himself.

They arrived at the hospital around five the next morning and were shocked when they saw me for the first time. I was lying flat on the bed. My hair had been shaved in a three-inch arc over each ear, exposing the area where doctors had drilled small holes into my head and attached Crutchfield tongs. The tongs were heavy, metallic, ice-tong-like things that attached to a rope, which then passed over a pulley and connected to a twenty-pound weight that hung freely. The point was to keep my head and neck as still as possible, but it also reinforced the seriousness of my injury. In this position, the only thing I could see was the ceiling. I called out to them, and they walked up to where I could see them. Mom grabbed my hand and started to cry. Dad looked down at me and asked how I was doing. It's funny how your mind automatically defaults to the standard phrases and questions in times of unimaginable stress.

"Okay," I said, doing my best to smile.

The doctor came in and asked to speak to my parents in the hallway. He explained that my vertebrae had been injured at the C5 and C6 level. There was nothing he could do to repair it. I was going to live, but I wasn't going to be able to walk again or have full use of my hands and arms. Most likely, I wouldn't live past the age of forty. My parents had a few questions for him. After answering them, he turned and left as they reentered my room. I could see the despair on their faces. I couldn't bear it. Somehow, I needed to do something.

"Hey," I said, "it's going to be okay, y'all. I'm going to be fine."

"But the doctor said you're paralyzed. You'll never be able to walk again. How's it going to be fine?" asked Mom.

"It just is," I said. "Whether I can walk or not, I'm going to be fine."

"But the doctor said..."

"I know what the doctor said, but he's not God. He can't see the future. I'm going to be okay. We all are. I promise."

It worked. At least, I thought it did. They all seemed to relax a little, especially Jody.

Since there wasn't much for anyone to do at this point, and since my family had been up all night—we all had—I suggested they get some rest and come back later. Around 7 a.m., they checked into a local motel beside the hospital. An hour later, they heard a knock on the door. Upon opening it, they were surprised to see Dr. Don Kellam, one of my dad's best friends and a fellow church member. He, too, had jumped in the car and driven through the night as soon as he'd heard the news about my accident. He grabbed my dad and hugged him.

"Bill," he said, "I just heard and came as fast as I could. I don't know what I can do to help. I'm not here to be your doctor, but I am here to be your friend. Let me know what I can do for you."

He was the first of several friends who would make the drive to Greenville that day. Overnight, word of my injury had traveled fast throughout our network of friends and family. As soon as my friends Andy and Sam heard, they impulsively jumped in Sam's white GTO and sped off to see me, arriving later that morning. They weren't allowed to see me because I was in the intensive-care unit. Instead, they spent time hanging out with "Bill," as they called my dad. They listened to his jokes and probably even a few of the quotes he loved to collect and share in times like these. He did his best to pass the time between updates from the doctor. He did his best to manage this family trauma.

In those days and weeks after the accident, I felt it was important to show confidence and optimism to my family and friends. I knew they were dealing with their own stuff; this was a traumatic experience that was bringing up a number of issues for each of them. I also knew they were worried about how this was affecting me. That was one thing I didn't want them to do. I didn't want them spending so much time worrying about me or how I was coping with all of this. I knew if I was depressed or freaked out, that would increase their stress exponentially. Better to put on a smile, exude confidence, and find ways to make light of a difficult situation.

Besides, I'm not much for self-pity. I don't do it very well. I don't like feeling depressed or fixating on worst-case scenarios. And I absolutely detest giving up. I'd much rather move on and figure out the next steps even if, in this case, I couldn't actually take a step. I didn't want to dwell on the fact that I was paralyzed. I wanted, instead, to focus on how to move on, how to adjust to living this new way and get out of the hospital.

Still, I had my moments of grief and fear, though I saved them for the nights when it was dark and quiet. It was the next best thing to crawling into my closet at home. I could be alone with my thoughts, fears, and questions. I could cry without upsetting anyone else. At night, I'd lie in my hospital bed feeling the heavy weight of my legs that wouldn't move, and I'd weep. I'd think of all the things I loved to do: playing tennis and golf, swimming, fishing, and playing basketball. I'd cry because I was pretty sure I couldn't do those things anymore, and I knew I would miss them. I'd think of the life I had before the accident: going to college, hanging out with my friends, working as a lifeguard, and preparing for my future career as a salesman (just like my dad). I'd cry because it felt like all that was over. It was like dying in a way, only I was still living. I also wondered what paralysis meant for my life. Could I really live with a disability? How would this affect my life? Would my friends still want to be with me? Would I ever date or get married? Have kids? It would be a whole new way of being. I wasn't sure what it meant for me.

Laying in the dark, I wondered why God had let this to happen to me. Had he led me to the swimming hole that day, knowing that I would be injured? The question came up more than a few times. Every time it did, I quickly rejected it because that would mean God had intended for me to be catastrophically injured, and that didn't fit with what I knew about God. I believed God was good and that he didn't want anything bad to happen to me or anyone else. There was no way God could have caused this. Besides, I knew the responsibility for my injury rested squarely on my shoulders. I was responsible for my own actions and decisions. I was the one who chose to go to the quarry that day. I was the one who dove headfirst into the water in my hurry to cover my nakedness, even when all my training begged me not to. No, the only one to blame for my injury was myself. My fault. Mea culpa.

MY IRON LUNG

Those first few weeks after my accident were awful. This wasn't solely because we were all still reeling from the psychological trauma of the experience. It was also because this was the early seventies, when the medical community didn't know much about spinal-cord injuries. Back then, people often didn't survive injuries like mine. The doctors said the main reason I had survived was because I was in great physical shape. In a sense, they didn't know what to do with me.

Nor did they realize the true nature of my injury. The doctors were sure that my injury was complete, meaning that my spinal cord had been completely severed, and there was no function or feeling whatsoever below the point of my injury. Magnetic Resonance Imaging (MRI) technology—the kind of thing that's commonly used today to diagnose injuries like mine—didn't exist yet. For the most part, the doctors had to guess the extent of my injury, and no evidence to the contrary seemed to budge them on their diagnosis. For example, there were no mobile X-ray units—those handy machines on wheels that allow the X-ray to be brought to the patient, rather than the other way around. Anytime the doctors needed an X-ray I had to be wheeled—tongs, pulleys, and all—through the hospital to the radiology unit. The motion of my gurney as it bumped over thresholds caused the weight that was hanging from my tongs to sway, pulling on my head, neck, and spine. The pain was excruciating, which meant that I *did* feel pain below my point of injury.

"Ouch!" I'd yell, then quickly follow it with an apology. I knew the personnel were doing the best they could and weren't trying to hurt me. Still, they looked at me with odd expressions. From their perspective, I shouldn't have been feeling any pain.

Things were also complicated because it takes someone with a spinal-cord injury longer to become medically stable, especially back then. I had to stay in the intensive-care unit longer than your average patient. In the meantime, people with critical emergency events, such as gunshot wounds and heart attacks, were being wheeled in, requiring the immediate attention of the nursing staff. It was a pretty intense environment, one that didn't allow much special attention from the nurses for my needs. One time, my urine bag got so full that it overflowed, spilling pee all over the floor. Mom, who was getting a quick lesson in advocacy, had returned from lunch and was furious to find that no one had even noticed the large puddle by my bed. But over time, she came to understand that the members of nursing staff were doing the best they could. They needed to focus on the emergency cases and on those patients who didn't have the luxury of family members who could help out.

What we didn't know was that my greatest ordeal—at least while in acute care—was yet to come. After two weeks in the Greenville hospital, the doctors decided I was stable enough to be moved to Charlotte, where I could be near family and friends. Their primary concern was my breathing, always a tricky issue for someone with a spinal-cord injury like mine. They wanted to be sure I could make the long drive.

Racing down I-40, lights and sirens blaring, my breathing remained stable. It was only after I was admitted to Charlotte Memorial Hospital (now Carolinas Medical Center) that I began to have problems breathing on my own. Up until this time, I had been using my chest muscles to compensate for my diaphragm—the muscle you use to breathe—which was now paralyzed. But after three weeks of doing this, my chest muscles, which weren't used to their new job yet, finally got tired and were losing their ability to support my lung function. Normally, the doctors would perform a tracheotomy to aid the breathing of someone with a spinal-cord injury, but my doctors didn't want to do that. This meant the only other option was to put me in an iron lung. It sounds crazy now, but even in 197,1 it was a little outside the norm to do this for someone who was paralyzed.

Iron lungs were a remnant of the polio epidemic, which spread primarily in the summer months from the 1920s to the 1950s throughout the United States. They were gargantuan pieces of equipment that looked like a space capsule lying on top of stilts. The person would be placed on their back in the tube with only their head sticking out of the end of it, while the machine used pressure to open and close the lungs slowly, rhythmically. By the time of my injury, very few hospitals had them anymore. In fact, the iron lung that I used was found in the hospital basement, left over from the time of Charlotte's polio tent hospital, a M.A.S.H.-type unit that was hurriedly built to accommodate the growing number of polio patients back in the forties.

The two weeks I spent in the iron lung were the toughest of all of my days since the accident. Huge, impenetrable, and swallowing up my body, the machine felt claustrophobic. There was no room to move the parts of my body that I still controlled. I couldn't even move my head since the weights and pulleys were still attached and hung down from the end of the machine. I felt completely helpless. Because I could only lie on my back, the nurses couldn't move my body or change the angle of my bed to relieve the constant pressure on my skin. While they did the best they could, reaching in under by body and trying to massage my skin, I still developed painful pressure sores. Worse, people with paralysis are at risk of developing "foot drop," a condition where the foot and toes point downward. As a result, I had to wear these special boots lined with sheepskin and designed to keep my feet in an upright position to prevent dropping. Unfortunately, the nurses didn't have much experience with the boots. They put them on incorrectly, and I developed pressure sores on both my heels and calves. Mom, however, did what she could to distract me and try to make the situation bearable, a role she had perfected over time.

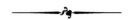

When we were little, we moved frequently as Dad worked his way up the ladder of General Foods. Right before my sixth birthday, we were living in Dallas, Texas, when severe thunderstorms broke out on Tuesday, April 2, 1957. Throughout the day, the rain pounded on the roof while thunder rattled the sky repeatedly, sending our dog, Jell-O, running for cover. By the afternoon, it had subsided, and Mom insisted that we go outside for a little while—with strict orders to stay on the back porch and out of the wet grass and mud—to run off some of the energy that had been building after being cooped up all day. After only ten minutes, my brothers and I heard a commotion next door and saw our neighbors talking excitedly and pointing off into the distance. We looked up and noticed the sky had turned an eerie dark gray. Turning in the direction our neighbors were pointing, we saw a massive funnel cloud rumbling in the distance. We were mesmerized, staring and watching as the tornado twisted and turned. At one point, it headed east, then, slowly and methodically, it changed course and wheeled in a new direction. We could see pieces of debris being picked up, spiraled through the funnel, then carelessly flung to the ground. We were simultaneously terrified and fascinated by this marvel, which we had only seen in pictures and on TV. The only thing that broke our attention was the sound of Mom calling us inside. For a second, none of us moved. We were transfixed by the storm's power.

As fascinated as we were, we were young enough to be oblivious to its potential danger. Mom used this to her advantage. Thinking quickly, she grabbed a sheet from the dryer and flung it over the dining room table.

"Hey, boys," she called, distracting us from the storm, "let's pretend we're going camping!" She forced a grin, doing her best to act as nonchalant as possible. We were easily diverted and hurried inside to hide under the "tent" she had made. As she shoved several toys under the table, she said, "Now you boys get everything ready for us in the tent while I make us some dinner for our 'campfire!'" Soon, we were focused on our mission while Mom continued to pretend that all was well, returning to the task of frying chicken for dinner. All the while, she watched the tornado wind its way toward our house. At one point, she watched as the storm picked up a school bus, circled it through its funnel, then carelessly cast it aside.

By this time, the tornado was only about a mile from our house and Mom was doing her best to figure out her next game plan. Dad, who was out of town, was calling in regularly to get updates. But as soon as Mom decided to corral us into a nearby closet, the funnel cloud suddenly changed course and wandered in the opposite direction. Mom continued to monitor the storm's path until it finally recoiled into the murky sky. All the while, my brothers and I played happily under the table, oblivious to mom's charade and the danger we had just escaped.

While we were able to escape the Dallas tornado, we had no choice but to endure the monotony of the iron lung. Mom did what she could, entertaining me with stories. Since I could only stare at the ceiling, she also hung a butterfly mobile and poster of a window above me, trying hard to keep my mind off my current situation. But it was hard. I was still in the ICU, and people around me kept dying. And that is what finally drove me to my breaking point. I had had enough and knew I had to get out of this iron lung and out of this place. As Tim Robbins' character in the *Shawshank Redemption* said, I needed "to get busy livin', or get busy dyin'," and for me, there was only one choice. The doctor said I couldn't come out of the iron lung until I learned to breathe on my own, so I insisted on practicing. Daily, the nurses would turn the power level down on the machine, and I would try to breathe by myself. First, one hour, then two, and so on. At first, it was both difficult and terrifying as I fought for every breath. Gradually, though, it got easier. Eventually I was able to go for hours with the machine turned off and, ultimately, to breathe on my own.

At the same time, I was steadily getting to eat again too. Since my accident, I'd been fed through a feeding tube in my stomach. In order to go to rehab, I also had to be able to eat normal food, which was fine by me. I had to go through the usual process of returning to solids: first the clear-liquid diet, then the full-liquid diet, before finally graduating to the grand prize: solid foods. For weeks, I fantasized about my first real meal, so when Mom asked me what I wanted, I was ready.

"Krispy Kreme donuts and corn on the cob," I said. And that's what I got. Sitting in my hospital room, breathing on my own, with bits of corn and melted butter running down my chin, I knew I had earned my one-way ticket out of the hospital. On to rehab. I was ready. It was time to get on with my life.

Chapter 4

Rehabilitation

Once the polio epidemic died down and the iron lungs went into storage, the people of Charlotte decided to convert their polio tent hospital into an actual brick-and-mortar hospital for children with cerebral palsy called the Charlotte Spastics Hospital. Its primary purpose was to provide custodial care for children with cerebral palsy when their families were too overwhelmed to do it themselves. It didn't even have a full-time doctor on staff, relying instead on one who stopped by periodically to give checkups and attend to minor illnesses.

By the 1960s, the hospital administrators decided it was time to expand the building to offer rehabilitation to children with disabilities, though they didn't know how they were going to raise the money to support this effort. Lucky for them, the state's Vocational Rehabilitation (VR) Department was looking for a rehabilitation hospital for adults. They offered to pour their resources into expanding the Spastics Hospital if the administrators would give them some say into the design and use of the new facilities. The hospital's administrators agreed, and construction soon began to surround the existing building. Charlotte Rehabilitation Hospital (CRH) was born.

The new rehab hospital was tethered to Charlotte Memorial Hospital by a long, gray, concrete underground tunnel. The leadership of CRH, being smart with their money, had developed an agreement with the acute-care hospital to share their institutional kitchen and laundry facilities, making the tunnel a handy way of transporting clean linens and warm meals to the rehab folks. But it also meant that people like me could be discharged from the acute hospital more quickly. Pre-tunnel, patients had to stay in the acute care setting until they were medically stable enough to leave and go forth into the world of rehab, which was often in a completely separate facility. But with the tunnel, patients could be discharged sooner since doctors were assured that if a crisis developed, the patient could be whisked back to them lickety-split.

My ride through the tunnel came nine weeks after my accident. I was all decked out for the big event in my pajamas and a new form of head gear: the halo. Just before being transferred, the doctors had removed the tongs, finally freeing me from traction. The process of taking the screws out wasn't painful so much as weird. The tongs were immediately replaced by a four-poster, a vest-like contraption with a high collar that kept my neck and chin up, since after weeks in traction, my muscles weren't strong enough to hold up my head on their own. Still, it was far better than the tongs.

I remember being rolled down to the elevators, going down to the basement level, and then continuing the journey through the beige, dimly-lit tunnel. The metallic gurney wheels echoed as they bumped and rattled along the way. At the end of the tunnel was another elevator and a sign that said, "Welcome to Charlotte Rehabilitation Hospital." As the doors to the first floor opened, I felt as if I was arriving on a whole new planet. The first thing I noticed was the walls. They were no longer the sterile, bland, white-washed hospital walls. Instead, they were brightly painted and covered with pictures and announcements of upcoming events and activities. The hallways were wide and open, and there was an energy about the place that was fueled by hope, goals, and progress. It was no longer about emergencies, death, and the need to treat the next life-threatening situation that blasted through the doors.

The staff greeted me warmly and helped me get settled. They wasted no time in explaining how rehab works. Gone were the days of lying around in my hospital bed. From day one, rehab would be a pressure-packed schedule of therapy, counseling, and activities designed to get me back to functioning as much and as quickly as possible. There was going to be very little sittin' around time. All I could say was, "Amen," to that. I couldn't take lying in a hospital bed and staring at butterflies one minute longer.

Good thing, because the rehab day started promptly at seven in the morning when breakfast was delivered to my room. In rehab, every moment of the day had the potential to serve as therapy, including mealtime. The staff was soon teaching me to use a universal cuff to hold utensils and shovel food into my mouth. It was awkward and messy, but I didn't starve. The therapists assured me that over time, I'd get the hang of it. After breakfast it was time to get dressed. This was another opportunity for therapy, as the occupational therapists helped me learn to do as much as I could to dress myself. I already figured there was no way I was going to be able to put pants on by myself; that was going to be a two-person effort. But with practice, I was able to learn to stick my arms in a shirt and flip it over my head. It was a small victory, but I was learning quickly that you use what you have and take what you can get when it comes to adjusting to a disability.

By 9 a.m. I was meeting with the physical therapist, whose job it was to help me regain as much mobility as possible.

"Are you going to help me learn to drive this thing?" I asked, nodding toward my wheelchair. The therapist looked at me and smiled.

"That's the plan anyway," she said. "Let's start by seeing what you can do now." She led me through a series of exercises to get a sense of my current level of functioning, which, when it came to my legs, was nil. "We can definitely work on those wrists and arms," she said. Funny, because my doctor back in Greenville had said the same thing before they put me on the ambulance bound for Charlotte. He had detected a slight movement in my wrists and thought there was a chance I would regain some use of them. The therapist busily wrote notes in my chart and prescribed a grueling schedule of exercises and activities.

"You're going to be with me for three hours a day, except on weekends, so get ready to work," she said as she reviewed the schedule with me. After lying in bed for nine straight weeks, I was weak and wondered how much I'd be able to actually do. I already knew my equilibrium was shot. You know that dizzy feeling you get when you stand up too fast? The first time the doctors helped me sit up, I had that feeling times ten. Everything was spinning, and I had a hard time catching my breath. For the first couple of weeks, I had to take things very slowly. I didn't have much endurance, and I tired quickly. I'd get so winded that the therapists would have to lean back my wheelchair to the point that my head would be resting on their stomachs so that I could catch my breath. It was slow going.

The rest of my day was filled with education classes that attempted to prepare us for a life with paralysis. I also had more occupational therapy, counseling, and therapeutic recreation (TR), which became my favorite time of day. Initially, the days were so full I was exhausted and ready for bed by 7:30 p.m. Unfortunately, there was no rest for the weary since that was the time for my personal care. The nurse would help me to get completely undressed. She'd then do what's called a "bowel program." When you're paralyzed, your muscles to push poop out on their own are impaired, which means that you have to have someone—usually a caregiver or attendant—manually stimulate the bowels in order to get the poop out. After nine weeks of this, I was starting to get used to it, though I'll admit it took some time to accept. Once she was done, the nurse would transfer me to a gurney, cover me up with a blanket, and wheel me down the hall past other patients, visitors, and the nurses' station. I'd wave, and they'd wave back. Sometimes I was the only person in the shower room, but it was more common for two or three other patients to be there as well. Although the nurses would pull a curtain between us, you could still see each other as the nurses removed our blankets and hosed us down using long spray nozzles. It felt like being in a car wash. I always came away clean, albeit slightly more humble.

What kept me going in the midst of my busy rehab schedule was time hanging out with my fellow rehab patients. It was my favorite part of the day. I was fed up with lying in bed. Plus, I hadn't spent much time with anyone except family, a few friends, and the staff. That nine-week period in ICU had been like a social drought. I was primed and ready to interact with people, spending as much time as possible away from my room. I'd hang out in the common area and invite someone to play board games, roll up to the nurses' station to chat, or visit other patients in their rooms.

Not everyone wanted out of their room as much as I did. There were some who preferred to stay in bed, leaving only when the staff made them. They chose to stay in their rooms for different reasons. Some were introverts who needed a break from the fully loaded rehab schedule and all the interaction that was required. Others were painfully shy or overcome by shame from their new disability and didn't want others to see them. There were a few, too, who were in the process of giving up, unable to deal with the profound change that had happened in their lives. They were the ones who, after rehab, would go home or to a nursing home and stay there. It was tough to see people turn away from life, especially the ones who were around my age and still had their whole lives ahead of them.

I found I had a knack for helping to raise their spirits and talk them through the dark times. I seemed able to sense when someone needed to talk or when they were feeling particularly low. It was then that my optimism and humor were a clear benefit to others. Optimism and humor kept me going and if sharing them with others was beneficial, then that was a bonus.

Like everyone else, the rehab staff appreciated my optimism and enthusiasm, even if they weren't buying it. In team meetings, when the doctors, nurses, therapists, social workers, and counselors all got together to discuss each patient's progress and treatment plan, the word that kept coming up to describe me was "euphoric," which, in their eyes, was not a compliment. To them, I was perhaps a little too cheerful, a little too optimistic. They thought I was putting up a really good front and wondered how long I could keep it up. They knew that this was a big deal for a twenty-year-old kid but hadn't seen any signs that I had really acknowledged that.

From my perspective, it wasn't that I was trying to gloss over what had happened or put on a happy face. At that point in time, I was doing my best to get through rehabilitation and get on with my life. Plus, I couldn't see the point of getting down about my disability. Depression was never my strong suit. Also, I didn't trust that there was some formula or schedule for how I was supposed to deal with this. The staff kept spouting the five stages of grief made famous by Elizabeth Kübler-Ross, but that seemed too easy and academic. It would have been different if they had sustained a traumatic injury and were talking from experience. But with the exception of one staff member who had polio, the rest were nondisabled. I recognized that they knew a lot about the physical impact of trauma and how the body would heal and how to improve function. But when it came to the emotional piece, that was more amorphous and difficult to pin down. I was going to have to figure it out for myself.

In other respects, the staff thought I was doing exceptionally well. They could tell I was highly motivated and continually noted my progress. I was achieving more milestones than many people with a similar injury, like learning to feed and partially dress myself. They chalked that up to my young age, my physical strength, my high level of motivation, my faith, and, ironically, my optimism. They also gave a lot of kudos to my family, who were continually supportive and visited daily. There were some patients who waited days or weeks to see a familiar face.

Still, Diane, my social worker, kept a close eye on me. I'd swing by her office periodically to discuss my progress and my plan for going home. She knew enough to keep the conversation light, asking how things were going in physical therapy or how my latest home visit had gone. But as we talked, she'd expertly watch for a sign that my cheerful exterior was starting to crack, knowing that it would happen only when I was good and ready. She knew that I had to figure it out for myself and in my own time. She understood it would happen only when I was ready to emerge from the deepest recesses of my closet space.

One morning, Dad came by my room carrying a piece of paper and some tape.

"Look what I brought," he said. Without waiting for a response, he turned the page over for me to see. It looked like one of the sale signs he often made to advertise the latest General Foods product in the local grocery stores, with its neat printing in colored markers. But instead of featuring Jell-O or Sanka or Log Cabin Syrup, the sign simply held an inspirational quote. I wasn't totally surprised; of course Dad would bring his quotes into rehab. He was never one to miss an opportunity. "I thought I'd put it on the back of your chair," he explained.

"That's great, Dad, but I won't be able to see it," I said.

"That's okay. It's not for you," he grinned. "It's for everybody else."

From then on, he'd bring in a new sign each week. Over time, the staff, and even the other patients and their families, would look forward to seeing the latest offering. I'd even catch people repeating the quote to others as I rolled through the hallways. But he saved the best for last. Toward the end of my rehab, Dad brought in the sign that became the fan favorite throughout the hospital: "I am not afraid of tomorrow because I have seen yesterday, and I love today."

DAD

Mom came to visit me every day, sometimes twice a day, bringing my favorite home-baked snacks and offering to run errands. In between, she tried to stay busy working in her garden or volunteering in the community. Meanwhile, Dad visited every day that he was in town but otherwise stayed busy with his job. Neither of them were going to church. They were both doing their best to ignore the spiritual crisis that was rumbling just below the surface. Our pastor and other church members visited us often in the hospital, checking in to see if there was any way they could help. My parents always greeted them graciously, updating them on my progress and asking after other people in the church, though they never accepted offers to return to church, citing the need to be by my side. But I saw the look of betrayal, loss, and fear in the eyes of my parents. My accident had called into question the very tenets on which they had based their lives, especially for my dad, who had toiled long and hard for God under the expectation that he and his family would be protected in return.

Dad's concept of God began early on in life when his parents attended a Presbyterian church in Virginia. There, the minister preached your standard hell, fire, and damnation message: if you're good, then God will look after you and reward you with a ticket to heaven, but if you're bad, well, hang on and keep your head down because it ain't gonna be pretty.

Coming from an adult, one with a seemingly tight connection with God, that was pretty scary stuff for a kid, and it had a significant impact on Dad. Luckily, it was balanced a bit by his mother who believed that you didn't need someone, not even a minister, to tell you how to be spiritual. What mattered was how well you treated people. Over time, Dad took the messages of these two significant authority figures and blended them to create the mantra "do your best," which would stay with him from then on.

Still, the preacher's words carried more weight than the rest, which soon became problematic. When my dad was eight years old, his dad left him, his mother, and his younger sister and never came back. Dad was devastated. He didn't understand why his father had deserted him. He couldn't explain why his family life was crumbling when he had been trying to do his best and be good. He sat for hours, talking with God and asking, "Why is this happening, God?" But it was going to get worse. With my grandfather gone, my grandmother didn't have the funds or the wherewithal to support her children. My dad was given the option of living with his grandmother or in an orphanage. It was bad enough that his father had left him, but now his mother was sending him away too, possibly even to an orphanage. His sense of abandonment was almost unbearable. While he didn't end up in an orphanage, he did get shuffled from one relative to another. In the midst of this, he struggled to recover and to understand why God had abandoned him and broken up his family.

On the night of December 7, 1941, Dad was sitting in a stadium, cheering on his high school football team when the announcer interrupted the game to report that Japan had attacked Pearl Harbor. By then, Dad was really unhappy. He was struggling in school, he hated his job plucking feathers off of chickens for a local processing plant, and he continued to miss his family. So he "suddenly became very patriotic," as he puts it, and ran off to join the navy. He was just seventeen.

On the eve of his first sojourn out to sea, as the ship was still safely docked in New Orleans, Dad went out with his friends for one last night on the town. Since his friends were more interested in chasing women, Dad, who wasn't totally comfortable with women yet and had never dated, bought a pint of rum and a Coke and held his own solitary going-away party. It was his first experience with drinking—one that he liked. The alcohol made his body relax and his mind forget his troubles. He drank some more, giving in and letting the rum carry him away to a better place. It was only when he felt someone poking his shoulder and calling him loudly to return to the ship that he realized he had drunk so much that he had passed out. It would be many, many years later before my dad could point back to that night and recognize it as the beginning of his life as an alcoholic.

It turned out that life as a navy gunner didn't make my dad any happier, but at least now he could turn to booze to cover up the pain. By then, he was probably starting to realize that he was drinking too much. He began a type of negotiation process with himself.

"If I can just get out of the navy and go to college for four years, then I'll be happy," he told himself. Upon discharge from the navy, he enrolled in The College of William and Mary in Virginia. He completed his degree and, during the process, met my mom, who was also a student. "If I can just get married and have babies, then I'll be happy and I won't have to drink so much." He and Mom got married and had three boys, who were all almost exactly two years apart (my mother later suffered a miscarriage during her fourth pregnancy). Dad adored us, but he still wasn't happy. So he kept drinking. And he kept bargaining with himself and God.

As much as he was drinking, Dad was still able to begin a successful career as a salesman with General Foods. The company was growing steadily with its offerings of new-fangled convenience foods, like Jell-O, which would soon be used to create an endless number of congealed salads, and Minute Rice, which defied tradition and suddenly gave women an extra hour of free time. My family loved it because we got to try many of these new products before they hit the market. We were drinking Tang long before the astronauts and showing our friends the wonders of Cheez Whiz. With their convenience and innovation, these products could sell themselves, and, indeed, housewives everywhere were buying them in droves. However, Dad's engaging personality and down-to-earth approach gave him an edge and a knack for selling stuff. As a result, he quickly moved through the company ranks, from local salesman to regional manager.

Me, Oogie, and Jody posing in one of Dad's marketing displays

Throughout this period, Dad had taken a long hiatus from the church and the God that he wasn't sure he could trust. However, once he had a family he decided it was time to rejoin the church. We began at the First Presbyterian Church in Wilson, North Carolina, but we weren't there long before Dad was promoted to the company's Institutional Development Division, and we moved to Dallas. By now, the situation with Dad's drinking was intensifying, both because he was drinking more and because he now had to hide it from his family and his coworkers. He had become what is called a functional drinker, which means he could do his job and be a fairly good dad and husband without anyone suspecting that he had a drinking problem. He'd have a few drinks with coworkers at sales meeting events or the one drink "to relax" after getting home from work—nothing out of the ordinary. But behind closed doors, he'd drink from one of the many stashes hidden in his briefcase, his desk, his car, or the shed behind the house. He must have been pretty good; none of us had a clue.

In fact, we thought our dad was pretty great. Everyone did. He was popular among his coworkers, our church members, and even my friends. He was sociable and easygoing. He was funny too, armed with an intelligence and wit that was both casual and insightful. My friends liked to hang out at my house, not just because we had a steady supply of General Foods snacks, which Dad kept in the trunk of his car—Double Bubble, Tootsie Rolls, or Nik-L-Nips—but also because he took a genuine interest in their lives, good-naturedly ribbing them and always careful to follow up on previous conversations about girlfriends or parent issues or the class they were struggling with in school. He was never "Mr. Johnson" to them. He was always "Bill."

Part of what made my dad "Bill" was his "Billisms," these pithy quotes that he liked to collect and throw out at us when the timing was right or when the mood happened to strike him. They were the offspring of his original mantra "do your best," and he had files—and a mind—full of 'em. Still does.

"He who hesitates is lost," he'd say when one of us was taking too long to make a decision. "You snooze, you lose," we'd hear whenever my brothers or I were moving too slowly, especially in the mornings. But his favorite was always the phrase he had posted on the back of my wheelchair: "I am not afraid of tomorrow, for I have seen yesterday, and I love today." It spoke of optimism and encouragement, of survival and hope, things he certainly knew a lot about and figured everyone else needed too. As such, that quote was everywhere in our house: plaques, paperweights, and signs. Mom even cut out a version of the quote done in calligraphy, glued it to a seashell, covered it with glaze, and then set it out on a table in the living room—a constant message of inspiration.

But while Dad freely offered these sayings to help one of us, they weren't doing much for him—nor were his continued attempts to bargain with God. He decided to change tactics. The voice of his childhood preacher still echoing in his head, Dad figured that he needed to get closer to God. He reasoned that doing so would free him of his addiction, and he'd finally be happy. He sat down with two ministers in Dallas one morning and announced that he wanted to become a minister. The ministers were really good with him. They patiently listened to Dad tell his story. And while he was careful never to divulge the darkness that surrounded him, I'm guessing the ministers sensed it and recognized the longing within, the search for redemption that lay below the surface. Together, they expertly and carefully explained that while not everyone is called to ordained ministry, there were many opportunities for him to get more involved in the church as a way of connecting with God.

I'm pretty sure those two Dallas ministers had no idea what their words would mean to someone with an addictive personality. They could never have predicted the impact of that message on my dad. Soon after, Dad was, as he'll tell you, working in the church "full force, anytime they had the doors open." He taught Sunday school. He became a deacon and then an elder. He handled the money for the Wednesday night dinners. He worked with the youth group. He even preached a few sermons. Whenever we moved, Dad always had a three-point game plan for settling into a new town: find a supermarket, a school, and a Presbyterian church. Before our boxes were unpacked, Dad was already establishing himself in the new congregation. He had found a new addiction, hoping desperately that it would replace the old one. It didn't. He was still an alcoholic, albeit a very busy and well-churched alcoholic. And he was still unhappy, still left wondering why God was letting him down when he was working so, so hard for him.

Thus, when I got injured, my father decided that God had betrayed him. As he saw it, since he had kept his bargain with God, God, for his part, was supposed to do right by Dad, which included keeping his wife and kids safe. Yet his wife had lost a baby, Oogie had come home from Vietnam with emotional scars that he couldn't reveal, and I was facing a life with paralysis.

"That's it, God," Dad thought. "I'm done with you."

CHAPTER 6

WHY NOT ME?

One Friday night in September, while I was still in rehab, fans at Memorial Stadium were in a frenzy as they watched the Garinger High School football team take its rival to the last seconds of the game. Garinger was preparing to go for another touchdown and secure its victory when its star player, Phil Hughston, went to tackle an opposing player. As he did, he made a critical mistake—going in with his head down—and when he made contact with the other guy, his neck snapped. Phil instantly hit the ground. Within seconds, he was surrounded by players, coaches, and trainers, all of whom could tell that Phil was gravely injured. People throughout the stadium grew silent as they watched emergency personnel go through the same motions they had with me—keeping his chin steady, wrapping his neck with the collar, and moving him gingerly, quickly, into the waiting ambulance. He was rushed to Charlotte Memorial, just a tunnel ride away from me.

Phil's injury was much more serious than mine had been. It had been higher up on his spine, which meant that even more of his upper torso, including his diaphragm, was paralyzed. This meant that, from the moment of impact, Phil was unable to breathe on his own. As soon as the doctors were able to stabilize him, he was placed in the iron long. My iron lung.

By Saturday, there was a lot of talk about Phil around our unit, both because some of us knew Phil and because all the news media were carrying his story. The community was rallying around him the way they had done for me. As soon as I heard about him, I felt the need to go visit him, knowing that our injuries were similar. I understood the darkness that comes from sustaining a traumatic injury, and more so, I knew what it was like to have to lay in that iron lung contraption day after day. I remembered how bored and hopeless it felt at times, and I thought I could at least offer a distraction. The next morning I had someone push me through the long tunnel and back up to the intensive-care unit, where I had spent so many days and nights. I greeted all of the staff, who remembered me, and who seemed implicitly to understand why I was there as they nodded in the direction of Phil's room.

As soon as I rolled in, I was taken back to those agonizing days in the lung—that huge machine, the sounds of the motor, the look on Phil's face as he stared up toward the ceiling. I recognized all of it.

"Hey, Phil. My name's Mark," I called out, knowing he couldn't see me. I didn't have the benefit of those who could stand tall enough to be in his line of sight.

"Hi," he said, weakly.

"Looks like you're getting the star treatment like I did. I got to spend some quality time in that thing too."

"You did?" he asked.

"Yeah."

"It sucks." I could hear it in his voice—the fear, the hopelessness, and the isolation. I started to get a little teary and realized those feelings hadn't gone away for me either.

"Yeah," I said, pausing to keep my voice steady. "The good news is that it doesn't last forever. Eventually, you'll get out too."

"Huh," he said softly.

Since his family had warned me that he was pretty weak and couldn't handle much, I stayed and talked with him for only a few minutes. Actually, I did most of the talking, telling a bit of my story of the iron lung and the wheelchair and rehab. I knew that, less than forty-eight hours after being injured, there was only so much that he could take just now. He needed a lot more time to settle into, and then come out of, the shock, before we could really talk. But I wanted to at least let him know that he wasn't alone. I wanted him to know that I knew what he was going through.

"Hey, I'm only a tunnel ride away. I'll come back in a few days to check on you and see how you're doing. Meanwhile, you might want to have your mom hang a mobile or something up on the ceiling. It helps to be able to stare at something besides those ceiling tiles."

"Good idea," he said.

The next day, Diane came looking for me in the common room.

"Hi, Mark."

"Hey."

"I heard you went and visited Phil yesterday."

"Yeah. I figured we had a lot in common, you know. Both young. Both quadriplegics. Both in an iron lung. I wanted to reach out to him."

"That was a great idea," she said. Then she hesitated, and I could tell something was up. "It's just that I've got some sad news." She paused, looking at me. "Phil died today."

"Wow. I talked to him yesterday!" Something knotted up inside me.

"I know. That's what makes it so hard to believe." She paused. "And so incredibly sad."

"But we were both dealing with the same things, both in the lung."

"I know. His injury was a more severe than yours was. He was never going to be able to breathe on his own."

"Man." It was all I could say. I was too struck by the thought that Phil had died from an injury that was similar to mine. I remembered my doctors saying they couldn't believe that I had not only lived, but was doing so well, given the number of people who didn't survive injuries like mine. I'd never really understood what they meant until now. Why had I survived? And why hadn't Phil?

Chapter 7

Mom

Three weeks after Phil Hughston died, my rehab team said that I was ready to go home. I could not have agreed more. I was ready to be done with hospitals for a while. I'd spent an entire summer, and most of a fall season, surrounded by hospital walls. I couldn't wait to be in my own house, with my own stuff, and finally create some space from the accident and its aftermath. Plus, I wanted to see what life in a wheelchair was going to be like. "Let's do this," I thought.

Driving home that first day from rehab, my excitement about returning home was mixed with a sense of awkwardness. It was that feeling you get when you're returning to a familiar place after being gone a very long time. You know you've changed and grown in the time you've been away, and you wonder whether that old familiar place will have the capacity to encompass your new self, and, in my case, a new wheelchair.

When we arrived at the house that first afternoon, I sat in the passenger seat and waited while Dad got out of the car and pulled my wheelchair out of the trunk. The chair was a large, adult-width semi-recliner chair with pneumatic tires, which were kind of like bicycle tires. In other words, it was a big, bulky thing, which required a lot of strength and a good deal of finesse to be able to pull it out of the trunk without damaging your car, your body, or your ego. But after several practice runs with my weekend home visits, Dad was starting to get the hang of it. He wheeled it over to me, lifted me out of the car, and sat me down as Mom was pulling my suitcase out of the backseat. It was early Friday afternoon, in that quiet time that comes before the kids get home from school and the neighbors get home from work.

Returning to a split-level home in a wheelchair means, essentially, that you're relegated to the ground-level floor, except for the times when people are available to help lift you and your chair up and down stairs. I wheeled along the driveway and around to the back entrance, following Dad who was carrying my suitcase. As we reached the back porch, Dad stepped to the side and gestured ceremoniously toward the new ramp that led to the door.

"You like it?" he asked. "In honor of this occasion, the guys at the church came over and built this last Saturday. Now you don't have to worry about any steps back here. You can come and go as you please through your own private entrance."

"That's great, Dad," I said as I wheeled myself up the ramp and through the door.

My parents had done their best to create the illusion that I was "on my own," recognizing that my dreams had not included living in their basement. My "private entrance" led into the downstairs den where there was a TV, a couch, and a recliner. To the right was a short hallway that led to my bathroom, which was still being converted and not quite ready for my wheelchair, and then my bedroom. The tiny room was completely overwhelmed by the hospital bed that had been brought in for me. This was not the somewhat restrained and streamlined hospital bed of present. No, this thing was a behemoth, an enormous iron structure with a hand crank and large metal casters that threatened to take over the room, and possibly the entire house. Even with it shoved into the corner, it still didn't leave a lot of room for my wheelchair. Over the bed hung a sling and a trapeze, which would help me transfer in and out of bed, or otherwise start my career as a circus performer. To the right of the bed I noticed that someone had built shelves along the wall.

"That's so you don't have to worry about reaching into the closet or messing with opening drawers. You can grab the supplies and some of the clothes you need," Mom explained. I could tell they had thought a lot about this, probably anticipating this day as much as I had. As if to demonstrate their purpose, Mom unpacked some of the stuff from my suitcase and set it neatly on the shelves, then turned and studied me for a minute.

"Well," she sighed, "I'll go upstairs to start working on dinner and leave you to get settled in."

"Okay," I said, "sounds good." She turned and walked up the stairs as Dad came in with another suitcase.

"The only thing we haven't finished yet is the shower. We're still working to modify it so that your chair will fit in it," he said.

"Guess I'll be taking bird baths for a while, unless you wanna take me out back and hose me down every day," I responded.

"Don't tempt me," he said before turning and walking upstairs.

I sat and looked around my new room. This room had originally been Dad's office until Oogie had gotten older and taken it over as his bedroom. I'd never really considered it much since I hadn't spent a lot of time in it or ever planned to. It was the smallest of the rooms in our house. It had one window that looked out onto the front lawn, although, given that this was the lower level of a split-level house, the most you could see was a couple of bushes and the sky. And that's if you were standing, which, of course, I wasn't. But it beat the fake window poster and mobile I'd been forced to stare at all those weeks lying flat in the hospital.

Figuring there was plenty of time to unpack later, I turned to head out toward the den, but the foot rests of my wheelchair hit the wall, leaving a nice nick in the wood paneling.

"Shoot!" I muttered. I propelled the chair forward a bit, then tried again to turn, this time clearing the wall by a few inches. I took a deep breath. This was going to take some getting used to.

Mom was my constant companion in those early weeks and months after I returned home. Dad was on the road, Jody was starting his freshman year at the University of North Carolina at Chapel Hill, and Oogie was living in Charleston, South Carolina, where he was attending Baptist College. When Dad was home, he was always available to help with my care and give Mom a break, but this was usually only on weekends. That left the bulk of my care to Mom, who never complained and was firmly committed to doing whatever it took to help me. Every morning, she came down to see if I was awake yet, though what I didn't know was that in the time it took for her to walk from her room to my room, she was quickly brushing tears from her eyes, not wanting me to see the grief that greeted her each morning. She became very good at helping me get dressed and then transfer out of bed. Since I couldn't make it up to the kitchen, she would bring breakfast downstairs for both of us. We'd sit together on the back porch and watch the community of birds who came daily to feast from her many bird feeders in the midst of the backyard garden she had spent so much time designing. Twice a day, I'd go out to roll around my neighborhood, trying to increase my upper body strength. My wheelchair was heavy and bulky—a far cry from the streamlined manual wheelchairs that people enjoy today. I had to exert a lot of effort to get just a few feet.

Mom's capacity to think creatively and explore new territory served us well. There was significant downtime back then, and the days could get long. We didn't have an accessible van, and it was hard for Mom to lift me in and out of the car each time we went somewhere. As a result, we spent a lot of time at home. Mom always had ideas for how to fill up the time. She was especially curious and eager to help me figure out what I could do given my disability. She set up a base of operations for me—a table on the back porch—to which she would bring her many ideas and experiments. Under her guidance, I tried painting, using a small easel that she set up on the table. The experiment wasn't totally a bust as we discovered that I had inherited a little of her talent. She brought me a typewriter, which I used to plunk out letters to family and friends. I started out by writing thank-you letters to many of the people who had come to visit or who had otherwise shown their support. We also put together puzzles and did crafts. When we were tired of being inside, we'd head out to the backyard where

I'd practice archery. Our backyard was big enough that I could shoot at trees and not have to worry about endangering anyone with an errant shot. Good thing since there were so many.

Mom's ability to make the most of things was honed in the midst of her peripatetic childhood. Her father was an astrophysicist for the Smithsonian Institution's Astrophysical Observatory who specialized in studying the sun, primarily the variations in its radiation and heat that reaches the earth. The Observatory was still a rather new venture for the Smithsonian, having been established in 1889, and the Institution was working to establish field stations around the world that would provide variety in their data and observations. These stations had to be in areas where the sky and air were clear and there was little rainfall, which usually meant remote mountains in desert regions. My grandfather was assigned to the station at Mount Montezuma in Antofagasta, Chile—a dry, desolate area—where my grandparents were housed in a ramshackle tin house, and where my mom was born in 1925. Tragically, however, the Spanish flu epidemic of 1918 was still holding on in some parts of the world, including this distant area of Chile, and my grandmother contracted it and did not survive. She died when Mom was only one year old.

Soon after, the National Geographic Society partnered with the Smithsonian to set up a new station on Mount Brukkaros, a volcanic mountain that lay in the midst of the desert in what is now Namibia, and chose my grandfather to set it up and run it. My grandmother's sister—my great aunt—was apparently really concerned about this. She wasn't sure how well it would work for a widower to travel to a remote country with an infant, especially when he was going to be occupied with such a hefty project. She offered to accompany my grandfather on the expedition to help care for my mom and keep up the house. Somehow, they decided instead to get married. Thus, when Mom was just eighteen months old, she sailed out of New York's harbor on a ship bound for Africa, accompanied by her father and Pauline, the woman who was now both her aunt and stepmother. Traveling with them was Fred Greeley, another scientist who would be working with my grandfather at the observatory.

In April, 1930, The National Geographic Magazine published a story about the three-year Mount Brukkaros expedition titled "Keeping House for the

Shepherds of the Sun." Written by Pauline, it gives a vivid description of what life in this remote African region was like for this adventurous woman and the toddler she was now raising. They were completely isolated, living by themselves at the top of a mountain, surrounded by a vast desert. The nearest community was the Hottentot village of Beerseba, which consisted of grass huts, one Lutheran church, and a missionary family's house. It was from here that Mom's family was able to recruit servants who were paid with money as well as rations of tobacco, flour, corn meal, sugar, tea, and soap. Otherwise, the nearest city was Keetsmanshoop, a distance of more than sixty miles through desert and over rivers that couldn't be crossed during the rainy season.

As a result, my step-grandmother had to be very creative when it came to entertaining and caring for my mom. They hiked around the mountain, enough that Mom became expert at climbing over rocks, exploring the terrain, and learning about the native plants and animals, such as springbok and ostriches. They skipped rope, danced, went on picnics, and made games out of household chores and cooking. Through all of this, Mom learned to be fearless and adventurous, traits there were critical in an area that was, at times, unforgiving and which included a number of threats like the black ringhal, a cobra that spit poison and showed up often around their home site.

In 1930, my grandfather completed his assignment at Mount Brukkaros, and the family returned to the States. They set up house in Chevy Chase, Maryland. Mom started going to a local public school where it became apparent pretty quickly that she was going to have a hard time learning. She was dyslexic, struggling with both numbers and words, although it would be many years before there was a name for this condition. Meanwhile, Mom's parents and the school tried everything to teach her to read. Finally, when she was in the third grade, Pauline, as enterprising as always, found a Swedish woman to tutor Mom, which did the trick. Mom was finally able to read.

Soon after that, my grandfather was assigned to work at the observatory on Mount St. Katherine, also known as Mount Sinai, in Egypt for three months. Whether it was because he wanted to give Mom a break from school, spend some time alone with his first child, or for some other reason entirely, he chose to take only my mom with him on this expedition. She was thrilled with opportunity to miss school and go off on another adventure. By now, Mom was old enough to hold her own in these exotic, remote locations, and she wasted no time exploring the Egyptian land and its wildlife as her dad continued to watch the sun.

When this was done, they returned to Chevy Chase. By that time, Mom was about ten and had spent enough time watching her father observe the world and its universe to begin to formulate her own questions about the world, particularly in matters of religion. She knew that her parents had both been raised to go to church when they were young but had stopped going by the time Mom was born. She also noticed that even though they didn't go to church, her family still celebrated the major holidays. Christmas meant a tree and presents, even on a remote desert mountain; Easter meant a new dress and shoes. Mom, being the curious child that she was, wondered why her family celebrated these two major Christian holidays when they didn't go to church. Her parents explained that they wanted their children to be able to make their own choices about whether to attend church. That suited Mom, who had already been scoping out local churches, and she announced confidently that she was going to begin attending the local Episcopal church, largely because it was within walking distance. Her parents fully supported her decision, even if they chose not to accompany her. Unafraid to attend church on her own, Mom instead found the experience to be exhilarating. She relished the opportunity to be the explorer this time, mimicking her father as she observed the church's practices and asked questions about God and Christianity. When the family relocated to Silver City, New Mexico, where her father worked at the Tyrone Observatory, one of the first things that Mom did was find a nearby church to attend.

Two years later, the family returned to Chevy Chase, and Mom graduated from high school. She then enrolled in The College of William and Mary in nearby Richmond, majoring in art and costume design and hoping to one day to be a fashion designer. On the day of enrollment, she was standing in line to get her class schedule when a cute boy with a mop of curly hair and a lot of personality started flirting with her. He gave her his phone number and casually said, "Call me." She didn't. All those moves to exotic places had made it difficult for Mom to make friends, and she was painfully shy, particularly around boys. A few weeks later, she was sitting on a bench, enjoying the cool spring breeze, when a friend of hers walked up and handed her a wadded-up chewing gum wrapper.

"Here," she said, "this is from some guy named Bill Johnson." Surprised, Mom opened the wrapper to find a single nickel. Summoning up the courage, she used it to call Bill, who instantly asked her out for a date. A year later, in 1947, they were married, and Mom gave up her dream of a career in fashion to begin their family.

Being raised by an adventurous set of parents and exposed to the world certainly rubbed off on Mom in other ways too. She was never a girly girl. As kids my friends and I loved to run through the woods near our home and kill water moccasins and copperhead snakes, and though we would carry them back triumphantly and with great fanfare, we knew that there was only one house where we could take them. No one else's parents were willing to have dead snakes brought to their doorsteps. Mom, however, would take the reptile from our hands and, without flinching, nail it to a tree and skin it, grinning as she handed us our trophy. Having three boys came easily to her.

Mom also grew up to be creative and enterprising. She loved to paint, sew, make designs with seashells, and do other types of arts and crafts. Mom also loved to blend her creativity with her role as family historian, creating endless scrapbooks that chronicled our life as a family, and collages she had put together of family photos, graduation pictures, and memorabilia from our various accomplishments that hung on our walls for all to see.

Over time, Mom discovered ways to use her creative talent to help others. She volunteered with local church groups to sew blankets and clothes for people in need or to make gifts for holiday bazaars. Eventually, she joined a group called Church Women United, an interdenominational group of women who felt called to address poverty and other issues both at home and abroad. Mom enjoyed getting to work beside other members of the community, including women from other races and socioeconomic levels. She got along well with them, forming bonds and developing relationships that would last for many years. In doing this, she began to really understand the needs of the people in her community and her ability to affect change. She had discovered the real meaning of church.

One day, it was raining, and Mom and I were trying to decide what to do with the day.

"Do you want to paint?" Mom asked.

"Yeah, let's paint my bed," I said.

"Okay, what color do you want to paint it?"

"Orange," I said.

And so it was that, after an afternoon's work, Mom and I stepped back to admire my bed. It was still clunky, but now it was also orange. Fluorescent orange.

There are very few ways to camouflage a large, iron hospital bed with a hand crank, particularly when it is sitting in your house instead of a hospital room. It just stands out. And there's certainly no way to make it cool. As I figured it, you might as well claim it and make it your own. The neon orange could serve as my mark, my way of transforming a situation that I had not signed up for. Sure it drew even more attention to this symbol of my disability, but people were going to notice it anyway—might as well make it interesting. And might as well try to connect it to those images that provided a truer sense of who I was at the time, paralyzed or not. Like the posters of Blood, Sweat & Tears; Chicago; Creedence Clearwater Revival; The Eagles; and Pink Floyd. And, more importantly, the poster of Raquel Welch, whose sexy stare followed my every move, and who never seemed to notice the wheelchair. Or even the orange bed.

NEW WHEELS

We were learning that it's expensive to have a disability. Besides the costs of my hospital and rehab stays, there was the price tag for the wheelchair, adaptive devices, like my universal cuff, and medical supplies to help me pee and poop. There were also the costs of modifying things like doors, the bathroom, and my bedroom in order to accommodate my wheelchair and enable me to take showers, lift myself out of bed, etc. But by far the biggest cost was for a wheelchair-accessible van that was required if I wanted to ever leave my house, which I surely did. Dad's insurance had helped with most of the medical and rehab stuff, but we were totally on our own when it came to modifying the house and getting the van.

This was the cue for which our friends and family had been so desperate. From the moment they heard about my accident, they had wanted to be able to *do* something. They wanted to visit or drive or cook or run errands or do laundry—anything to feel like they were helping, anything to feel in control again. The ripple effects of my accident had run wide circles around the community. This was especially true by the time I got home, when reality was dawning on most of us that paralysis was going to be a long-term gig. (I wouldn't say permanent—I always held out hope for a cure—but certainly long term.) Until then, most people had been hoping it was a temporary thing, a minor blip on the radar screen. Now it was clear that we were in this for the long haul, and everyone needed something to do to feel more in control.

When they heard that I needed an accessible van, my community sprang into action, launching a wave of fundraisers. The Charlotte Grocery Manufacturer's Association to which Dad belonged set up the Special Mark Johnson Fund and committee to raise donations. The local volunteer fire department also began fundraising. At the time of my accident, my family attended Carmel Presbyterian Church, which my parents had helped start, so the church members organized a bazaar and gathered donations. Our close family friends wrote personal checks and/or collected funds from their personal and professional networks.

During the Thanksgiving break, my friends—Andy, Robert, Rick, and Wes—came home from college. We shared a special bond and not just because we had grown up together. During high school, we had been part of a YMCA group we lovingly named "The Misfits" to emphasize that anyone could join us. With the support of our youth director, Carl Manfield, we had converted one of the Y gyms into a dance club where high-school students could hang out on Friday nights. After a year, the club was one of the Y's most successful programs, and we had developed lifelong bonds with each other. I always looked forward to seeing my Misfit friends.

While they were home, the guys got together to write a letter seeking donations for the van. They were careful to emphasize they didn't want anyone to "respond out of pity or obligation" but to make a gift that was "an expression of friendship." Toward the end of the letter, they wrote:

> Mark has a sign on the back of his wheelchair that says, "I am not afraid of tomorrow, for I have seen yesterday, and I love today." It is our wish that with our gift, Mark can realize all that he means to us and, maybe in our small way, make his love for today a little stronger and his outlook for tomorrow brighter.

Within weeks, they began receiving dozens of letters and cards, all stuffed with cash or checks. They were hoping to collect at least five hundred dollars, a pretty sizable amount at the time.

On the afternoon of Christmas Eve, I heard a knock at the door and soon heard the footsteps of multiple people coming down the stairs. Andy, Wes, Rick, Robert, Sam, and several other friends appeared in the den where I had been sitting.

"Hey, Mark," said Andy.

"Hey, y'all." I said. I could tell something was up. I had just seen them a few days earlier, and we hadn't planned on getting together today. "What are you elves up to?"

Andy smiled and looked around at the others. "We came by to wish you a merry Christmas and to give you this," he said as Wes walked over and handed me a large envelope. I used my teeth to rip open the top of the envelope and poured out its contents onto my lap. There were about two dozen Christmas cards, each from various friends. I started to read through them when I noticed a check in the pile. I picked it up and saw that it was a check for more than one thousand dollars.

"You guys have been busy," I said.

"That's from all of your friends, Mark," said Robert. "We wanted to help you get that van."

"Thanks, y'all. That's really great."

By mid-January, 1972, we had plenty of money to get me mobile. The community had raised enough money to buy a van—a Chevy Sportvan—and someone had even made a donation specifically to cover the costs of gas for an entire year. The van didn't have a wheelchair lift. Instead, we propped up boards—and later a folding ramp—so that someone could push me up into the van. It also didn't have hand controls, which meant that I couldn't drive it and instead had to sit in the back. Still, I knew the van signaled freedom, and as long as it could get me out of the house, I didn't care who drove or where I sat. I was happy.

Immediately, we went to work to customize the van and make it mine. This was the time when it was cool to have a van, and while this wasn't a Volkswagon van—the ultrahip and iconic van of the time—the Space

Vehicle was pretty close. It was a good start toward helping me fit into my peer group again. It was painted a vibrant thunderbolt orange. I picked the color. Not only would it fit well with the colorful patterns of the hippy counterculture that were popular at the time, but it matched the equally funky, outspoken, unexpected orange color of my hospital bed. A pattern was emerging, and so was my signature color. Mom sewed tie-dyed curtains for the back windows while Oogie hung paneling inside and fitted the van with an eight-track tape player. It was as cool as any other van on the planet. I was set to go.

POOPING ON MYSELF

By early spring, our family was ready for a break from the stress of the past year and decided to go to the beach. Growing up, we had gone every year, although the trips had become less frequent as my brothers and I got busy doing other things. But now we felt a need to reestablish a sense of normalcy, to return to the sand and the surf that was so much a part of our life as a family. As soon as we had agreed on a date, Dad called the rental agency and learned that a cottage was available. He booked it and smiled. Immediately, there was a difference in the Johnson household. We had something to look forward to.

On our first day of vacation, we spent the early morning fishing, though none of us caught anything worth keeping. Afterward, we hung out on the beach playing horseshoes and watching people body surf until Mom called us in for lunch. Jody helped push me through the sand and up to the house, where we found that she had created a real feast: fried chicken, baked beans, cole slaw, fresh silver queen corn, sliced tomatoes, and fresh peach pie. Starving, we rushed toward the table.

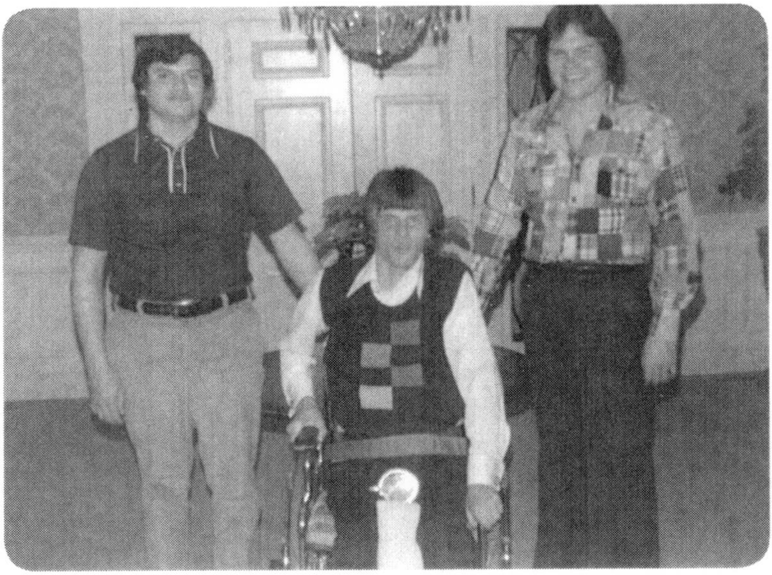

My brothers, Jody (left) and Oogie, did a lot to support me after the accident

"Unh, unh!" Mom called out, "Not until you wash that sand off! I don't want you tracking sand through this house."

We obligingly turned and went back out to the porch, where we took turns running our feet and hands and my wheelchair under the outside faucet. Jody checked around my chair, brushing sand off the tires and foot rests. Once we passed Mom's inspection, we were allowed to come in and sit at the table. We immediately began to dig in.

Our stomachs full, we retired to the living room to play board games and wait out the afternoon heat. Jody transferred me to the couch so that I could take the pressure off my butt for a while. My therapists had insisted that I do these kinds of things every day to prevent pressure sores. Over the next couple of hours, we talked, watched baseball, and visited with some friends who were also in town. It was a relaxing afternoon until the moment when I noticed a familiar sensation and realized that I needed to poop. Immediately.

With spinal cord injuries, especially the injuries that are as high up the spinal cord as mine, you can't usually tell when you have to poop.

The spinal cord, since it's paralyzed, can't send the requisite signals to control your urges to poop. Usually this isn't a problem because you've got your bowel program routine—although the frequency depends on the individual—but you can still have accidents on rare occasions, particularly if there's a difference in your diet. In this case, I imagine it had something to do with eating too much fresh tomato and corn. Either way, it was about to happen right here on the beach-house couch and in front of my family and our friends. I started to panic, looking quickly around the room to figure out what to do. My eyes settled on Jody. I trusted him. For the past two summers, he'd spent a lot of time helping to take care of me. He'd know what to do, and better yet, he'd be low-key about it since he was never one for making a big scene about anything.

"Hey, Jody," I said, as casually as I could. "Come 'ere."

Jody got up from his chair and came toward me. As he got closer, I motioned for him to lean down so that I could whisper to him.

"I'm having a bowel movement. Get me outta here," I said.

A flash of panic flickered across his face, but he acted instantly, scooping me up off the couch and carrying me toward the bedroom.

"What's up?" Mom called after us.

"Nothing, Mom," Jody said. "Just helping Mark with something." He was walking as fast as he could. Unfortunately, with each step my body bounced in his arms, creating pressure on my bowels and causing the poop to start to flow. I was pooping in my shorts as my brother carried me through the house, and there wasn't anything either of us could do about it.

"Hurry," I said, but I knew that Jody didn't need any convincing. He knew exactly what was happening and was walking as fast as he could.

By the time we reached the bedroom, my shorts and underwear were soaked, and the smell of poop surrounded us. Jody gently laid me on the bed and started to pull my shorts off. There was poop everywhere.

"Go get a towel or something," I said.

He walked into the bathroom and came back with three or four towels. He scooted them under me and then quietly, methodically, worked to clean me up. He took my shorts and underwear and wrapped them up tightly in a towel without bothering to clean them out. Then he carried me into the bathroom, sat me in chair in the tub, and cleaned me up, washing the remaining remnants of poop down the drain. Neither of us spoke.

As he was helping me pull on clean underwear and shorts, I looked at him and saw that he was crying.

"Hey, I'm sorry…" I started, but then I realized that I was crying too.

"No, man, this is not your fault," Jody insisted. "You couldn't help it." He hugged me. He was crying harder now. "This, this whole thing… it sucks. It just sucks. and there's not a thing we can do about it," he choked out.

We continued to cry, then Jody let go of me and got up from the bed. He walked over to where he had laid the towel with the dirty clothes and picked up the pile. I expected him to take it into the bathroom, but instead, he started to head toward the door.

"What're you doing?" I asked.

"I'm getting rid of these," he said, walking quickly out the door.

I heard the back door open and then close. I looked out the window to see Jody walking with determination toward the beach, the clothes and towel wadded up into a ball in his hands. He walked all the way up to the shoreline and stopped. He stared out across the water and took a deep breath. Then, with one great, graceful thrust, he hurled the ball through the air and into the deep blue sea.

LACK OF FOCUS

After the incident at the beach, I realized I wasn't happy with my life. I was an almost twenty-one-year-old guy who was living with his parents. I wasn't going to school, I didn't have any goals or plans, and I had to rely on people to do my personal stuff like bathing, dressing, and pooping. And while I had this great new van, I couldn't go anywhere on my own because I hadn't learned to drive yet. I was dependent on people to drive me, but most of my friends were off at college, and I didn't want to bug my mom and Jody for a ride all the time. Needless to say, I didn't go many places. This was hard for a guy who had always stayed busy. I'm not saying I was Type A, but I always had something going on, whether it was playing basketball with my friends or working as a lifeguard. And even after my injury, I stayed pretty busy in rehab. Certainly, Mom had done her best to keep me occupied once I got home, but she could only do so much. I was going a little stir crazy with all of this free time on my hands.

I was also keenly aware that I didn't have a girlfriend, unlike most of my friends. I'd gone through high school without dating anyone, too scared to ask anyone out, including Janet Fitch, the girl that every guy had a crush on. By the time I got to college, I had finally started to date a little. Actually, that sounds too active and intentional on my part. I should instead say that I allowed myself to be paired up via blind dates or invitations to Sadie Hawkins dances. While none of these ended in long-lasting relationships, I did discover that some women might actually be attracted to me—a complete revelation and big boost for my confidence. Eventually, I even gathered up the nerve to ask a woman out all by myself. Her nickname was "Mouse" —I don't remember her real name—and we connected over a shared love of sports and The Beach Boys. We ended up dating for about four or five months—my longest-running relationship at the time—until I was injured. After I got out of rehab, Mouse had come to visit me. It was an awkward meeting, and I finally ended the relationship, realizing that we hadn't been together long enough for either of us to feel the need to try to make this work. Plus, my self-esteem was a bit of a mess at the time; these were not the makings of a healthy relationship.

I was getting used to the new way that my body looked, felt, and worked, though I still didn't like it. Because my legs couldn't move, my muscles were starting to atrophy, losing the strength and shape that had come with years and years of running, basketball, playing tennis, and other activities. This was a bitter pill to swallow. I found myself feeling self-conscious and tried to stop, realizing that negative body issues were part of what had gotten me here in the first place. But it's hard when you see people looking at you because you're different. The staring thing gets old quick.

I didn't have many outlets for my growing frustration. One night, Dad and I were sitting in the downstairs den. Mom had fixed dinner for us—ham, macaroni and cheese, salad, and rolls—but then had gone off to take a much-needed break while Dad and I ate dinner and watched The Bob Newhart Show. During a commercial break, Dad took a bite of the macaroni and cheese and made a face.

"Ah, heck," he said, "she did it again."

"What?"

"She cooked the macaroni and cheese too long, so now the cheese is hard and gummy. She always does that!" he said, looking disgusted.

Mom was actually a really good cook and worked hard to make great meals for us. I knew Dad was looking for a reason to pick at her. "No, she doesn't," I said.

He looked up, surprised. "Yes, she does," he insisted. "She did the same thing the last time she made macaroni and cheese."

I could feel myself getting angry. "Dad! Knock it off! Stop picking on Mom. You do it all the time," I said.

"No, I don't."

"Yes, Dad, you do. You pick on her and you criticize her, and I'm tired of it. Really sick of it."

"Well, sometimes she doesn't think about what she's doing, and she makes mistakes. I'm just pointing 'em out to her," he replied.

"But you act as if you never make mistakes. You act as if you always do the right thing, and she's the only one who ever makes mistakes. But you make mistakes too, Dad. You're not perfect."

Dad studied me carefully, seeming to sense that this argument was not about Mom and her overcooked macaroni and cheese. "Mark, calm down," he said. "I didn't mean to upset you."

"No, Dad, I will not calm down! I won't! I'm tired of this, and I've had it!"

I set my plate on the table next to me, wheeled around, and rolled into my room, slamming the door behind me. I sat, breathing heavily, feeling tears slide down my cheeks. I knew what Dad knew. This was not about Mom's cooking or even about how Dad treated her. This was me being angry about my situation, about having to live with my parents instead of a college dorm, of spending my days doing puzzles and archery rather than going to class and hanging out with my friends. This was about the anger that was there just under the surface. I knew the only person who could handle it was my dad. He understood anger. He understood having to adjust to the curveballs that life throws your way. He understood loss.

Chapter 11

Making a Commitment to Service

In those days, I was watching a lot of television. I had never watched a lot of TV before my accident. I was usually hanging out with my friends or playing some sort of sport. But after my accident, watching television became a primary way to pass the time and be entertained. By then, most of my friends were away at school, although a few of them still lived locally and would come over. Plus, the doctors had said that I couldn't spend all my time in the wheelchair because it would put too much pressure on my butt and possibly cause pressure sores. Periodically, my parents would help me get into bed so that I could lay down. Thus, watching the television became a way of passing the time, especially since I didn't like to read. Over time, I developed an interest in a variety of shows, although I particularly loved *All in the Family*, *Hawaii Five-O*, and *Sanford and Son*. I ended up watching so much TV that I got a gig with Neilsen to monitor commercials. They would send me a schedule for when certain commercials were supposed to appear, and I kept a record of whether they were shown and when. It was the network's way of making sure the local stations were airing the commercials according to schedule. In my head, it justified the amount of television that I was watching and provided a small amount of money for my rainy day fund.

One night, I was watching *Ironside*, one of my favorite shows. Raymond Burr, who would go on to become most noted for his role as Perry Mason, played the part of Robert Ironside, a shrewd, twenty-year veteran detective for the San Francisco Police Department. Ironside had been shot and paralyzed by a sniper, but he continued to investigate and solve crimes from his wheelchair using a really great modified police truck, and he always got the bad guy. The show was groundbreaking, both because its main character had a disability and because the show's message was that the character could go on with life as usual, even with a disability. Although I'd been a fan of the show before my injury, in those off moments when I happened to catch an episode, now that I was also using a wheelchair, it was cool to see someone with a disability portrayed on TV, especially in such a positive light. Ironside was making the most of his life, and I liked that.

During a commercial break, an announcer began talking about Billy Graham, our hometown hero, and the fact that he was coming to Charlotte to host a crusade. The ad was filled with images of people looking ecstatic as Billy preached with his familiar southern drawl that invited you in to sit awhile with him and Jesus as you drank lemonade. It showed pictures of people flocking to the stage to give their lives to Christ and being prayed over by Billy and his team members. It featured brief testimonies of people whose lives had been changed by the experience. The announcer reported that the crusade would be held April 5–9, 1972, and that a special service for youth would be held that Friday, when Billy would be preaching on "Hope for the Young and Searching." By the time *Ironside* came back on, I was no longer paying attention. I was already envisioning myself at the crusade, sitting and listening to Billy. I was young. I was searching. "I need to be at that crusade," I thought.

It was getting close to a year since my accident, and my parents still hadn't gone back to church. They were both still traumatized, but more to the point, they still felt like God was to blame for what had happened to me. Dad, in particular, could get pretty riled up about the fact that God had broken his promise, as if he had entered into some sort of divine gentleman's agreement. This was a bit disconcerting for me. My parents had gone to church pretty faithfully. They were always off to some church meeting or activity or Wednesday-night dinner. It was part of who they were and part of who we were as a family. It was weird to be in their house and not have anywhere to go on Sunday morning. It was even stranger to have everyone act as if this was all a matter of routine when it wasn't. Church members would come by, and my parents were always glad to see them. Whenever the subject of coming back to church came up, they would politely explain that they had some issues to work out with God right now and weren't quite ready to come back. End of discussion.

I wasn't going to church either, though not because I was part of their boycott. I was still at the point in my life where I went to church because my parents did, if they did. I hadn't really started to develop my own spiritual identity. I still had regular conversations with God when I was on my own at night, still wrestled with the fact that I had a disability and that life had taken a major detour from the path I had planned to follow. But otherwise, I didn't really know what I thought about God, and I wasn't quite sure where I stood with him. Hopefully, Billy could help me sort it out.

The billboard outside the Charlotte Coliseum and auditorium announcing the crusade...and an upcoming Elvis concert

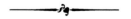

On the day of the crusade, Dad dropped me off at the Coliseum, and I did my best to merge into the crowd of people who were making their way past the fountains that lined the entrance. It was slow going. I was pushing myself in my manual chair, which was never a fast process, and there was a boatload of people, mostly my age, mostly fresh faced and eager for a spiritual experience. As I entered the Coliseum, one of the ushers pointed me toward the front, where there was a section reserved for people with disabilities, within about twenty feet of the stage. Going to concerts, I'd always wanted first-row seats, though this wasn't really what I'd had in mind. I gradually made my way toward the cluster of people in wheelchairs and found a parking spot. Around me, people were praying, reading their Bibles, talking, or singing along with the music that was playing on the loudspeakers. The energy in the room was made up of anticipation and hope, and probably a little anxiety. Coming to meet the Lord under these conditions was pretty awesome. I was certainly feeling butterflies in the pit of my stomach.

After a while, Cliff Barrows, Graham's favorite song leader, came up on stage to lead the choir and the crowd through a number of well-chosen hymns. The crowd started cheering and clapping, grateful for the start of the crusade. The choir began singing "Just As I Am" as people raised their arms in ecstasy, closed their eyes, and began singing the familiar verses. After several more hymns, Barrow introduced one of the pastors of a local church and invited him to address the crowd. I knew this was a trademark of the Graham crusades. Billy was not just into saving souls and then heading on to the next town. He was also about infrastructure, recognizing that those newly won souls would need local churches and a community to support them. He understood what a boon his crusades were to the attendance of local churches. He always invited local church leaders to help plan and lead the crusades, pray with people during the altar calls to begin to connect with the new converts, and provide a study guide and information about local churches as people were leaving. It was an approach that was both considerate and respectful of the people and community. I thought that was cool.

After the pastor spoke, Beverly Shea took the stage, and it was then that the energy of the crowd ascended to a whole new level. Beverly, a

Grammy-Award-winning baritone known as "America's beloved gospel singer," traveled regularly with Graham. Although he was more of an icon for older generations, the youth in the building seemed just as excited to hear him sing such favorites as "How Great Thou Art" and "The Wonder of It All." As the last notes played and Beverly sat down, Barrows introduced Billy, who walked onto the stage with his Bible tucked under his arm, wearing that homely, deferential, "aw shucks" grin that made him so likable and so trustworthy. Yet, at the same time, he stood with a confidence that owned not only the stage but the entire auditorium and everyone in it.

Billy started with general remarks to the crowd before opening up his Bible and reading several passages. He then began to preach and tell stories. He was funny, self-deprecating, but authoritative, and though by now he was fifty-four years old he was still able to tell stories and preach in a style that was accessible to the youth in the crowd. Billy started out speaking in carefully measured, conversational tones, then gradually gained speed, intensity and volume. With each word I was right there with him, feeling the growing restlessness in the pit of my stomach.

He started off telling the story of Daniel, the Old Testament prophet. Daniel and three of his friends, all members of the Jewish nobility, were only in their early teens when they were captured by the Babylonians after the destruction of Jerusalem. Because of their dashing good looks and sharp minds, they were chosen for the dubious honor of being advisors to the royal court. The Babylonians were hopeful that they could integrate the boys into the new culture and raise them to worship the pagan gods and otherwise participate in pagan culture. But things didn't quite work out the way the Babylonians had planned. Though traumatized by the separation from his family and homeland, Daniel didn't give up, instead developing a successful career interpreting dreams. Neither did he and his friends give in to the demands of their captors. When they refused to worship the pagan gods, Daniel's three friends, who had been given the Babylonian names Shadrach, Meshach, and Abednego, were thrown into the furnace before being miraculously saved. Daniel was later thrown into the now-famous lion's den, but he, too, was saved by a miracle, causing the king to declare that everyone worship "the God of Daniel."

Daniel, Billy explained, had made his own decision to follow God, whereas many youth today believe in God only because their parents do.

"When will you make your own decision to follow God?" he challenged.

"Good point," I thought. Until now, I had been following in my parents' footsteps. I hadn't made my own personal commitment to Christ. Score one for Billy.

Billy went on to talk about how Daniel was also committed to living his life for God no matter what the circumstance, no matter what happened to him. According to Billy, Daniel stayed true to God and true to himself, never giving up in the face of trauma, and never letting the expectations and practices of the rest of the world influence him. He was even brave enough to stand up to the Babylonian king when the consequence was death by lion. Yet many young people today, he said, wander aimlessly, giving in to peer and other social pressures to conform and live according to someone else's expectations and standards. In the end, they never really learn who they are meant to be, which is behind a lot of the problems in our society.

"Who are you searching for?" Billy asked the crowd. "Who are you living for? I am asking you tonight to enlist in the army of Christ. I am asking you to give yourself to him and let him change your life. And I believe if we can get enough young people to Jesus Christ, that we can go out and change Mecklenburg County. We can change North Carolina if we can get enough young people living for and dedicated to Christ."

Barrows stood up and led the choir in a quiet hymn. As he did, Billy said, "As the choir sings, I invite you to come and commit your life to Christ." He then began to pray, asking God to work in the hearts of these young people and encouraged us to come forward. Slowly, gradually, people began to stand up and make their way toward the stage. Some were tentative about it, while others walked purposefully up to pray with one of the many volunteers who now stood in front of the stage. While Billy prayed and people walked by me, I sat thinking about what he had said. I knew it was time for me to make my own decision to believe in Jesus Christ. That was a given. But I was also really taken by what Billy had said about Daniel. He had lived his life fully no matter what happened, even after a huge trauma. Had I been doing that? Since my accident, not really. I'd just been getting by. And Daniel hadn't let all those nasty social pressures get to him, even when his life was threatened. Meanwhile, I'd spent my life worrying about what others thought about me and whether I fit in. Maybe it was time for me to give that up too. I wondered. Perhaps Billy was helping me understand how to do that, by believing in God in a way that was meaningful, purposeful, and which helped me focus on what mattered, ignoring all the extraneous stuff. It seemed to all make sense. Those butterflies in my stomach were really doing dances now.

I started to make my way slowly to the stage, again trying to merge with the crowd that had gathered at its base. Luckily, since I was sitting in front, I didn't have far to go. Eventually, a volunteer approached me and offered to pray with me. As he kneeled down and began to pray, I closed my eyes and silently committed my life to God in a way that was new and different. And mine.

Score two for Billy. And God.

A Fork in the Road

I'd like to say that after the crusade, everything fell into place for me and that I accepted my life with a disability and felt comfortable with who I was and had a clear sense of purpose in my life. I'd like to say that, but it wouldn't be true.

The crusade had been a watershed moment in terms of my spirituality. I now felt a direct connection with God, one that was my own. I was beginning to explore what that meant for me, particularly as I worked on the Bible studies that the Crusade staff had given us after the event. Moreover, I was working hard to conquer my self-consciousness and get past other people's prejudices about my disability. That part was going to take some time.

The piece that was still missing for me concerned living life fully. I knew I wanted to be like Daniel and not let any obstacles, real or imagined, get in my way. But I wasn't sure what that meant for me.

I was spending much of my time at the rehab hospital. I had to go for outpatient therapy, where I continued to work on building my upper body strength and improving the function of my hands, wrists, and arms. I also went to see Dr. Asreal, my urologist. While in the hospital, I would make it a point to stop by and greet the many staff members who had helped me through my rehab and some of the patients who were still there.

I had also started working there as a volunteer, calling bingo every Wednesday for both current and former patients. I can't say that I was much of a bingo man prior to my injury. And it wasn't that I caught bingo fever after my injury either. But it was a good rehab activity, particularly for people who needed to work on their dexterity. Trying to pick up those little chips and put them on a specific square can be a real challenge if you don't have full use of your fingers or wrists. Also, it was a great way to network with other people with injuries. It was better than a support group, which the hospital employees were always trying to start. There, you had to talk about your problems and share your feelings, but bingo was like our own version of a support group. You could come and hang out with people. You could work on your dexterity. You could laugh at my jokes and shoot the breeze. And you could even shout out "bingo!" when you needed a release. In the end, you left feeling better than when you came. In my mind, that seemed like a better way to do group therapy.

I grew to love my time at the hospital. I loved that I didn't have to explain myself to others and that I could get anywhere I needed to go without encountering an obstacle. It felt like home, with a very large and diverse family. I started to wonder if this was where God wanted me to be. But I wasn't sure even of this. Since the crusade, I'd been feeling a growing restlessness inside. I was sure that God was working in me, but I didn't know exactly what that meant; this was the first time I'd been in tune with my spiritual life. I was still toddling around like a two-year-old trying to find my way in the world.

Two months after seeing Billy Graham, I woke up on a summer morning feeling a bit on edge. I wasn't very talkative at breakfast and went through my morning workout with less enthusiasm than usual. I wasn't really sure what was bugging me, but I could tell that something was off kilter. After lunch, I headed to the hospital to volunteer. When I got there, I decided to stop by Diane's office. I propelled myself down the hallway and into her office to find her sitting at her desk.

We chatted for a bit about some of the new patients and about an outing that she was planning. I talked about the progress I was making in outpatient therapy and the Bible study lessons I'd been working on since the crusade. I was talking fast and offering too much detail. I was starting to feel that edge turning to anxiety, and I wanted to cover it up with words. But it didn't matter because Diane was one step ahead of me. When I stopped to take a breath she made her move.

"So what's next?"

"I don't know. Professional Bingo caller?"

She laughed, but didn't budge. "No, seriously, Mark, what are you going to do next?"

"I was thinking about going back to school. I've missed a year, so I'll have to retake some of my core classes, but then I've got two years to finish."

"That's true. Do you think you'll go back to East Carolina?"

"Probably not," I said, though it hadn't even occurred to me to leave Charlotte. At least not right away. "I probably need to stick around here for a while. My parents have done all that work to get their house ready for me. Oogie's getting ready to come home from school, and Jody's been helping out. I'll probably go to Piedmont College or somewhere local." I took a deep breath. My anxiety was rising.

"That sounds good," Diane said. "What do you think you want to study? Are you going to continue to study business?"

I breathed in. "Well, I'm actually thinking of making a change."

"Really? What kind of change?"

"Well, I was thinking about studying counseling. You know, maybe get a degree in counseling instead." This time, I took a deep breath. That anxiety was not going away. I knew Diane was watching me.

"Interesting," she said. "What would you do with a counseling degree?"

"Well, I was thinking I might come back here and work. You know, I'm pretty good at talking with the other patients. They seem to respond well. And I think I could help them, especially since I'm injured, and I've been through rehab and everything they're going through. I think they would like being able to talk with someone who's been there. You know?"

I smiled, trying to appear confident, hoping that the anxiety, which had now turned to panic, didn't show.

She paused, studying me carefully.

"That's a great idea, Mark. It's true you'd make a great counselor. It's commendable that you want to help others like yourself who'll be going through rehab. But you're not ready."

I stared at her. I tried to inhale deeply, but now there were only short, shallow breaths available. The panic was taking up too much space.

"You've got to grow up, in a manner of speaking. You've got to go out and live in the world and really feel what it's like to live with a disability. You need to experience what it's like to use a wheelchair and get around town and deal with people's attitudes and find your place in the world. You need to figure out who you are and where you fit in. Until you've figured that out, and until you've come full circle and adjusted to life in society, outside the comfort of this hospital, you won't have much to say that's of any value to someone in your position right now."

I tried to breathe, but there was no breath. I tried to speak, but there were no words. Instead, there were only tears as my body began to release the grief and panic and fear that now spilled forth into Diane's office. I sobbed, my shoulders heaving uncontrollably. At first I tried to fight it, but then I understood that this had been building up inside of me for more than a year, and now that I finally had a release for it I needed to let it run its course.

Diane waited patiently while I cried. At one point, she got up and brought over a box of tissues, setting it down next to me. After a few minutes, I looked up at her. When I did, I saw a mixture of relief and empathy in her expression.

"That's been building up in there for a good while I think, hasn't it?" she asked.

"Yeah," I said. The tears were still coming.

"What are you feeling?"

I paused to wipe my eyes with a tissue. "I'm scared. I don't know what I'm going to do with my life," I said.

"Well, what were your goals before you were injured?" she asked.

"I was going to be a salesman like my dad, and I was going to get married and have a family and all those other things that adults do."

"You can still do all of those things. You can do anything you want except walk up and down stairs."

"But I don't know how. I don't know how I'm going to do all of that in a wheelchair."

"It's about making adjustments. You can do all those thing; you simply have to be creative and willing to make some modifications."

I looked at her. She could tell I didn't believe her.

"Mark, you've done great up to now. You've worked hard and come a long way, farther than a lot of people. And I know you want to stay here. I know it's safe and you do well and know who you are here. But you can't stay here. You've got to go and figure things out for a while. Then you can come back and share what you've learned with other patients."

I breathed in and noticed that I felt calmer and more open.

"I'll do my best," was all I could say.

"I know you will. Keep me posted, and let me know how you're doing."

"I will," I said, and started to wheel myself toward the door. I paused and turned back toward her.

"Diane, thanks. Thanks for everything," I said.

"You're welcome, Mark. I'm glad I could help. Keep me posted because I can't wait to hear about what you do next," she said.

I smiled and headed out the door.

SECTION 2

BECOMING AWARE

"An individual has not started living until he can rise above the narrow confines of his individualistic concerns to the broader concerns of all humanity."

—Martin Luther King Jr.,
"Conquering Self-Centeredness," 1957

BACK TO SCHOOL

Not long after my talk with Diane, I was having dinner with my family when Oogie made an announcement.

"I'm not going back to Baptist College this fall," he said. "I don't think I'm built to be a full-time student," he explained. "I think I'd rather go to Central Piedmont Community College part time and get a job."

"You mean Centipede?" I joked, referring to the name for the college used by locals.

Oogie laughed and nodded.

"That sounds good," Dad said. "You should talk to Joe. He'd probably be willing to set you up again at Decca." My parents were very close to Joe and Carol Voynow, who owned a distributing company for Decca Records. Growing up, Joe always had a summer job waiting for me and my brothers. This didn't work well for me as I preferred something the outdoors. Oogie and Jody, on the other hand, both worked there for multiple summers. Oogie ended up making a career of working for the company for eighteen years.

"I was thinking that, too," said Oogie.

"You planning on starting this fall?" I asked.

"Yep."

I hesitated. "Well, what if I go with you?" They all looked at me. "I've been thinking about it, and I think I'm ready to go back to school. It's time."

My parents looked at each other. "Seems like a good idea," Mom said.

"Yeah, maybe you might actually apply yourself this time around," said Dad.

"Oogie and I could ride together," I said. "I'd just have to have a schedule that's similar to his. And I'd have to take a lot of the basic courses over because of my grades at ECU."

"What would you study?" Dad asked.

"I think I want to be a guidance counselor and work with junior-high kids. You know, that's such an important time for kids, right as they're hitting puberty. Their bodies are changing, and they're so awkward and insecure about themselves. I think I'd like to see if I could help kids avoid all that ugly stuff, or at least get through it a little better." I turned to Oogie. "Would you be up for riding together?"

"You bet."

School was never my strength. I always preferred to talk to my friends instead of doing work, just as I always chose to play basketball rather than finish my homework. This may have been because of my social nature, but it also could have been because I wasn't inclined toward academics. Of the three boys in our family, Jody was the one with the natural academic talent and good grades, while Oogie and I struggled to get by in school.

I did pretty well in math, but I had a really hard time reading. The comprehension piece was difficult—I'd read a passage but couldn't tell you much about what I'd read—but so was the actual task of reading words on a page. Words didn't flow for me the way they did for my classmates. This made reading out loud in class a complex trauma. I'd do anything to avoid being called on in class. "Please, Lord, please don't make me read out loud," I'd pray fervently, begging God to spare me the humiliation. Other subjects, like social studies and history—anything that required reading—were difficult for me too. My report cards revealed the difficulty time after time.

Lucky for me, during my eighth-grade year, I was in the right place at the right time. As the school year began, my parents received a brochure and letter from the principal. He explained that the governor was developing a progressive educational program that was designed to help eighth grade students "of average or above-average potential who, for one reason or another, are below grade-level in basic skills—reading, writing, and arithmetic. These are students of promise, whose intelligence well qualifies them for success in high school, college, and later life, but whose academic achievement up to this point does not." In other words, it was for us underachievers. The brochure went on to explain that the school was intended "to remedy educational deficiencies and to equip its students with the skills and attitudes they need for success in school and adult life." The North Carolina Advancement School, as it was called, had been developed by John Ehle, Special Assistant to the Governor for Educational and Cultural Affairs. Ehle went on to establish the North Carolina Film Board, the North Carolina School of Science and Math, and other innovative programs for the time. The residential school was located in Winston-Salem, an hour away from our house. The inaugural class was slated to begin in January, 1965, the winter of my eighth-grade year, and the principal thought I might be a good candidate for such a program.

It didn't take long for my parents to consider this invitation. They both agreed that a little discipline would go a long way in getting me to focus and improve my performance at school. They sat me down, showed me the letter and brochure, and explained whey attending the Advancement School would be good for me. They weren't going to push me into it and gave me time to consider whether I wanted to go. I thought about it for a bit. It was no secret that I could do better at school. I was tired of the anxiety at report-card time. Up until now, I had been able to slide by, but it was getting harder and harder to do that. I was ready to try anything. Plus, I was more than a little intrigued by the fact that this invitation suggested that I was a "student of promise." I'd never thought of myself like that and was curious to see if there was something there or if it was simply a good sales pitch. Though I worried about missing my friends and the start of track season, I decided to sign on to this new adventure. My parents were excited and secretly relieved.

The Advancement School turned out to be a great thing for me. The teacher-student ratio was smaller, and I thrived under the additional attention and efforts to keep me focused on my work. The school used a reward system to encourage us. After several weeks, I had earned a jacket and other cool things. It felt like an extended camp. We slept in bunk beds and had time to hang out, play basketball, and watch movies. We all shared the camaraderie that comes from being together on an adventure for an extended period of time.

The bonus was I no longer dreaded progress reports. I worked hard and excelled. I felt confident in my efforts. The reports from my teachers were laudatory and positive. Several even wrote that I handled myself well in front of a group and was a "natural leader." My parents were pleased with the progress reports as was my principal.

I left the Advancement School with a mixture of curiosity and trepidation, wondering whether I could go back to my old school and do well. I was worried that I couldn't. In the end, I did better. My teachers noticed some progress, though not enough to produce the same glowing reports I had received from teachers at the Advancement School. I went back to being a slightly less-than-average student, making it clear that I thrived only under certain conditions. I hoped that these conditions were in place for me to return to school after my injury. They seemed to be, particularly given that I was determined to make life better. For the first time in my life, I was excited about going back to school. I had a sense that enthusiasm would make a difference this time around.

As predicted, I was going to have to retake basic courses at Centipede. My 1.9 GPA at East Carolina University hadn't really impressed the administration officials, and they didn't accept many of my transfer credits. Thus, my schedule at Centipede was all about the basics. I was able to piece together a schedule that fit Oogie's schedule. Together, we'd ride to campus, which was small and easy enough to navigate in a wheelchair. Oogie would push me to my classroom, then after class, I'd wait for him to come get me or meet him in the parking lot.

My grades were much better this go round, and once the semester was over, I had enough credits to transfer to the University of North Carolina at Charlotte in January, where I could really get to work on my major in guidance counseling. By then, Oogie had decided, after three attempts, that he was not the college type. He made the liberating decision to hang it up and see where he could best make his mark. He moved to Virginia Beach, where he worked full-time for Decca Records, keeping the military bases stocked with the latest tunes. I was sorry to see him go but glad he would now have the chance to find his own niche.

With Oogie leaving, I needed a new chauffeur. My friend, Jim, reconnected me with Jan, who had gone to my high school and hung out at the pool where I was a lifeguard. A student at UNCC, she readily agreed to take over driving duties. Jan was a vivacious, free-spirited, Italian girl who came from a family of five kids, a rare thing in the South. Growing up in such a large family, Jan had learned to talk fast in order to be heard and would pepper me with rapid-fire questions as we drove the forty-minute route to school each day.

"How do you write with a pen, turn the pages on a book? If you could drive, how would you do it?" Jan was always curious and never shy. I loved her friendly, eager spirit and was always willing to answer her questions.

Jan was a tiny thing who couldn't have weighed more than one hundred pounds. The first day she helped me down the ramp of my van, I thought for sure I was going to go careening into the car next to us; easing me gradually down a ramp in my hunk of a chair could be a challenge. Both of my brothers had mastered it, but they were built for it. Jan was not. But somehow, we both managed to make it to class and back home every day without any major mishaps.

Chapter 14

Learning to Drive Again

For Christmas of 1972, my parents surprised me with hand controls for the van.

"We think it's time you learned to drive," said Dad. He and Lloyd Threatt figured out how to install them in the van. The next Saturday, Dad drove me out to an abandoned airport. The wide-open tarmacs allowed plenty of room for error. It had been over two years since I'd driven a car, and this was the first time in my life I'd used hand controls, which were basically sticks that allowed me to use hands, rather than feet, to push the brakes and accelerator. Dad lifted me out of my chair, swung me over, and plopped me into the driver's seat. It was weird to be sitting at the steering wheel again after all this time. I practiced grabbing the hand controls a couple of times—pull to accelerate, push to brake—before Dad turned the ignition and the van's motor began to rumble.

To anyone watching, I'm sure it would have looked like a teenager's first time before the wheel of a stick-shift car, with all the fits and starts. After about thirty minutes, however, I started to get the hang of it, and by the end of the hour, I was driving up and down the runways without incident. Rounding corners proved to be the trickiest part of driving; my limited dexterity prevented me from making the single, fluid motions that create smooth turns. Those jerky turns would become part of my signature driving style.

Now that I could drive myself, Dad removed the driver's seat from the van so that I could roll up to the steering wheel in my wheelchair. However, my chair made me taller, which meant that I had to duck to keep from hitting the ceiling, and even then I was viewing the road at an odd angle from the top of the windshield.

"I think it's time we got this van modified to fit you," my dad said, laughing. He and Lloyd started searching for a body shop that could modify the van. These days, there's an entire industry dedicated to modifying vehicles for people who used wheelchairs. In 1973, however, very few shops knew how to do this, and the ones that did weren't in Charlotte. However, the two finally found a couple of body shop mechanics who were willing to participate in this grand experiment. Dad and Lloyd started things off by installing a lift on the van so that I wouldn't have to go up and down a ramp anymore. Instead, I could push my chair onto the platform, then push a button that caused the mechanized lift to raise me up to the level of van and swing me in. It turned out that was the easy part of the modification process.

To give me enough headroom, the body shop guys cut out a section of the floor of the van that was just under the driver's seat, and installed a lowered floor, creating a kind of trough. In order to drive, I had to remove my footrests, then roll my chair up to the driver's area and hold onto the side of the van as my chair slid down into the trough, otherwise I'd start sliding out of my chair. The real trick, however, was getting out. The trough was deep enough that it took some strength to get my chair out. I couldn't simply back out of it. Instead, I'd have to rock my body back and forth to create some momentum, then hang onto the side of the van and swing my chair up and out of the trough, which didn't always work. As a result, I found myself looking for hills to park on whenever possible; that way, I had gravity on my side when it came to getting out of the trough. Once I was safely out of the trough and ready to leave the van, I'd use a pulley system my dad and I created to get my feet back on the footrests. When all was said and done, it took roughly ten minutes for me to exit the van.

Hills also came in handy when it came to closing the sliding door. This van didn't have a door that closed automatically, so Oogie tied a rope to the handle that enabled me to close and open it from the inside. Since that wasn't always easy to do, I got creative. One day, my friend, Skeet, was visiting, and Mom asked us to run to the store. When we got to my van, Skeet opened the passenger door and got in while I rode up the lift and rolled over to the steering wheel. As I was working with the pulley, Skeet turned toward the side door, which I'd left open.

"Do you want me to close the door?" he asked.

"Nah," I said. "Get in and watch!"

Skeet looked at me questioningly, but sat back down and waited. I revved up the van and backed out of the driveway, then gradually began to pick up speed. I traveled about twenty feet before suddenly hitting the brakes. Together we watched as the door slid closed with a loud "ca-thunk!" I looked at Skeet and smiled mischievously. He started laughing and shaking his head.

"Son of a gun!" he said. "That is just like you to figure that out!"

Sitting in my thunderbolt-orange van

BECOMING A COUNSELOR

In 1973, Congress passed major legislation designed to address the specific needs and rights of Americans with disabilities. Called the Rehabilitation Act—or the Rehab Act, for short—it started with employment in an effort to help people with disabilities get jobs. But Section 504 of the Act took things even further by declaring that "no otherwise qualified individual with a disability in the United States...shall, solely by reason of her or his disability, be excluded from the participation in, be denied the benefits of, or be subjected to discrimination" by any program receiving federal funds. This meant that people with disabilities had the right to access public spaces, such as libraries, schools, post offices, and airports, and that it was up to the property owner to make that happen. Passage of the Act marked the first time that we as a nation agreed that people with disabilities had civil rights worth protecting in the same way that blacks and women and people of other races and religions did, making the Rehab Act the cousin of the Civil Rights Act of 1964. It was a great moment, one that was worthy of much collective fanfare, but it was completely lost on me.

Now a senior with a full class load at the University of North Carolina at Charlotte, I was too busy to pay attention to events at the national level. Plus, my social life had picked back up, and I was also starting to volunteer a lot more at Charlotte Rehabilitation Hospital (CHR). I was still calling bingo and checking in on new and former patients. I enjoyed that connection with my peers. I liked being able to help others who were adjusting to a life with spinal-cord injury. Others noticed this as well. A Vocational Rehabilitation counselor who had an office at CRH approached me one day and asked me to start a support group at CRH for people with SCI.

"There's this whole group of people who could really benefit from getting together on a regular basis, and you'd do a great job of leading it," he said.

"Thanks," I said, "and I agree with you on the need for a support group, but I don't have time right now to lead it, especially since I'm getting ready to graduate and then start graduate school." The support group idea would have to wait, at least if it was going to involve me.

I was glad I passed on the support group. Once graduate school started, my life got even more hectic because the classes were harder and required more reading, which still was not easy. I had to do an internship and chose to serve as a counselor at a local junior high school. Being around all those gangly, insecure, hormone-driven kids, I felt completely in my element. I understood their awkwardness, their search for self, and their need to fit in. I could still relate to the pain of feeling like you didn't fit in, though now I understood it in a whole new way. The kids seemed to be comfortable with me as well as fascinated by my chair. Sometimes, the chair was even helpful in breaking the ice with the kids who were shy or working overtime to keep their distance. With it, I could crack jokes or tell my story or find some other way to establish some sense of trust. It also worked well because it placed me at eye level with some of them, unlike all of the other adults who towered over them. I sensed that working with these kids was the right career path for me.

My internship experience formed the basis for my master's thesis, which explored who or what makes the most effective counselor. Using extensive research and surveys, I looked at guidance counseling, rehab counseling, addiction counseling, and many other areas to test my theory and gather data. In the end, I concluded that the person who makes the most effective counselor is one who has "been there, done that," so to speak. It's the person who has struggled with addiction, survived a sexual assault, lived with a disability, or, in my case, still remembered what it was like to navigate the awkward years of adolescence. All of my research proved that people respond best to advice and support when it comes from someone who has intimate knowledge of the subject matter and can share his or her experiences. My thesis was very well received; not only was it published, but I was invited to fly to Canada to present it at a conference. Mom accompanied me and sat in the audience, proud of her son who had come so far from the Advancement School.

My career plans changed on a December afternoon, during one of my volunteer shifts at CRH. I was playing checkers in the common room with a recently injured patient when Mr. Thompson, the hospital administrator, came in and waved me over.

"Hey, Mark, can I talk to you in my office?" he asked.

"Sure," I said. Curious, I rolled down the hallway with him to his office, and once inside, waited to hear what he had to say.

"I wanted to let you know we've got a counseling position open here, and I wanted to ask you to consider taking it," he said.

"You know that I'm planning to be a guidance counselor and work with junior-high kids, right?"

"Sure, sure. And I certainly understand if that's what you really want to do. But I'm asking because I know that you would make a great counselor. I've seen the work you've done as a volunteer all these years. The patients respond to you better than they respond to most of the staff, and I know it's because they see that you have an injury too. You know exactly what they're going through. I'm confident that you'd be a great addition to our team here and would love it if you would consider working here."

"Can I think about it?"

"Absolutely. Why don't you take a few days to think about it and then let me know what you decide?"

For the next two days, I struggled to make a decision, going back and forth. I'd been so sure about my career path and sure that I should work with kids. I'd even started making a list of the schools where I most wanted to work. But this job offer felt right. Obviously, I loved working with people with disabilities; all my volunteer time was proof of that. I'd still be using the counseling skills I'd been honing in graduate school, which meant it wouldn't be a complete change in course. Plus, I couldn't believe how this job opportunity was being handed to me. Maybe this was what I was supposed to do with my life, and all of my life experiences had been leading up to this. "Perhaps this is where God wants me to be," I thought. Then I thought some more.

Three days after our initial meeting, I went into Mr. Thomas's office.

"I'll take the job," I said, smiling.

He stood up, looking both relieved and excited. "That's great news, Mark. I think you'll be a great asset."

Not the Problem

Settling into the new job, I found that I really liked working for CRH, and for the most part, I enjoyed working as a counselor. I liked being able to work with patients and knew that I could offer them what no other counselor at CRH could: my own experience with a disability. That meant a lot to people who were struggling with new injuries and having to carve out new identities that now included their disabilities. The job was easy. It felt like I was doing the same thing I'd been doing as a volunteer all these years, only now I got to hang out with people full time, and I had this title that gave me some added clout with the staff who had known me before as a patient.

Now that I was working at CRH, I finally had the time and space to start up that support group. I posted flyers around the hallways, visited current patients, and sent letters to former patients, inviting them all to the first meeting. We started out with eight people, then the next time we met we had twelve, but over time, it evened out to about five members who showed up on a regular basis. For the first couple of months the meetings were focused on letting the members talk about whatever was going on with them. They talked a lot about their feelings about being disabled, which usually meant depression, anger, fear, or even shame. And they described their roadblocks, those things that kept them from being able to do the things they once loved or to move forward in their lives, and how they couldn't get past them. It was the same thing I was hearing from the people I met with on an individual basis.

But over time, all this began to wear on me. I started to realize that while I could empathize with people and what they were feeling, in general, I didn't have a lot of patience for talking about feelings. I couldn't hack it when people wanted to complain just for the sake of complaining. It drove me nuts when anyone wanted to wallow in self-pity. It was fine to be sad or angry or scared, and I understood that many people were legitimately depressed and would need the help of a psychiatrist or other counselor to work through that. But I realized that I wasn't the right guy for that job.

In the midst of this process, however, I had another epiphany. I started to understand that a lot of my clients and peers were feeling shame or sadness or anger because they thought that by having a disability, they were the problem. They talked about being stared at and being condescended and being excluded. They were sad because they had lost friends or were treated differently by family members. They were frustrated when they were denied access to certain places and couldn't get jobs. As I listened to them, I began to understand that they weren't the problem. Instead, it was society that was the problem. It was the social attitudes that said that having a disability is somehow a bad thing or shameful that was the problem. It was the prejudice and intolerance that caused people with disabilities to feel angry, depressed, and alienated. Up until now, I'd been too busy with my own efforts to assimilate into society, feeling like it was up to me to make everybody feel okay about my disability and that it was my problem to figure out how to overcome inaccessible buildings and other obstacles I encountered each day. But now I got it. Now I could really feel the injustice of it all. And now I wanted to do something about it. Not only that, I wanted other people with disabilities to do something about it too. Sitting and complaining about it wasn't going to do any of us any good. It was going to take action to shift this paradigm. Luckily, my parents had set good examples.

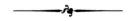

Carmel Presbyterian Church came into existence right in the middle of the Civil Rights movement, which made the process of starting a new church—one that was responsive to the needs of its community—very interesting. Living in the South, we were right in the thick of it. Already, Martin Luther King Jr. had been preaching in Atlanta, and Rosa Parks had refused to give up her bus seat in Montgomery. But the issue grew more intense and closer to home when four young African-American college students sat down at the Woolworth's lunch counter in Greensboro, North Carolina, an hour and a half away from us. They sat peacefully at the counter where only white people were allowed to eat, knowing this seemingly small act of defiance would signify their growing dissatisfaction with having to stand while eating. We watched with growing interest as the students showed up for a second day, then a third, and then a fourth, each time accompanied by more and more people, both for and against them. Ultimately, the protest was ended by a bomb scare, though within days, similar protests began showing up in neighboring cities, including ours.

Our minister was a young guy with a lot of energy and a great wit about him, a progressive thinker who was willing to take some risks. He spent time talking with people and really trying to capture the pulse of the neighborhoods that surrounded Carmel. Over time, he discovered that the community really needed another pre-school to accommodate the growing number of young families that were moving into town. On the surface, that seemed to be something that Carmel and its members could do. But there was more to it. Our pastor made it clear that if we were really going to meet the needs of the people who lived and worked around us, we needed to create a school that was integrated. Suddenly, the issue was no longer simple.

As an elder on the Session, the church's governing body, Dad helped make decisions about its direction and role as a new church in the community. Not surprisingly, he and his colleagues spent many a meeting discussing and debating this idea of an integrated school. They all understood the implications of opening up the church's doors to African-Americans, though they didn't agree on whether it should be done. Over time, word spread through the congregation that the minister—and even some members of the Session—wanted to set up an integrated school, which would most likely lead to an integrated congregation. Sides began to form. My parents supported the minister and were staunchly in favor of integrating both church and school. This wasn't because they had developed a close friendship with our pastor and his wife, but because they believed strongly in the need to treat everyone with dignity and respect, and saw the school's potential benefits to the community.

Late one evening, after several hours of debate on the subject, the Session cast its vote to determine whether or not to support the proposal for the integrated school. After all the votes were counted, the chairman announced that the Session had voted in favor of supporting the school by a margin of only one vote. It was a mixed victory for the school's supporters. While they got the school they felt so passionately about, there was now significant division within the congregation. But for my parents, the worst part was that many of the opponents blamed the minister for forcing integration onto the church. A few even went as far as heckling the minister and making life difficult for both him and his family. My parents could not abide seeing their minister and friend treated in such a way by fellow Christians, particularly when he was trying to do the right thing. They stayed as long as they could, doing their best to support him, but after a while, they left Carmel and began attending Sharon Presbyterian Church, which was within walking distance from our house.

I started to push back with my clients and the support-group members, trying to get them to own their own personal power for change. During one group meeting, several people were complaining about Eastland Mall, a new mall that was opening up to much fanfare. It was the largest mall in the state and the first one to feature a food court. The mall also included a movie theater. However, it had stairs leading down to the entrance and no ramp for wheelchair access.

"Those stinking stairs!" said Lee. "It makes me so mad! I wanted to see *The Deer Hunter*."

"Me, too! I wanted to see *The Promise*," said Debbie.

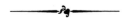

"I don't even understand how a new movie theater could be built with no access," said Lee.

"I know. It's really frustrating," added Madelyn.

I sat and listened, then took a deep, slow breath. "So what are we going to do about it?"

They stared at me.

"What do you think we should do?" asked Debbie.

"I'm asking you. What do you think we should do?" I countered.

"We could make them carry us down and up the stairs," suggested Gordon.

"That's true," I said.

"But we shouldn't have to," said Lee.

"Exactly," I said.

"Aren't there building codes that require them to include access?" asked Lee.

"Yep," I said.

"Why don't we report them to the city for code violations?" suggested Lee. I could tell he was starting to get excited.

"Sounds good," I agreed. "Are you volunteering for the job?"

He looked around at everyone. "Sure," Lee shrugged. "Why not?"

"Great!" I said.

Within days of our meeting, Lee had submitted a letter on behalf of our group to the City of Charlotte, asking them to address the theater's code violation. After a month had gone by with no response, we called the City but got passed from one employee to another, never getting a clear answer. We then sent a letter to both the City and the Eastland Mall management, asking for a ramp to be installed. Again, we waited for a response that never came. After making a second round of phone calls, we got a variety of responses.

"Yes, we've received your letter and are working on a response. Please check back in another week or two," said one mall employee.

"We're looking into your request to see what options are available and what the costs are," said another.

After more phone calls, we finally received a letter from Howard Phillips, the mall's manager, in which he announced that the mall was going through with plans to build a ramp. We were pleased but guarded; we were learning that we couldn't take them at their word until we saw actual results. Sure enough, three months later, there was neither a ramp nor any signs of construction of said ramp. When we called Mr. Phillips' office, he explained that the mall was waiting for the materials to be delivered.

"How long can that take?" asked Lee.

"Not that long," said Gordon.

We decided it was time for Plan B. And so it was that one Tuesday evening, nine of us showed up at the theater. Several reporters from local media showed up at the same time, thanks to our group's well-timed phone calls. The next day, the following article appeared in The Charlotte Observer:

> "'Wheel-In': Handicapped Want Ramp at Theater"
>
> Nine Charlotteans confined to wheelchairs conducted a "wheel-in" Tuesday night at the Eastland Mall Cinema theaters to demonstrate for a ramp for the handicapped.
>
> The nine, all members of the local chapter of the National Spinal-Cord Injury Foundation, rolled up to the theater entrance twenty minutes before show-time for "The Promise."
>
> Without assistance, there was no way for them to get down a flight of stairs into the lobby. They later got help from the mall and theater personnel.
>
> Mark Johnson, 27, of 4021 Rutherford Dr., president of the foundation's Metrolina chapter, said that was the point of the demonstration.

> Johnson said the paraplegics wanted to emphasize that no ramp for the handicapped had been built at the theaters despite a July, 1978 letter from mall manager Howard Phillips promising construction would begin "as soon as materials are delivered."
>
> "It's been a year and no ramp," said Johnson. "In the meantime they have built the new Sears & Roebuck store (at the mall)." Phillips was not available for comment.
>
> Without a ramp, paraplegics have to wait until someone can carry their wheelchairs down the steps, Johnson said. The lack of a ramp violates N. C. law, he said, and means wheelchair occupants could be trapped inside in a fire.
>
> Theater Manager Mike Malmstrom passed out tickets and told Johnson he would call for maintenance workers to help carry the wheelchairs down the stairs.
>
> Malmstrom refused to comment on the lack of a ramp. "That is the mall's responsibility, not the theater's," he said.
>
> County police officer J. H. Newsom, working off duty at the mall, Malmstrom, a mall maintenance worker, and a youngster lifted the nine chairs.

The article elicited a strong response from the community in support of our request. Several days later, I received a call from Mr. Phillips who reported that the mall had determined that a ramp would not fit in the available space, so they were going to install a lift instead. Mr. Phillips was quick to emphasize that work on the lift had already begun. Our support group celebrated by going to see *Superman* the day the work was completed, again with reporters in tow. The members relished the fact that we had been successful in doing something about the barriers we faced, while I celebrated the action we'd taken and the members' willingness to do something about the discrimination we faced. They were starting to understand that we were not the problem. And, hopefully, so was everyone else.

MR. HANDICAPPED

At the end of my first year with CRH, I scheduled a meeting with Mr. Thompson.

"How's it going, Mark? How'd you like your first year with us?" he asked.

"Overall, it's been good," I said.

"That thing with the movie theater was great, Mark. People are still talking about what a great protest that was."

"Thanks. And yeah, I was really excited about that too. That's actually what I wanted to talk to you about. I'd like to know if I can revise my job description a bit."

"Really? In what way?"

"I'd like to keep doing counseling, but I'd like to blend it with some community education. There's a lot that the community doesn't know about disability. I'd like to be able to work more in the community to raise awareness and educate people and address some of the barriers we're seeing." I took a deep breath, realizing how much I wanted this.

"Do you think you can do both things?" said Mr. Thomas.

"Definitely. I'll continue to meet with people individually and run the support group. But I get the sense that what people really need after awhile is something to do about what they're feeling and the barriers they face. And that's where the community education would come in because I'd be helping people to get involved in their community and do something constructive with their feelings of frustration. The people that were involved in the movie-theater protest came away more empowered and upbeat than I've ever seen them. I think the same could be true for others."

"Sounds like you've thought this through," he said. "And, in general, I'm in support of it. It would be a great way to link us to the community and provide a way for our patients to get involved in something after rehabilitation." He paused. "But I have to say that my main concern is the funding. You know, right now your position as a counselor is funded by insurance billing. If we change your job description, we'd be giving up half of the funding for your position, and we'd have to find the extra funds in the budget." He paused, thinking it over, before looking up and smiling. "Why don't you come up with a draft of your new job description and some goals, and I'll run it by the board?"

"Great!" I said. "Thanks, Mr. Thompson."

With the hospital board's blessing, I was off and running, thrilled to be focused on activities that raised awareness, fostered dialogue, brought people together, and created change. I had so many ideas and things I wanted to accomplish. Plus, I'll admit that it was a relief not to have to be a full-time counselor anymore.

I started paying even more attention to local politics and issues, showing up at City Hall meetings when necessary to address topics that related to disability. The city's leaders began to listen to what I had to say, and I developed a certain level of credibility and respect. Capitalizing on this, I approached *The Charlotte Observer* with a few ideas, and they responded by inviting me to be a weekly guest columnist. This seemed like an ironic twist of fate, given my tenuous relationship with the written word, but it turned out that I had a knack for writing. I particularly liked to write about attitudes and the ways in which they perpetuated barriers for people with disabilities. As the result of our partnership, the newspaper began doing more stories about disability issues (often at my nudging), and often came to me for a quote or picture. After several of my columns and stories were published, I was invited to cohost a segment of *Good Morning Carolina*, which aired just before Captain Kangaroo. I even modeled clothes by Joseph A. Bank in a fashion show sponsored by CRH. In a very short amount of time, I had become Mr. Handicapped Charlotte.

While all of this exposure provided a lot more material for Mom's scrapbook—and a nice benefit to CRH—the obvious benefit was the platform it gave me to raise certain issues. I talked about the need to get involved in one's community and offered suggestions for ways to do that; I described the barriers that existed for people with disabilities; I explained the significance of Section 504, which I now fully understood; and I encouraged people to communicate with and have compassion for one's neighbors.

Our support group, too, was increasingly getting more exposure, and soon we were invited to form the Metrolina Chapter of the National Paraplegia Foundation (NPF). Empowered by our new, official-sounding name, we started getting even more involved in our community, monitoring accessibility issues throughout the city. We concentrated on handicapped parking spaces, addressing the need for additional spaces, and publicly taking on the rude nondisabled drivers who parked in the ones that existed. We went to the city and petitioned for curb cuts on downtown sidewalks and, after a series of meetings, the city council voted to create a program that would install a certain amount of curb cuts every year until, eventually, all of the city's sidewalks were accessible. Inspired, we then made the case for accessible public transportation and recreation and began to get that too. With each accomplishment, we found that people in the community were starting to see beyond our disabilities and address us in new and more positive ways. It appeared that we were starting to redefine the problem, at least in Charlotte. Community education and advocacy were working. I had finally found my niche.

RETURNING TO CHURCH

On a bright Sunday morning three years after my accident, Mom woke up, showered, and helped me with my morning routine. She then got dressed, shouted a quick good-bye, and headed out to her car. As she walked along the sidewalk, she stopped for a moment to admire her double delight hybrid tea roses, whose mixture of creamy white and strawberry red always made her smile. She made a mental note to cut some of them later and take them to a neighbor who'd been sick. Then she got into the car, drove to the end of our street, took a left onto Sharon Road, and drove the half mile to Sharon Presbyterian Church. Getting out, she nodded a greeting to the people she didn't know and stopped to speak to the ones she did. She entered the sanctuary, found a place to sit—up close and on the right side of the aisle, where she always like to sit— and settled in. She took a quick look around at the familiar sanctuary, noting some recent renovations that had been made and appreciating the large spring flower arrangement that stood near the pulpit. It was a vibrant mix of lilies, tulips, carnations, and—her favorite—gardenias. Lastly, she took a deep breath, bowed her head, and began to pray. She had finally returned to church.

Mom's decision to go back to church had been a process. She'd had time to recover from the trauma of my accident and see that I was not only going to be okay, but that I was finding my place in the world with a disability. Likewise, she'd watched Oogie enough to know that he would never share his experiences in Vietnam, but would at least be able to return to moments of pleasure and fulfillment in his career and family life. At the same time, she'd continued to watch the unfolding drama of my dad, whose drinking had increased. During all this, however, she had never given up prayer, instead using it to raise her loved ones up to God. In doing so, she had found that God had not abandoned her during this time of loss, but had, in fact, been present the whole time, grieving with her and offering her comfort.

Tentatively, she'd scheduled a meeting with the new pastor at Sharon. In meeting with him, she explained that she had no more issues with God, but she still wasn't sure about the church. After leaving two churches because of unrest, she wasn't sure what to do next. She wanted to return to church, feeling the need for that community and shared experience, but didn't want to have to leave again. The pastor quietly listened to her talk, then pointed to his Bible for a response.

"You might find it helpful to read the first chapter of First Corinthians, Betty," he said, flipping the pages. "The church in Corinth was dealing with many of the same things that you're talking about. People were arguing, there were divisions and factions in the church, and its members were even arguing about who the better minister was. But Paul scolded them and reminded them that their devotion and loyalty should be to Jesus Christ. If they all focused on Jesus, they would understand what they have in common and see that division was completely unnecessary. Then they'd be free to worship God."

Mom looked at him, concentrating on his words.

"Betty," he said, "I know you've been through a lot. But if you'll place your focus and loyalty on Jesus Christ, then you will always know where you belong and what to do. We ministers will come and go, and we'll probably make many mistakes along the way, but Jesus will always be there for you, offering his perfect love."

Mom smiled, knowing that he had delivered the answer she was looking for. The very next Sunday, she sat amid her fellow congregants of Sharon, feeling very much at home.

Dad, for his part, was still keeping his distance from God. True, his anger had subsided in the years since my accident, but he still hadn't forgiven God for what had happened to me. I'm guessing, too, that my injury really summed up for him all the other ways in which he thought God had betrayed him: his father's—and even his mother's—abandonment, Mom's miscarriage, the alcoholism, Oogie's war experience, politics and divisions in the church, and the many physical ailments that plagued him throughout life. He was dealing with a type of spiritual paralysis for which the only rehab was time and, possibly, the prayers of others. When Mom announced she was returning to church, Dad neither protested nor offered to accompany her. It would be another year before he would be ready to reenter the sanctuary doors.

As for me, matters of faith were all relative. I still felt a greater connection to God since Billy Graham's crusade. I now had my own direct relationship with God rather than a relationship via my parents. But I can't say I prayed on a regular basis, nor did I feel compelled to go to church, except at Christmas and Easter. My faith was still maturing and was most likely in its tween years. Still, I was happy for Mom. I knew her return to church meant good things for all of us.

IT'S MY RIGHT

Although the Rehab Act had been passed three years earlier, by 1976, President Nixon and his cabinet still had not issued the regulations necessary to implement Section 504, which disability advocates agreed was the most important piece of the entire Act. The Secretary of Health, Education, and Welfare (HEW, now the Department of Health and Human Services) was particularly concerned about the costs and administrative support necessary to implement and enforce 504 and refused to issue regulations. Thus, during the '76 presidential campaign, advocates pressured the candidates to make implementation of Section 504 a priority. When Democratic candidate Jimmy Carter agreed to support 504, the American Coalition of Citizens with Disabilities began a national effort to support his bid for president, and when he won, they expected swift action on 504. Not wasting any time, two days after Carter was sworn in, disability advocates met with the new HEW Secretary Joseph Califano to request immediate implementation of 504. Unfortunately, Califano had some of the same reservations as his predecessor, and it became clear that there would be continued delays.

Angered, advocates scheduled a series of protests in ten cities across the nation— including Chicago, Denver, New York, and Washington, DC— in April, 1977. By far the longest protest was held in San Francisco, where more than 150 advocates stormed the local federal building and staged a sit-in that lasted twenty-eight days. The response from the community was impressive. The mayor instructed the local police to leave the protesters alone. Groups such as the Black Panthers were allowed to bring food and water into the building, and attendants were allowed to come and go freely to provide care for the people inside. After twenty-five days, one of the leaders, Judy Heumann, traveled with a group to DC to meet with Secretary Califano. When he refused to meet with them, they staged a protest on his front lawn that lasted another twenty-five days. Finally, Califano gave in and signed the 504 regulations as protesters sang "We Shall Overcome" in solidarity with black Americans, who had to fight similar battles for their civil rights in the recent past.

With 504 regulations now in place, cities across the nation had to assess their infrastructure and practices to see what it would take to comply with the law. It was up to them to make sure that public programs and services were accessible to people with disabilities. Given our recent accomplishments, the city of Charlotte asked the Metrolina Chapter to partner with them in this effort. We agreed and began working with city officials to evaluate the city for access and develop a transition plan.

At the same time, the national disability community started talking about the need for more independent living centers throughout the country, which led to an amendment to the Rehab Act by Congress in 1978. The first center had been founded by Ed Roberts, Hale Zukas, and Jan McEwan in Berkeley, California, in 1972. It provided peer support, information and referrals, community education, and other key services to people with disabilities. What made them groundbreaking, as well as effective, was that the centers were consumer-controlled; they were run and controlled entirely by people with disabilities. The Rehab Act amendment, which provided funding for many new centers, acknowledged the importance of these centers in assisting people with disabilities to find services and housing and otherwise live as independently as possible.

As the Rehab Act funds began to flow into North Carolina, the state's Vocational Rehabilitation (VR) Department tried to figure out where to establish the first independent living (IL) center in North Carolina. This was new territory for them since the state hadn't had any centers up to that point. I was sitting in my office one day when John Dalrymple, a VR administrator, called me up.

"Hi, Mark."

"Hey."

"I've got an opportunity for you and the Metrolina Chapter!" he announced.

"Oh, yeah? What's that?"

"The state wants to apply for IL funding and is looking for groups to help start a center. I was thinking that the Metrolina Chapter should apply for one of the grants to set up one in Charlotte."

"But we're a support and advocacy group, John," I said. "We don't have staff or offices or anything to run a center."

"I know. That's what the grant money is for. Besides, Metrolina is the most active support group in the state. Y'all are really the best group to apply."

I paused, taking this all in. "It sounds great, but I need to talk with the other members about it and see what they want to do."

"No problem. Get back to me as soon as you can."

"Will do," I said, hanging up.

When I reported all of this to the group at our next meeting, they thought it was a great opportunity. They were familiar with some of the history of IL centers and relished the idea of starting one up in Charlotte. And while they understood what a big job it would be to get going, they also remembered that we had been able to get the state's largest mall to install a lift in its movie theater. They knew we'd fought successfully to get accessible parking spaces, curb cuts, and some accessible transportation. They celebrated when we partnered with the city to help implement 504. All of this had come from a support group. They knew what they were capable of, and they were confident that we could do it.

As John had predicted, approval of our grant application came easily. After a small celebration, we started meeting to plan the set up of the center. We had to make decisions about budgets, office space, staffing, and a host of other details. Starting up a center was new territory for us, but we did research, took a trip to Berkeley, invited some experts from the community to advise us, and got some technical assistance from Lex Frieden, a leader in the movement. There were many long meetings and even more late nights.

While this was happening, we were still working with the city to develop its 504 transition plan. Our research revealed that Charlotte had no accessible recreation centers. I know many people assumed that people with disabilities couldn't play competitive sports or participate in recreation programs, yet Charlotte was home to the Charlotte Tarwheels, a wheelchair basketball team that traveled around the country to compete. Ironically, the team practiced at my church because they couldn't get into any of the city's rec centers. Timing, however, was in our favor, as the city was prepared to break ground on a new recreation center not far from my house. We scrambled to get a meeting with the recreation officials, who soon agreed to make the new center accessible.

Thus, in May of 1980, the Metrolina Chapter of the National Paraplegia Foundation held the grand opening of the Metrolina Independent Living Center, the first in the state. Four months later, in partnership with the Parks and Recreation Department, we did the same for the Marion Diehl Recreation Center, which was billed as Charlotte's first center to provide "year-round recreational programs for persons with or without disabilities." People with disabilities in Charlotte now had a place to go to get help from their peers as well as a place to hang out and play.

As we were learning, there would always be more work to do and more issues to address, but for now, we celebrated.

CHAPTER 20

SUSAN

My wife's powers of recollection about the story of how we met are stronger than mine, so I'll defer to her…

According to Susan, we met soon after she began her internship in the speech therapy department at CRH. We crossed paths in the cafeteria and struck up a conversation. Although I'd like to write that she was immediately attracted to me, it's probably truer to say that she was fascinated by me. She didn't know much about spinal-cord injuries and had never met anyone in a wheelchair with a job. A few weeks later, Susan saw me at a staff party and began peppering me with questions about my injury, my job, and my life in a chair. It was like being with Jan all over again, though by now I was used to it. People have always been curious. As we talked, though, I realized that I was starting to develop a crush on Susan. She was cute, driven, smart, and funny, and we seemed to have a lot in common, especially our love of sports and anything to do with water. But I also knew I wasn't going to do anything about my feelings, at least not at that point in time. Not only was she dating someone, but I was shy.

When it came to dating, my injury kind of complicated matters to say the least. While before my injury, I was just awkward around women, now I wasn't sure if women would be attracted to me because I had a disability. Cautiously, I had asked out a few women to test the waters and was pleasantly surprised when they said yes. Then one day, I met Joan, a lovely, young physical-therapy student who was doing her internship at CRH. She thought I was funny and laughed at my jokes. Before my insecurities could get the best of me, I asked her out, and she accepted. Our relationship heated up pretty quickly. We spent as much time together as possible and were soon talking about serious things, using words like "love" and "marriage." But she didn't know how her family would react to the news that I wasn't Jewish, so almost as quickly as it had started, our relationship ended. I was devastated. Joan had been both my first love and the first real relationship I'd had with a woman since being in a wheelchair. I plunged into the usual melancholy and depression that follows the end of one's first love, moping around the house and convinced that I would never fall in love again. My parents, who had never seen me this way, did their best to console me, but they couldn't help. Only time and space in my virtual closet would help me recover.

I kept my feelings for Susan tucked in my back pocket. We continued to run into each other at work or at other parties, and each time we talked, she'd ask more questions, and I felt a greater connection with her. One December day, I rolled into the cafeteria to find Susan serving food in the cafeteria. After her internship had ended, Susan wanted to continue working at CRH, but the hospital didn't have any positions available for speech therapists. Susan agreed to work various odd jobs instead—filing medical records or serving lunch in the cafeteria—to maintain her connection to CRH and wait for a job opening. On this particular day, she was sporting a cheery red Santa hat, and she carried it off with a great sense of humor and flair.

"Any woman who can wear a hat like that I need to date," I thought to myself. But all I could say to her was, "Love the hat!" Susan laughed and waved at me as I rolled toward my table.

Three months later, Susan realized that she couldn't continue to support herself working odd jobs at CRH. She needed to complete a year of clinical fellowship in order to get her Masters degree in speech pathology and went to work for an organization in Charlotte that helped people with developmental disabilities. She continued to hang out with her friends from CRH, and one night, she showed up at a party I attended. As soon as she saw me, she waved and eagerly came over to sit next to me, which I took to be a good sign. I felt my confidence level beginning to rise. We began to talk, and while other people came and went, she stayed right next to me for the next hour. "Another good sign," I thought to myself, giving a further boost to the confidence index. Finally, I wrangled together the nerves that had been jangling about for the past nine months and corralled them into a question.

"So would you like to go out some time?"

She smiled. "Sure," she replied.

"Wow! Great!" I said. "What would you like to do?"

"I don't know. What do you think we should do?"

"How about going to see Steve Martin in concert? He's playing at Carowinds this weekend, and I've got tickets," I said, trying hard to look casual about this. She paused for a split second, long enough for me to pick up a particular vibe.

"Let me guess," I said. "You don't like Steve Martin."

She gave an awkward smile. "Not really…"

"Seriously? C'mon, he's really funny. How can you not like Steve with his banjo and King Tut act? Plus, we can go early and hang out at the park."

She smiled. "Okay. I'm up for it," she said. It wasn't the full-spirited gushing response I'd hoped for, but I knew I had an opening and was willing to go for it.

"Great. I'll come by Saturday and pick you up," I said, and turned to roll away, feeling both successful and suddenly self-conscious, as I tried to figure out exactly how one wheels off in a way that's sexy and suave.

As soon as I left, Susan sought out her girlfriends. "Wow! Mark Johnson just asked me out on a date!" she gushed. "What do I do?"

"What do you mean, 'what do you do'?" asked her friend, Bonnie. "What'd you say to him?"

"I said, 'yes!'"

"Well then, go out with him!"

"But I don't know how to date someone in a wheelchair," answered Susan.

"The same way you do anybody else."

In 1976, Carowinds, Charlotte's primary amusement park, debuted its newest and biggest roller coaster, Thunder Road. Featuring a moonshine theme, the coaster boasted twin tracks that allowed two trains to race each other up, down, and around the park at various points, even crisscrossing the border between North and South Carolina. The new ride opened to great fanfare, as NASCAR stars Bobby Allison and David Pearson came out to greet fans and be among the first to ride the coaster, and the local Alcohol, Tobacco, and Firearms office donated two moonshine stills—both of which had been confiscated during raids in the North Carolina mountains—to be placed at the entrance and exit of the ride.

Three years later, Thunder Road was still one of the park's biggest draws, for which people waited an hour or more to ride. Susan and I had already spent an hour around the park when we stopped to watch people on the new coaster. By then, we were starting to overcome that first-date awkwardness and settle into an easy rhythm together.

I watched Susan as she followed the path of the train, her face filled with excitement as she vicariously enjoyed the ride.

"Go ride it," I said, nudging her with my arm. She looked down at me, still smiling.

"You wanna go ride it?" she asked.

"No, I'm saying you should go ride it."

"No way, that wouldn't be any fun. I want you to come with me," she said.

"I can't."

"Do you like roller coasters?" she asked.

"I love 'em. Always have."

"Then you're riding this one," she said, and she turned and began walking purposefully toward the line, pulling my arm to indicate that I should follow her. As we headed toward the gate, people passed us in their hurry to get in line. Several of them looked back at me quizzically. I returned their stare with an equally quizzical gaze; I had no idea what was about to happen. As we neared the gate, a park official approached us and asked if we were planning to ride the roller coaster. When we said yes, he indicated that we should follow him as he led us around the gate, through a side entrance, and to the front of the line. Susan looked at me and smiled again.

"Cool," she said.

"Just one of the many perks," I said.

I could hear the progress of the train enough to know that it had almost completed its path and would soon be coming to pick us up. I wasn't really sure what was going to happen next and started to get nervous. Susan, however, remained completely calm and confident. When the train came to a stop in front of us, she immediately turned, bent down over me, and started to lift me up, as if she'd done this a million times. She hadn't, and I felt myself sliding toward the ground, but she quickly readjusted her weight and was able to lift me high enough to clear the ground and the top of the train car. I was too shocked to put up much of a fight or say anything as she turned and sat me down on the seat of the train. She quickly tightened the seat belt around me, then sat down and buckled her own belt. She turned to me, beaming, though very much out of breath. "We're off!" she exclaimed.

The train soon lurched its way out of the station and zoomed up and down the hills and loops of the mammoth coaster. Like any roller coaster, the ride was both exhilarating and terrifying, although I enjoyed the added thrill that comes with not being able to control your lower body. I was getting a crash course in gravity and learning really quickly how much you use your lower body to stabilize yourself in situations like this. In the beginning, I flopped around a good bit as we hurtled through space, though eventually, I figured out that I had the perfect excuse to hold onto Susan in a combined attempt to maintain my balance and make my first move. As I leaned over to her, she smiled and didn't seem to mind. If anything, she seemed triumphant that we were both on this thing, both sharing the thrill of Thunder Road.

TIME FOR A CHANGE

After that first date, our relationship quickly gained traction. I was still living with my parents, so we spent a lot of time at Susan's place. We'd hang out with her roommate, watch movies, or cook dinner together. Since her bedroom was upstairs, the only place that we could make out was on her couch. For the most part, this worked okay because Susan and her roommate, Karen, who also had a boyfriend, had worked out a schedule that allowed each couple to be in the apartment alone. Still, Karen and Kevin would come in at the end of the evening and find us in various positions on the couch, which was always embarrassing.

One night, Kevin teased, saying, "I'm tired of coming in here and finding y'all on the couch."

"Well, get Mark up the stairs to my room and we won't have a problem," Susan countered.

And the next time I was over, he did, lifting me up over his shoulder and hauling me up the steps. As Susan watched, she suddenly realized that she was strong enough to do the same thing. Two nights later, as we sat cuddled together on the couch, Susan asked, "You want to go up to my room?"

"How?" I asked. "Kevin's not here."

"I'll carry you," she said. She stood up, lifted me up, and headed toward the stairs.

"Whoa! Are you sure you can do this?" I asked.

"Absolutely," she responded.

Slowly, she climbed the steps. I could tell this was challenging for her, but she seemed determined. By about the third step, though, she started giggling.

"What's so funny?" I asked.

"Nothing." Then she started to laugh harder as she went up each step.

"What?!"

"Nothing," she breathed in the midst of her laughter.

"Stop it!" I said.

"I…I can't," she said. Still laughing, she reached the top step and carried me to her room, laid me on her bed, then bent over in a heap of laughter.

"Are you okay?" I asked.

"Yes, I just…" she tried, but she was still laughing. Finally composing herself, she said, "I'm sorry. That's what I do when I'm carrying something heavy. I start laughing, and I can't stop."

I rolled my eyes. "Great," I said.

Sure enough, every time she carried or dragged me upstairs, she would end up in a heap of giggles. It had a way of sucking the romance out of the moment, but we always seemed to recover enough to enjoy our hard-won privacy.

Eventually, Susan and Karen moved to a duplex closer to CHR and built a ramp for me to use. I not only appreciated it, but also took it as a good sign for our relationship.

Our first real conflict came when Susan's sister, Peggy, invited us to stay for the weekend in Atlanta.

"Let's go," said Susan. "It'll be a lot of fun. Peg and Tim want to take us to the lake."

"It sounds great, but I can't," I answered.

"Why not?"

"Because I've got to do my bowel program, and I won't have anyone to do that for me. And Peg's house isn't accessible. Plus, there's too much stuff to bring with me."

"Well, teach me to do your bowel program."

I grimaced. "You don't wanna do that. It's gross."

She looked exasperated. "Please. I work in a hospital. Not to mention the fact that my dad used to have me sew his hand up when he'd cut it. If I can do that, your bowel program will be easy." I hesitated. "C'mon," she said, "teach me what to do so we can go to Atlanta."

"I'm not sure..." I said.

"You know what, Mark, life's too short," she said, which made me laugh for a moment. That sounded a lot like a Bill-ism. But she didn't catch it and kept talking. "And you know, we're both too active to let this kind of thing stop us. If we're going to have a relationship, we've got to be able to figure out how to make it work so that you can travel and do stuff."

"I don't know. I'm not comfortable with the thought of you doing my bowel program for me."

I looked at her and saw the disappointment on her face.

"I think you need to think about what's important to you. Do you really want to be independent? Do you really want to be able to live your own life?"

"Yeah, I just don't think I can go to Atlanta," I said, sighing. I really wasn't sure what to do.

Susan stood up to leave.

"Where are you going?" I asked.

"Home. I need to think for a while."

"Why?"

She paused. "Because this is hard, Mark. Having a relationship with you is hard. We have to plan everything, and think ten steps ahead of everything, and there are things we can't do together. It's hard, and it's really frustrating."

"And I'm sure my lack of flexibility isn't helping," I said, trying to smile.

"You're right. It isn't," she said and walked out the door.

I sat alone in the den, feeling the silence and emptiness. Susan was right. This whole injury thing was still hard and frustrating even ten years later. And trying to have a romantic relationship with someone made it scary too. I knew I couldn't do all the things that nondisabled people could do, and I recognized that Susan or any other romantic partner could easily walk away if it got to be too much. I didn't want this relationship to end, and I especially didn't want it to end because of something related to my disability.

But I wondered, too, if Susan was right about the whole bowel program thing. I'd been doing the same routine for ten years; it was now a part of me and who I was. It had become almost sacred. I started to wonder, though, if maybe I could change up my routine or have someone else help me. That would be a revelation, especially since it would open up opportunities for travel and other activities. But that left the real question: was I willing to make changes in my routine? And was I willing to let others, like Susan, help me with them? If it meant continuing my relationship with Susan and having a full life, then the answer was absolutely.

CHAPTER 22

TAKING CONTROL

Slowly, tentatively, I made some changes in my routine, from how long I'd sit up in my wheelchair to the frequency of my bowel programs. Susan was delighted, not only because it meant we could go places or do more things, but also because she saw how the changes were affecting me. I was starting, albeit gradually, to take control. I was learning that I could question medical advice and that I could control my personal care routine instead of being controlled by it. With a simple change, we had cracked the dam and were waiting to see how the flood would unfold.

It didn't take long for the waters to rise. Susan, especially, wasn't going to sit back and wait for more change to take place, not when she saw that I was primed.

"Mark, when are you going to move out of your parent's house?" she asked one evening as we lay together on her bed.

"I don't know. I haven't thought much about it," I said.

"Well, I think you need to think about it. You're twenty-nine years old."

"You're right," I said.

"Look at your personal care routine—something you'd done the same way for ten years—and changed it. Look at how much that's freed you up to go out and do things."

"I'm not sure if I'm ready to move," I said.

"When are you going to be ready? Isn't ten years enough for you to figure out how to live on your own with a disability?"

Ouch. She was so right. Here I was, almost thirty, ten years post-injury, and I was still living with my parents, still relying on them to take care of me. It was a simple case of inertia. It's not that I didn't want to live on my own, but after living with them for a decade, it was just easiest to keep doing the same thing. I was comfortable.

But for my sake, and for the sake of our relationship, I knew that I needed to figure out a way to live on my own. I started visiting various apartment buildings and was surprised to find a two-bedroom condo that was reasonably accessible for a wheelchair and had easy access to the parking lot. The condo was located in the Franciscan Terrace community, a stone's throw away from Billy Graham's childhood home, which seemed like a nice connection. It was also close to work. I purchased it, in part, using some of the money I'd earned from Nielsen. Watching all that television had finally paid off.

Once I had a house, I asked around for a roommate. A friend connected me with a guy who was willing to pay a smaller portion of the rent in exchange for providing some attendant care. I also hired an attendant for morning and evening routines.

My parents knew little about all of this. I'd been careful not to say too much until all the details were in place. I knew they'd be concerned and that it represented a significant change for them. They'd structured their lives around me. I started with Mom, knowing she would be the easier one to tell. She took it well, asking a lot of questions to make sure I had covered my bases. I could tell she'd wanted this for me for a long time, but I knew she would also be sad to see me leave the nest. Hopefully, this time would stick. I asked her to break the news to Dad. I didn't relish the thought of having to discuss it with him, knowing he would ask even more questions than Mom and really press me to make sure I was ready.

"No way," she said. "You need to tell him yourself."

Living on my own for the first time in ten years, and for the first time with a disability, was groundbreaking. I felt like I was throwing off this veil of dependence and fear that had slowly, stealthily, and subconsciously crept over me. I realized I had been treading water rather than trying to see if I could still swim. That's not to take away from what my parents did for me. They exhibited the greatest act of love by taking me in and devoting their lives to caring for me. They sacrificed to do that. But after a while, we had all gotten too comfortable with the setup and never questioned it. Moving into my own condo meant that we were all getting our lives back and that Susan and I could finally be a true couple.

Living on my own was also an adventure—one that was mostly good. For the most part, my roommate was as reliable as any single, twenty-something guy can be. Usually, he was around to back up my attendants, but there were the few odd times when he left me hanging, and I had to get creative. Mom came by several times a week and kept my freezer stuffed with home-cooked meals. Susan and some of my other friends checked in regularly to make sure I had what I needed.

The condo really ignited my relationship with Susan. We had privacy for when we needed it, but we also had a place to entertain friends and have parties. For the first time, we were getting to see what life was like together as a couple because we had a place of our own. It proved to Susan—and to me—that I could be independent, which did great things for my self-confidence and self-reliance.

CHAPTER 23

FEAR

The first time I met Susan's mother, Sally, was soon after Susan had surgery to correct a synchronized swimming injury. In the 50s, when Susan and her twin sister, Peg, were in school, synchronized swimming was one of the few competitive sports available to women; it would be another twenty years before Title IX leveled the playing field (pun intended) for girls of all ages. As such, both Susan and Peg had donned the sparkly white swim caps with big, bold flowers on them and competed on their high school's team. Susan brought her usual intensity to her performances, and during one particularly dramatic move, she lifted her arm in a quick, sweeping motion and dislocated her shoulder. It must not have been a serious injury because Susan tolerated the pain and went about her busy lifestyle. But after many years, the pain had begun to interfere with her activities, and she was finally getting it repaired. Sally came up from Florida to help take care of her.

Up to now, Susan had told her parents very little about me. They knew we were dating and that I had a disability. She certainly hadn't told them that we were starting to get serious. I think she knew intuitively that my disability would be an issue for them. Her father, Tom, was the owner of a thriving imports car business that was the reward for his hard work, determination, and business savvy. Tom had managed his family much like he managed his business. He liked efficiency. When his twins were growing up, he had insisted that they wear matching outfits, participate in the same activities, and share the same friends. It was easier and neater that way. Even when he and Sally had a third daughter, Marianne, who was two years younger than the twins, he decided that she, too, could share everything with her sisters. It just made sense to him.

There were many times when Susan's and her father's strong personalities clashed, resulting in heated disagreements between them. This was especially the case when Susan announced her intention to develop a career as a speech pathologist. A businessman to the core, Tom didn't understand the value of a rehabilitation career. He thought his daughter's talents could be put to better use. But Susan was passionate about her career choice and had decided that she press ahead despite her father's concerns.

While her parents had been kept in the dark about our relationship, there were other family members that Susan kept in the loop. Peg knew the most about the development of our relationship since she and Susan talked often. Peg and her husband, Tim, came to Charlotte twice, and we went to see them. If they had any initial discomfort about my disability, it disappeared very quickly because we got along great and developed a very comfortable rapport. Additionally, Susan's Aunt Judy lived in Charlotte along with her husband, Dave, their daughter, Becky, and son, David. Susan was very close to her extended family and had lived with them for a time when she first moved to Charlotte. They invited us to their house many times for dinner, and over time, I developed a very easy relationship with them. Aunt Judy did her best to put in a good word about me to Susan's parents, but Susan continued to edit a lot of the news about our relationship when talking with them.

With her mother in her house, though, it was harder for Susan to hide the reality of our relationship. She couldn't hide the ramp that led to the door of her duplex. I'm sure that must have been a surprise to her mom and was a sign of Susan's commitment to me. I came over several times to have dinner with them, and from our interactions, I'm sure Sally figured out that we had a strong connection. Sally and I seemed to get along well. She was easy to talk to and always pleasant. I got the sense that she liked me as a person, but I could tell she wasn't really comfortable with the fact that I was in a wheelchair.

This, however, was not enough to deter Susan. As our relationship continued to progress, she decided that it was time for me to meet her family. In late November of 1979, she called her parents and announced that she wanted me to come home with her for Christmas.

"Absolutely not," said her father.

"What? Why?" asked Susan.

"Because he isn't a member of this family, and he doesn't need to be here while we celebrate Christmas."

"But, Dad, I love him, and we're really starting to get serious. I want you to meet him."

"I don't care if you think you're getting serious with him. He is not welcome here for Christmas."

"But, Dad, that's not fair!"

"I don't care about what's fair."

"But, Mom," said Susan, "you met him when you were up here. You saw what a great guy he is."

"He's a very nice young man, Susan," she responded. "I…well, he's just not your type."

"My type? What do you mean?"

"She means that you're an active woman with a lot going for you," said her father.

"So?"

"So he's handicapped, and you've got no business dating someone when you've got no future with him."

"Your father's right, Susan," said her mom.

"I don't know what you're talking about. I'm really starting to think that we do have a future together."

"If you married him, you'd be taking care of him," said her dad. "You'd be his caregiver, not his wife."

"Susan, it's too much of a burden to be with a man like that. We're concerned about you," added her mother.

"But..." said Susan.

"This is not who you are," implored her father. "Go find someone who's more like you."

Susan had underestimated her parents' dissatisfaction and was really caught off guard by how adamantly they opposed our relationship. I think she'd counted on having a chance for them to get to know me and see that our relationship could be as rich and full as any, but it was becoming clear that they didn't want such an opportunity. Their visions of people with disabilities were limited solely to people who needed to be cared for and weren't active, and they didn't want me anywhere in the picture.

Although Susan continued to defend and plea for our relationship at her parents' home during Christmas—without me there—they would not budge, and this disturbed her greatly. She was used to disagreeing with her parents, particularly her dad. Often, she got her way, but even in the times when she didn't, she was able to live with it. This, however, was different. Susan recognized that marrying me would be a lifelong decision, and she wanted her parents to be not only supportive, but also happy for her. For us. She didn't know if this was going to be possible, but she also didn't like the alternatives: break up with me or alienate her parents. It seemed like an impossible situation.

What made matters worse was that my parents also began pressuring Susan to end our relationship. It's not that they didn't like Susan—they absolutely loved her—but they were concerned about me. I'm sure that they wondered if Susan really understood the realities of my life—the planning, the arrangements, the care, the costs—and whether she was really committed for the long haul. And they had seen my pain after Joan had left and knew the pain of losing Susan would be much greater.

"You're a great woman and we love you dearly," said my dad to her one day, "but it's a lot of work to take care of Mark and you don't want to be tied down. You should find someone who's as active as you are and go and have a good life." Although my parents, I think, were testing Susan, I'm sure that this only added to the pressure she was getting from her parents, and it was all getting to be too much for her.

In January, Susan and I were in her kitchen fixing dinner, preparing for a quiet Friday night together. As she moved about the room checking the spaghetti and putting together a salad, I could tell she was restless and that her mind was somewhere else while I was talking about my brother's upcoming wedding.

"So, what do you think?" I asked.

"About what?" she said.

"About Oogie's wedding."

"What about it?"

"Um, hello? Did you not hear me talking for the past five minutes? Oogie and Mandy have set their wedding date for June, and I want you to come with me."

"Oh." She looked intently at the carrots she was chopping. "June? That's really far off."

"No, it's not. It's just five months from now." I smiled, trying to lighten up the mood, which seemed to be growing heavier by the second. But she didn't answer.

"Hey," I said, rolling up next to her and tapping her arm so that she would look at me. "What's wrong?"

"Nothing's the matter," she responded as she quickly moved away toward the refrigerator. "Why?"

"You don't seem like yourself today. You seem really far away."

She sighed. "I've got a lot on my mind right now."

"Is that thing with your parents still bothering you?"

"Yeah."

"Well, like I said, it's okay. Maybe they need time, and I can wait."

"I know," she said, offering a soft smile. "You've been really understanding about all this." She sighed again. "But I think I've got to figure some things out."

"Like what?" This didn't sound good.

"I don't know." She walked over and sat down at the table, still holding the jar of olives she had plucked from the fridge. I rolled over next to her. "I'm just feeling a lot of pressure right now."

"From who?"

"From everyone."

"Including me?"

"Yeah. You and my parents mostly."

"What..."

"And it's not that you're doing anything wrong. I mean, I love you, and you're great to me. But I know that you want to be with me, and I know that my parents don't want me to be with you, and I feel like I'm caught in the middle. I need to figure out what I want."

"Don't you know what you want?"

"I thought I did, but now I'm not so sure."

"What does that mean?"

She stared at the table for a long time, then finally looked up. There were tears in her eyes. "I think we need to take a break for a while."

"A break?"

"Yeah. I think I need some time to myself to figure out what I want."

"Are you breaking up with me?" I could hardly believe it.

"Yeah. I am."

After we broke up, Susan turned to her friends for comfort. In particular, she turned to her roommate, Karen, and Mary, her former clinical supervisor who had also become one of Susan's closest friends and confidantes. Besides spending a lot of time with Susan at work, Mary had spent a lot of time with us as a couple, so she knew me well and understood the depth of Susan's feelings for me. Susan spent a lot of time talking with her about the issues with her parents and the fact that she was now trying to figure out exactly who she was and what she wanted in life. Mary, for her part, spent a lot of time listening and offering insight and support when necessary. All of this was done over drinks and many dinners at their favorite bar, Whispers. Susan had completed her fellowship and had finally gotten the job she wanted as a speech therapist at CRH. Working together at CRH after we'd broken up was difficult to say the least. We saw each other as we passed in the halls, and while we still talked often, the dynamics were completely different. I knew that she still loved me, and she knew that I still loved her. But there was this great divide between us and neither of us knew how—or if—we were going to be able to cross it and be a couple again.

After about four or five months, Susan began slowly to reach out to me, inviting me for dinners and offering to come visit me in my condo. She missed me and wanted to reconnect, and over time, we gradually rekindled our romance, though it didn't have the same intensity as it did before. Susan was still trying to figure things out for herself and needed to maintain both distance and perspective. But what I didn't know was that she was thinking about moving away. Mary knew how much Susan wanted to work with people with brain injuries, and when a job posting showed up in *The Charlotte Observer*, Mary showed it to Susan. The position was at a trauma hospital that specialized in brain and spinal injuries, and Susan immediately followed up and applied for the job. When she was invited to go for an interview, she bought herself a nice new suit, went in with all the confidence of a young, talented, and driven woman, and got the job. Susan was still in the process of deciding whether to accept the position, primarily because it would require her to move all the way to Denver, Colorado. Susan didn't tell me this because she wanted it to be her decision. She did, however, call her parents to share her good news. Although they still didn't understand her career choice, they loved the idea of her moving to Denver, thinking it might spell the end of our relationship. They even offered to pay her moving expenses.

Chapter 24

Marriage Proposal

Although I was in the dark about Susan's potential move, I must have known that something was up because I decided one day that I was going to propose to Susan. I knew that our relationship hadn't yet returned to its glory days, but I loved Susan and knew for certain that I wanted to spend the rest of my life with her—I needed her to know that.

After a particularly wonderful Saturday that we'd spent together at the lake, and which had held several wonderful moments between us, I took a deep breath, turned to Susan, and held out an engagement ring.

"Susan, will you marry me?" I asked. I'd been practicing those words for days, getting a feel for how they felt, trying to get used to them, and trying to picture Susan's response.

She looked surprised, then concerned. She didn't say anything.

I tried to laugh though my stomach was in knots.

"I don't think I'm ready," she said, staring intently at me.

I laid the ring down. "Do you ever think you'll be ready?"

"I don't know. I mean, I love you very much," she said, taking my hand. "But I'm still trying to figure things out, and I know I'm not ready to make a commitment to you yet."

"I know," I sighed. "But I am, and I want you to know that. I love you, Susan, and I want to spend the rest of my life with you. And if you need time to think that over, well, I can live with that."

"I know," she said, bending down to kiss me. "And I love you for that."

A week later, Susan asked me to come over to her apartment. By the way she sounded on the phone, I could tell something was up.

"What's up?" I asked when I arrived.

"I need to tell you something."

"Sounds big."

"Yeah, it kind of is," she said, taking a deep breath. "I've been offered a job in Denver."

I was stunned. "Wow. Congratulations."

"Thanks," she said, waiting for the obvious next question.

"Are you going to take it?" I asked.

"Yes," she said. "I really want it. I mean, it sounds like such a great job for me. But I also really need it."

"Why's that?"

"I think it's going to help me figure some things out."

"How so?" I was starting to feel a little panicky.

She paused. "Well, I'm getting so much pressure from people, especially my parents, to date someone else and have a different job and live somewhere else. And I think I need to go and be alone and try this out for a while. Figure out what I want." She reached up and stroked my hair. "I don't think I can be really happy, with you or anyone else, until I do that." I looked up and saw tears in her eyes.

"Then it sounds like that's what you need to do," I said. "But just know I'll love you no matter who you end up deciding you are. And I'll miss you. Really miss you."

Before she left, I insisted on taking Susan to a jewelry store. "You wouldn't take the engagement ring I offered you, and I want you to have something to remind you of me," I said. Together, we picked out a beautiful butterfly ring. I thought it was an appropriate symbol of our love for each other, which had gone through many transitions and was now allowing her to fly free.

After Susan got settled in Denver, we talked on the phone every week and would send cards and letters back and forth. From the sound of things, she was doing well. She loved her job and was thrilled about working with people with brain injuries. She seemed to love Colorado, especially since it meant skiing and other sports that she loved. If she was dating anyone else, she didn't tell me.

Six months after she left Charlotte, I told her I wanted to come visit. I was curious to see her in her new environment and to see how her process of self-exploration was going. When I arrived and saw her waiting for me in the Denver airport, I felt a really powerful, physical sensation, realizing how much I still loved her. Apparently, the same was true for her. It was a really joyful reunion.

It was also fun to see Susan in her own environment. This woman, who had always appeared self-confident and assured, had a new sense about her, as if she was somehow more aware of and certain of herself. It looked like the six months in Denver had done her some good. She seemed to revel in showing me around town and introducing me to her local hangouts. I was seeing the life she had established for herself, far from the pressures of the people who wanted the best for her but didn't know how to give her the space she needed. It was almost as if she had needed to make the same move toward independence as I did, though for different reasons.

Two days after I arrived in Denver, we were sitting by the pool in her apartment complex. The night before, we had stayed out late celebrating our time together, so it was nice simply to sit in the sun and hang out for a while, putting off the fact that I would be returning to Charlotte tomorrow. After swimming a few laps, Susan got out and dried off when she turned to me.

"You know what?"

"No, what?"

"I've been thinking, and I've decided that I can't imagine living without you," she said.

Something inside me did a little back flip. "Are you saying you'll marry me?" I asked.

"Yes, I am!"

I laughed and shouted, "then *kneel*, woman, kneel!" She laughed, too, as she came and got down on one knee in front of me.

"Susan," I said, in the most officious tone I could muster, "will you marry me?"

"Yes," she said, giggling.

The people around us had figured out what was going on and began clapping as Susan raised up and kissed me, long and hard.

"But you've got to move to Denver," she whispered, smiling mischievously.

"Done," I said.

Over the next few months, there was the usual frenzied activity that comes with wedding preparations, with the added bonus of my preparing to relocate to Denver. Susan began looking at places to live for us while I gave notice to CRH and began looking at job opportunities in Denver. On top of all this, we both had to manage our parents' reactions to the news of our engagement.

Susan's parents reacted as we had expected they would. They were deeply disappointed and concerned this was not in Susan's best interest. They tried a number of times to change her mind, but after many heartfelt talks on the phone, they realized Susan had made up her mind. With that, her mom and dad insisted the wedding be held near their home in Sarasota, Florida. Peg and Marianne had both been married in Sarasota—in a joint ceremony, no less—and, in keeping with family tradition, what was good for one daughter was good for all three. It made things so much easier. But Susan stood her ground and refused to get married in Florida, explaining that the majority of our friends and family were located closer to Charlotte. Her parents relented and offered to pay for a small wedding reception, primarily for close friends and family members. We were expecting about a hundred and fifty people to attend the wedding, which meant at least half of them would not be able to attend the reception. But we agreed to this term since it was clear they were beginning to understand our love for each other, and it seemed like a reasonable compromise for having the wedding in Charlotte.

My parents, by contrast, were thrilled with the news of our engagement and were especially happy for me. They thought back to the grim predictions for my future. They could see Susan's commitment to me. It was more than they had dared to dream for me, and yet it was exactly what they had hoped.

What made our wedding particularly interesting was the fact that I was meeting my future father-in-law for the first time. While I had seen Sally a couple of times, each time she came to visit, Tom was always busy working and doing other things. I knew, of course, how he felt about his daughter marrying me and was both curious and nervous to see how this would play out.

My mom was actually the first member of my family to meet Tom. She was walking into the fellowship hall of Sharon Presbyterian Church, where the rehearsal and wedding were going to be held, when a tall man arrived at the same time and opened the door for her. Realizing that she didn't know him, she introduced herself and was surprised to learn that he was the father of the bride. He was very gracious to her and offered to help carry in decorations from her car. A few minutes later, I arrived and wheeled into the hall, where Tom and my mother were still talking.

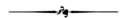

"Here's Mark, now," I heard Mom say as I came up next to her.

Tom stuck out his hand and shook mine. "I'm Tom Klinedinst," he said. "Nice to meet you."

"You too," I said. "Thanks for coming."

He nodded his head, "Oh, sure, sure. Glad we could be here. This is all very exciting." There wasn't a lot of feeling to back up his words, but I could tell he was trying. We continued to talk for a few minutes more—polite chitchat, really—until Susan came in. Tom lit up when he saw his daughter, and walked quickly over to greet her. I could tell he was happy to see her and was grateful for a break in our conversation. Honestly, I was too. This was going to take awhile.

In my scrapbook are many pictures from our wedding, which was a joyous ceremony, and our wedding reception, which was a great affair. But one picture captures a particular moment that occurred toward the end of the party. At one point, Tom called me over to a bank of public telephones that lined the hallway, indicating that there was a phone call for me. I took the receiver from him and put it to my ear.

"Hello?" I said.

"Mr. Johnson, this is Mr. Jones, from the Adam's Mark hotel. I'm calling to let you know that there's been a problem with your reservation tonight. I see that you've reserved the honeymoon suite, but unfortunately, it's been double-booked, and we're going to have to put you in a different room. I really apologize for the inconvenience, Mr. Johnson."

"What? No! I mean, I just got married, and this is going to be for our wedding night. It's really important that we have that suite."

Jody and Oogie, who'd been nearby, saw the concern on my face and came to stand next to me.

"I'm sorry, sir, but it's not available."

"Are you sure? I mean, I can't believe this would happen on our wedding night. What are we going to do?"

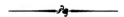

There was a pause on the phone before I suddenly heard the sound of my brother-in-law's voice.

"Mark, this is Tim. We're just kiddin' ya!" He started laughing. At that moment, I looked up to see Tom standing over me, laughing as well. He reached down and slapped me on the back.

"Welcome to the family!" he said.

Cutting the cake with Susan at our wedding reception

Following our wedding reception, our friends held an "after-wedding" party at my condo complex. They invited all of our friends and family, including the ones who hadn't been included in the reception, which gave us an opportunity to celebrate our marriage and say good-bye to everyone who knew us and loved us. Susan's parents even stopped by to meet our friends and join in the fun. The next day, Susan and I began our "honeymoon" by driving out to Denver with a van full of my belongings, ready to begin the next chapter of our lives together.

SECTION 3

GOING BEYOND AWARENESS

"If there is no struggle, there is no progress."

—Frederick Douglass,
"West India Emancipation" speech, 1857

WADE

After arriving in Denver and getting settled, I'd gone to Craig Hospital to see if they would be interested in creating a kind of advocacy position like I'd had at Charlotte Rehabilitation Hospital. I was convinced of the position's benefits, both to the hospital and the community, and thought a similar setup would work well at Craig, one of the country's leading rehabilitation hospitals for people with brain and spinal injuries. But Denver had two independent living centers—Atlantis and HAIL (or Holistic Approaches to Independent Living) —and Craig's leadership figured that was sufficient infrastructure for local advocacy services. Disappointed, I decided to head to the two centers next to check them out and see if either of them had a job to offer.

I went first to HAIL, which turned out to be a stroke of luck since they were in the process of setting up a new transitional living program and needed someone to coordinate it. Theresa Preda, who was HAIL's director, liked my work in Charlotte enough to hire me to get the program going. My job was focused on helping people—most of whom had been living with their families, though some had been in nursing homes—who wanted to live on their own. It was my job to help them think through how to get an apartment and set it up, how to use the city's transit system, and how to do basic things like shop for groceries. Many of them had never done these kinds of things for themselves.

Settling into the job, I began to understand why there were two independent living centers in one town. It turned out that there really was very little interaction between the two centers; in fact, the two centers didn't appear to get along well. From what I could tell, this seemed to be largely about a difference in advocacy style and approach. Atlantis was known for its radical politics and no-holds-barred civil disobedience tactics, while HAIL was the more well-mannered, play-by-the-rules kind of center. No doubt, HAIL appreciated the gains that Atlantis had made on behalf of people with disabilities, but it wasn't necessarily willing to follow in its footsteps when it came to pressing issues. HAIL was too polite to take risks.

The other difference seemed to be in the types of disabilities addressed by the two centers. Both centers were staffed by, and served, people with disabilities. However, Atlantis worked with people who had more severe disabilities, while HAIL seemed to be more comfortable with people with less severe disabilities. It seems there's a caste system in every culture. I thought this was fascinating, given what I'd heard about the legendary "Gang of Nineteen." They were a group of Atlantis members who had blocked buses and taken on the city's transit system, ultimately winning their fight for accessible public transportation. That must have been a powerful statement to have the most severely disabled claim such power and achieve such success. It made me curious to know more about Wade Blank, one of the founders of Atlantis. I'd met him a few times and could see how he had been typecast as the long-haired radical with a single-minded focus on transportation issues.

In the early part of 1965, the civil rights movement was reaching a climax. For the past two years, members of the Student Nonviolent Coordinating Committee (SNCC), a student civil rights group, had been trying to help black citizens in Alabama register to vote. However, white resistance to their efforts was intense, and the students were frequently arrested, beaten, and/or threatened with death. Realizing they needed help, the SNCC pleaded with the Reverend Doctor Martin Luther King Jr. to come and support their efforts. Dr. King responded by calling on his fellow civil rights leaders and other supporters to join him in a march from Selma to

Montgomery, the state's capitol. Several hundred people answered his call, and on March 7, they began marching. But as they crossed the Edmund Pettis Bridge the marchers encountered a wall of state troopers on the other side, who violently attacked them with billy clubs and tear gas in an episode that would become known as "Bloody Sunday." When the protestors tried to march again on March 9, they were again met with brutal resistance. Undaunted and determined, Dr. King planned a third march on March 21. This time, he issued a call to white seminary students, ministers, nuns, and other leaders of the church to join them, hoping their presence would provide some protection for the marchers.

At the time of the call, Wade Blank was a seminary student at McCormick Theological Seminary, in Chicago, Illinois. Following in the footsteps of his mother, a staunch conservative and deeply religious woman, Wade was a supporter of Barry Goldwater, who paid little attention to the civil rights movement. However, one day he returned to his dorm room to find his roommate, who was African-American and the first black man that Wade had ever known, shoving clothes into a backpack. When Wade asked where he was going, his roommate explained that he was traveling down to Alabama to march with Dr. King. Knowing Wade's conservative leanings, he then looked at Wade and dared him to go with him. Wade was torn. His first instinct was to back down from the dare; he wasn't really interested in going down south to make trouble. He also knew his fiancé, who shared his conservative leanings, wouldn't go for it. But he was afraid that if he didn't go, his roommate would think he was a racist. He decided to call his fiancé and discuss the idea with her, though she couldn't believe he was even considering the idea and threatened to break up with him if he decided to go. Hanging up with her, Wade felt trapped. He was starting to wonder if God, and not just his roommate, was challenging him to go. Finally, he made his decision. Returning to his dorm room, he surprised both himself and his roommate by accepting the challenge.

By the time Wade and his roommate made it down to Alabama, the marchers had successfully made it out of Selma and were now one day's march away from Montgomery. The two joined hundreds of people as they walked peacefully along the highway and participated in various chants and songs that the leaders would initiate from time to time. As they did, Wade talked with his roommate and other marchers, listening to their stories and reasons for marching, even as white citizens stood along the route and hurled insults and threats at the protestors. But rather than responding in kind, Wade was amazed to witness how the marchers met this violence with dignity, grace, and courage.

When they reached Montgomery and the capitol building, Wade listened with rapt attention as Dr. King gave his famous "How Long? Not Long!" speech. In it, Dr. King extolled the use of "nonviolent resistance" to address the struggles of oppressed people, even in the face of brutality as seen in Selma. More importantly, for Wade, Dr. King bathed his speech with spiritual phrases, making it clear that social justice work, particularly when it was addressed with grace and without violence, was the work of Christians everywhere.

By the time Wade returned to Chicago, he was a single man, since his fiancé had followed through on her threat and broken up with him. But he was also a changed man.

After Selma, Wade began taking courses in community organizing that were offered at McCormick. The classes included practical experience in low-income neighborhoods, giving the students a chance to connect with people who had little voice in the laws and policies that affected them. As a result, Wade began to develop a strong interest in working with people on the fringes of society, understanding what Jesus meant when he called on his disciples to serve "the least of these."

Upon graduating from seminary, Wade returned to his home state of Ohio to be ordained in the Presbyterian Church and began serving as the pastor of a local congregation. Initially, he loved his role in the church. He enjoyed getting to know the people in his parish, was popular among the teens and young adults, and relished the opportunities to minister to those in need. He loved exposing his members to the needs of their community and encouraging them to get involved. But, increasingly, Wade felt conflicted in his work. He resented having to keep his more wealthy parishioners happy, particularly when their ideas about the work of the church contrasted sharply with his, in order to keep the offering plate full on Sundays. This was especially true as America was getting more deeply involved in the Vietnam War. Wade believed that it was the church's duty to speak out against the Vietnam War, but many of his more conservative members disagreed. At times, these disagreements became problematic, both for Wade and the congregation. He moved to a couple of different churches during this time, trying to find the right fit for his pastoral style.

By 1970, Wade was serving a church in Akron, Ohio that was located just ten miles from Kent State University. Like college students across the country, many of the Kent State students were involved in anti-war protest activities, and Wade made an effort to reach out to them. Soon, the Students for a Democratic Society (SDS), a campus group that was involved both in the Civil Rights movement and the anti-war protests, began holding their meetings at his church and using its mimeograph machine to make copies of pamphlets and rally posters. Wade loved getting to know the students; he related to their passion and energy, their belief that what they had to say mattered, and their desire to affect change in the world in which they lived. He was happy to be able to offer church resources to support their activities, and for the most part, his congregation tolerated it.

On April 30, 1970, President Nixon announced that the United States was invading Cambodia. Outraged at this expansion of the war, the SDS students met in one of the church's Sunday-school rooms to plan a student rally on campus the next day. The rally was held around noon on Friday and resulted in a large turnout of more than five hundred students. Encouraged, the students decided to hold another rally on the following Monday to continue their protest. Unfortunately, on Friday evening, a riot broke out in the town, which escalated to the point that the mayor declared a state of emergency. By Saturday, the town leaders agreed to request assistance from the National Guard. The arrival of the Guard that Saturday evening only intensified the feelings of the protestors, who began rioting on the Kent State campus. At some point, someone set the school's ROTC building on fire, and more than one thousand students cheered as the building burned, while the Guard did its best to restore order and make arrests.

As the tension on campus continued to mount on Sunday, Wade worried about the members of SDS. He recognized the potential danger of combining the military with students who were young and convicted of the rightness of their cause, and he worried about their safety. In his sermon, he preached about Jesus' call to love one's enemies and admonished the congregation to pray for a peaceful end to the riots on campus. He then spent the afternoon tracking down the SDS members, who were busy planning the second rally for the next day. Wade did his best to persuade them to be safe, but otherwise all he had to offer them were his prayers.

On Monday, May 4, 1970, Wade periodically checked in with a couple of the students in between meetings with church members and other routine business of the day. Around 2 p.m., he was reading in his office when the phone rang. On the other line was one of the SDS members, who was clearly distraught. She reported that when more than two thousand students had shown up for the rally, the Guard had tried to disperse the crowd with tear gas. From there, the situation continued to escalate until the Guard began firing at the students, killing four of them and wounding nine others. While none of the SDS members were killed, Wade knew some of the students who were killed. He was both devastated and outraged.

To stay busy and find some way to express his feelings, Wade coordinated his own protest on campus, which was held a few days after the shootings. He set up a table with bowls of water and called on people to come and "wash their hands" of the killings that had taken place on campus and those that were continuing to occur in Vietnam and Cambodia. Several hundred people, including students, faculty, administrators, and community members, waited patiently, and silently, for their turn to dip their hands in the cool water. As they did, Wade prayed.

After the events at Kent State, Wade began to be hounded by the FBI, who had increased their attention on Kent State and anyone in the area involved in antiwar protests. At the same time, he was having a harder time dealing with the conservative politics of some of his parishioners, particularly the ones who blamed the students for the massacre. When an FBI agent told a member of his congregation that the church "should find another minister," and the member actually considered it, Wade became furious, quitting his job and never returning to parish ministry.

For a while, he and some friends ran a bookstore in Akron called "Alice's Restaurant;" it was the only bookstore in the region that sold copies of Mao's *Red Book*. He attended some national antiwar rallies and used his van to ferry draft dodgers to the Canadian border. He also returned to McCormick, where he got a Master's degree in the theology of rock music. Meanwhile, he prayed, listening to God and trying to discern what God wanted him to do next in his life. Through this process of listening, Wade began to sense that he was being called to do what he considered to be "real human service:" helping the people who were on the very fringes of society, the ones whom no one else was willing to help. To inaugurate this new phase in his life, he decided to leave Ohio and start fresh in a new city. He chose the city by throwing darts on a dart board where he'd written the names of various cities. His dart landed on a small piece of paper that simply said, "Denver."

When Wade arrived in the Mile-High City, he got a job as an orderly in a nursing home. He chose this deliberately, knowing that the job of an orderly required great patience and humility. It also provided access to the people who had been shut away by society, forced to receive care in an institution rather than in their own homes. Wade treated each person with great care and dignity, believing that he was finally ministering to the people who needed him the most. As he got to know the residents, and they realized that this orderly was willing to listen to what they had to say, Wade began to provide counseling to them on an informal basis, which got the attention of the nursing home administrator, Tom O'Halloran. He was impressed with Wade's concern for the residents, and when O'Halloran went to work for Heritage House, another nursing home, he took Wade with him and gave him the job of recruiter/activities director for the new "youth wing." Although there were only a handful of young people living in Heritage at the time, O'Halloran hoped that Wade, who sported the long hair and tinted glasses that were en vogue at the time, would relate to the youth and be able to recruit them from rehabilitation hospitals and other nursing homes. Wade was clearly good at his job, given that the program had sixty youth—and a waiting list for more—by the end of his first year.

Wade approached his job with great enthusiasm. He developed friendships and shared meals with the young residents, whose disabilities included cerebral palsy, muscular dystrophy, spinal-cord injuries, and developmental disabilities. He listened to their stories and learned they were all there, living in a nursing home in their late teens and early twenties, simply because they didn't have the services needed to support them at home. Recognizing that most of the youth would be living in this institution for the rest of their lives, Wade formed a residents committee and sought their input, wanting to be able to create an environment that reflected their age and interests. He did what he could to implement their suggestions, allowing them to stay up later than the curfew that had been set for the elderly residents of the home, setting up coed living arrangements when requested, letting them have small pets, and advocating for better food.

At first, Wade thought he could set up some great activities, give the residents some say in their care, and otherwise go home to his rock music. But over time, he began to understand the political implications of his work. After raising money to buy a used van, Wade started taking the youth into the community to rock concerts, bars, and ice cream shops, and during these outings, he noticed how the community reacted to people with disabilities, greeting them with stares, insensitive comments, and inaccessible buildings. These youth—who, except for their disabilities, were just like other young people their age—were clearly unwelcome outside the walls of the nursing home. However, things weren't much better within the walls either, as the hospital administrators—including O'Halloran—gradually began to deny more of his requests, sometimes even sabotage the work he was doing. Wade began to understand the economics of the situation: the administrators saw the youth for the Medicaid check that was paying for their care and nothing more. They were a commodity. As a result, the administrators were threatened by any efforts to give the residents a voice.

Wade began to understand that the youth were quite capable of living on their own in the community if they had the right support, such as an attendant who could come into their homes and provide care. But when he suggested that Heritage allow several of the young adults to live in an apartment and have the nursing-home staff check in on them as an experiment, O'Halloran fired him, then promptly erased all of the improvements he had made to the youth wing.

Wade was both furious and guilt-ridden. Almost all of the young adults living at Heritage House were there because he had recruited them and had promised them a place that would not only care for them, but listen to their needs and ideas. Now, however, the staff had taken away most of their privileges, torn down the posters that decorated their rooms, and implemented scare tactics to keep their protests at bay. The youth were living in an awful environment, and Wade felt responsible for getting them out. He began working tirelessly, applying for grants to rent apartments and pay attendants. With the help of Barry Rosenberg, another activist, Wade established the Atlantis Community. It was one of the first independent-living centers in the nation, for the purpose of promoting disability rights and coordinating attendant care and other support services for people in the community. Then, with the support of the state social services department, and over a six-month period, Wade arranged for nineteen severely disabled youth to get out of Heritage House and live in their own apartments. It was one of the first coordinated efforts to help people with disabilities transition from nursing homes to homes of their own in the community. This caught the attention of many people, including Hollywood, which produced a made-for-TV moving about Wade and the young adults of Heritage House, titled "When You Remember Me." Without intending to, Wade had added momentum to a movement.

INJUSTICE

After Wade had gotten all the youth out of Heritage Center, the Atlantis Community members settled into their new homes and began establishing their new lives. Like other people their age, they wanted jobs and hobbies; they wanted to go to church, visit their friends, and go to the movies. But as they started to try these things, they realized one of the biggest barriers to independent living was the Regional Transportation District (RTD), Denver's public transportation system, whose buses were inaccessible to wheelchair users. True, RTD did have a fleet of twelve minibuses that were designed to provide transportation for people with disabilities, but riding them required a forty-eight hour advance reservation, and they generally ran late by an hour or more—hardly the makings of independent living.

For more than two years, the members attempted to work with RTD to find a solution, but when it became clear that RTD was not interested in working with them, the Atlantis Community filed a lawsuit against the agency in 1977, calling for RTD to make all of its buses accessible. Given what he'd learned during the civil rights movement, Wade didn't expect to win the suit, but he knew it was the best option for getting the attention of the RTD leadership and showing that Atlantis was serious about the issue. While they waited the long months for a response to their suit, Wade prepared the Atlantis members for their next steps, just in case. And when the judge handed down the decision in June, 1978, ruling against them, the group was ready.

On the morning of Monday, July 5, 1978, during rush-hour traffic, Wade and about sixty other Atlantis members, attendants, and supporters met at the corner of Colfax and Broadway, the city's busiest intersection. Patiently, they waited for an RTD bus to pull up to the bus stop, and when it did, they poured out into the street and stood defiantly around it so that the bus couldn't move. When a second bus pulled up alongside the first bus in an effort to help, they surrounded it too. The police were called in but refused to arrest the protestors, afraid of any liability issues that might come from arresting people with disabilities. For the next two days, the group held their ground, while supporters brought in food for them.

Over the next eighteen months, Wade and the group—which was becoming known as the Gang of Nineteen, in honor of the first youth who were freed from Heritage House—continued their demonstrations. They struck at random times and places and used a variety of tactics, both to get attention and raise awareness about the need for accessible public transportation, such as sitting at bus stops with signs that read, "We'd like to get on the bus." They also made sure to show up at every RTD meeting and disrupt the proceedings, and in October, 1978, they took over RTD's administrative offices. Over time, the public grew more supportive of Wade and the Gang of Nineteen, and finally, in May, 1979, the RTD board voted to buy 127 new accessible buses and to retrofit its existing fleet of 250 fixed-route buses. They had won.

The impact of this victory was lost on me until my first Colorado winter. Those who have grown up around snow make fun of those of us who haven't. Just hearing that snow is on its way prompts us Southerners to buy bread and milk. At the sight of the first flake, we start closing things down, seldom leaving the house until things have thawed out.

Our first winter in Denver, Susan was much more adept at managing the snowy roadways, given that she'd seen her share of them while living in Illinois. I was at a greater disadvantage, both because of my lack of experience and because of my large, full-size van, which was less than nimble when it came to managing slick pavement and slushy highways. So it wasn't looking good when a snowstorm hit Denver in January, 1982. I sat looking out the window as the snowflakes kept coming, piling up high in our yard and driveway. I realized I was going to have to grin and bear it when it came to making the snowy ride to my downtown office.

I carefully navigated our slushy sidewalk and started up the van, then eased out onto our street and tried to get a feel for the road. When nothing happened the first mile, I began to gain more confidence and gradually sped up, though I was still driving well under the speed limit. But as I approached the next intersection, my back tires hit a patch of ice and the van started to skid. Panicked, I broke the first rule of driving and quickly turned the steering wheel to the left, which, of course, only made things worse. The van gained momentum as it slid across the ice, making it clear that I no longer had control of it, and veered into oncoming traffic, where I was broadsided.

"Ugh," I thought. "This can't be good." I was okay, but my van most definitely was not.

Indeed, the news from the mechanic was not good: both the van and my wheelchair lift had sustained significant damage, and it was going to take several weeks to fix everything. In the meantime, I was going to have to figure out how to get around without it. I was going to have to ride the public buses.

Thanks to Wade and the Gang of Nineteen, I had the option of riding one of RTD's fixed-route buses to work while my van was being repaired. But riding one of those from Westminster, where I lived, to downtown Denver took about one and a half hours since the bus stopped at every single bus stop. True, RTD offered a second option for suburban commuters—the express bus, a sleek, Greyhound-style bus that bypassed all those fixed route stops and sailed into downtown in a matter of thirty short minutes. It was, by far, the better option. Unfortunately, the express bus wasn't accessible. That left the fixed-route bus with its endless commute.

That first morning, my alarm clock went off two hours earlier than normal. I had plenty of time to roll down to the nearest bus stop and wait about ten minutes for the bus to arrive. Once on board there was nothing to do but hang out as the bus started and stopped its way toward downtown. There were thirty-seven stops. I know because I counted every last one of them. With each stop, and with each passing minute, I got more and more frustrated. I knew I should have had the option to ride the express bus and bypass these needless delays to my commute. I couldn't believe I had to endure this kind of mind-numbing commute—a clear waste of my time—simply because I used a wheelchair. I thought about all the other people with disabilities who had jobs or other reasons to commute into the city, the ones who couldn't afford to have their own van and who were also forced to endure this special kind of torture because the express buses weren't accessible. And I started to get angry.

It was then that I recalled Wade and his fixation on accessible transportation. I'd heard him say once that transportation could make or break you if you were a person with a disability, and I realized that he was right. Having access to transportation made all the difference in where you lived and whether you could get to work or to the doctor and whether you needed to take thirty minutes or an hour and thirty minutes to get somewhere. I finally understood what he'd been saying because now it was personal.

By the time I arrived at work, I was a man on a mission; I was going to do what it took to make all forms of transportation accessible to people with disabilities. I started talking to anyone who would listen, venting the frustration that had been building over thirty-seven bus stops. My coworkers listened patiently as I ranted, and some even shared their own stories of interminable commutes. A couple of people even suggested that I call Wade, knowing this was his bailiwick. In complete agreement, I picked up the phone and called him.

"Hey, Wade. It's Mark Johnson with HAIL."

"Hey, Mark. How can I help you?"

"I've just had my first experience with RTD, and I think I understand why you keep talking about transportation issues. I needed to ride the express bus to work, but it wasn't accessible, so I just spent an hour and a half on the fixed-route bus. It was torture. There's got to be a better way."

Wade chuckled, then asked, "What do you want to do about it?"

"Whatever it takes," I said.

Wade began to speak with intensity and excitement, clearly thrilled that I wanted to help. I learned later that he saw me as the perfect catch for his campaign to make all transportation accessible. While he sported the look and outspoken attitude of a young radical from the sixties—complete with long flowing hair, slogan t-shirts, and scruffy jeans—I was the clean-cut, soft-spoken, polite Southern boy with an endless supply of button-up shirts and pressed slacks. He recognized I could open additional doors. By combining our passion, we'd make the perfect team.

Wade spoke quickly, bringing me up to speed on the things that he and the folks from the Atlantis Community had been working on. After Denver had made its entire fleet of public buses accessible, two things had happened to raise the ire of Wade and his fellow advocates. First, RTD had hired a new director, who didn't know the history of the fight for accessible buses and had recently ordered eighty-nine new buses without lifts. Second, after President Reagan took office, the American Public Transit Association had sued Secretary of Transportation Andrew Lewis, arguing that the Section 504 rules were too costly. Reagan had agreed and decided that while states should try their best to make public transportation accessible, they should have the "local option" to determine whether that process was economically feasible. As a result, states had immediately begun to backpedal on their commitment to accessible transportation; in RTD's case, that meant going back on their commitment to keep ordering buses with lifts. Wade considered this a slap in the face to people with disabilities, and he and the members of Atlantis had begun showing up at RTD board meetings again to tell them that. Wade reported that the RTD board was planning to meet in the next month and wondered if I wanted to attend and present an argument for making all buses—including the express buses—accessible.

I talked with the folks at HAIL about my conversation with Wade and got my boss's okay to spend some time on this issue. I dove into the process of researching and developing a sound and thorough case that was sure to change the minds of the RTD board. I looked first to Seattle, a city that had already made a lot of progress in making public transportation accessible for people with disabilities, and gathered budgets and other data to show the impact on their system. From there, I started to collect data on the amount that RTD was spending on buses, what it would cost to purchase accessible buses, the cost amortized over the life of the vehicles, potential ridership, and the increase in income for RTD. I typed up a statement and supportive documentation, showing, in vivid detail, why this was the right thing to do for both RTD and the people of Denver. There was no way we could lose.

On the day of the RTD board meeting, I woke up extra early, pumped up and ready to make the case. When I arrived at the RTD headquarters, I saw Wade and a few others waiting for me.

"Nervous?" Wade asked, as he patted me on the back.

"Nah," I said, though I flashed a grin to indicate that I was, a little. I knew there was a lot riding on this, not only for me but for the rest of my peers.

Wade smiled back. "Go get 'em," he said.

We entered the meeting room and found seats together, then waited while the board reviewed the minutes and went over other items on the agenda, until finally they were ready to address our issue. I was the designated spokesperson for our group, and when the chairman called my name, I rolled down to the front and waited while a board member moved a chair out of the way so that I could roll up to the microphone sitting on the table. Confidently, I presented our case, taking time to look each board member in the eye in an effort to get their buy-in. I proudly referred to the charts and data that I'd prepared, and when I was done, I sat and waited to answer their questions. When there weren't any, the chairman called for a vote. One by one, the board members answered.

"Nay," voted the first member.

"Nay," said the second.

"Nay," added the third. On and on, they each, with the exception of a couple of allies, voted against the motion to purchase accessible fixed- and express-route buses in the future. Our motion was defeated.

I couldn't believe it. I sat, stunned, feeling like someone had ripped my heart out. Although I'd had to fight for issues in Charlotte, for the most part, we'd always gotten what we asked for once we'd made a solid argument. Slowly, I turned and rolled back up the aisle to where Wade was waiting for me.

"You alright?" he asked.

"I can't believe they voted against us," I said. "It doesn't make sense. There was all that data, all the numbers that showed how much money they'd be saving..."

Wade stood patiently while I ranted and raved, giving me the space to vent my rage. Finally, all I could do was shake my head and stare down at my feet. That's when Wade bent down in front of me and put his hand on my shoulder. In a soft but steady voice, he said, "Until there is an emotional change, no intellectual persuasion will work. Right now, they don't understand. They don't know what it means to be disabled. They don't know what it's like to have no access to transportation." He paused, waiting for me to look him squarely in the eye. When I did, he said, "We have to make them feel it."

I stared at him, not knowing what to say.

"C'mon over to my house tomorrow night, and we'll talk about what's next. Invite some of your colleagues from HAIL," he said. "We need everyone to be a part of this."

"All right," I said, feeling completely defeated. I wasn't sure what he had in mind, but I was willing to listen.

FIRST ARREST

Wade lived in an old, two-story brownstone just outside of downtown Denver. Because there were stairs leading up to his front door, he'd installed a lift. I didn't know too many people who had taken the time and money to install a lift in their homes—especially when they didn't have anyone with a disability living with them—and I was deeply impressed. After riding the lift up and rolling through the door, I was happy to see about fifteen or so people already gathered in Wade's living room and kitchen. It was an eclectic mix of people. There were some nondisabled people, although the majority had disabilities, including a few with fairly significant disabilities. I was glad to see some staff from HAIL there, including Barry Rosenberg, who had helped to cofound HAIL and was an old colleague of Wade's. I watched as the HAIL staffers tentatively started to connect with people from Atlantis. Moving in and among them was Wade, who was busy playing both host and ambassador, helping to forge connections between these two groups.

For the first hour, we sat around and ate spaghetti, discovering that Wade was a pretty good cook. The conversation was easy, and I could see that people were beginning to settle in and develop connections. After dinner, someone passed around glasses of Drambuie, and a few people sat sipping their drinks while Wade talked about what to do next with RTD.

"We've exhausted the formal process. We've made our case to the board, but they didn't want to hear it. It's time to bump it up," he proclaimed.

"What do you have in mind?" I asked.

"We've got to get the attention of RTD's director. He needs to understand the need for lifts on buses because he can help get the board members in line with us."

"But we've tried and tried to call him, and he never returns our calls," said Babs Johnson, who worked at Atlantis.

"Exactly," said Wade. "It's time that we demand that he meet with us." He smiled and looked around. "Anyone got an idea of how to do that?"

"I say we go in, take over the building, and not leave until we get our meeting," said Larry Ruiz, member of the original Gang of Nineteen. "That's what worked for us before." Several people around the room voiced their support for this idea.

"That's good," agreed Wade. "He needs to see that we're serious. He needs to feel it." He thought for a minute. "Let's start with a quick press conference, tell everyone that RTD has reneged on their promise of accessible transportation, then head up to the director's office and stage a sit-in. The press will already be there and can cover it all."

Everyone agreed that this was a good plan. When Wade asked who was interested in participating, almost everyone raised a hand, including me.

"Just remember that you could get arrested," said Babs. "We've been down this road before. I want to make sure that some of you who are new to this kind of work are up for that."

Wade and a few of the Atlantis members gave some quick, impromptu training on civil disobedience, including how to be arrested. They encouraged us to travel lightly, since the police would be required to confiscate and catalog everything that you had with you, and said that we really only needed to have our IDs with us. As they talked, a few of us who were new to this looked around at each other and chuckled nervously.

"Hey," said Wade, acknowledging the fear in the room. "If things start to heat up, and you want to leave, then leave" added Wade. "Don't feel like there are any expectations on you. Do what you're comfortable with, and we'll take it from there."

On January 5, 1982, I woke up well ahead of my alarm clock, feeling both excited and nervous about the events of the day. I didn't know what it would hold or what the outcome of our action would be. While Wade had warned us about the possibility of arrest, I didn't think that would happen to me. I was here to help out and add my voice to the protest, and that was about as far as I'd thought about it.

Around 1 p.m. we met around the corner from the RTD headquarters to give everyone time to show up and go over last minute plans. We knew that to make the biggest impact, we needed to show up as one united group, all at the same time. Wade was keyed up, walking purposefully back and forth between people to make sure everyone knew what to do. As I rolled up, he saw me and smiled, walking quickly over to me.

"Hey, Mark!"

"Hey."

"Ready for your first action?" he said.

I exhaled. "Sure, where do you need me?"

"In the front," he said.

"Sounds good to me," I said.

When all thirty of us were fully assembled, Wade gave us a few last-minute instructions and his own brand of a pep talk, then turned and led us down the street. As we made our way toward RTD, people on the street turned and stared at our eclectic mix of folks, clearly unsure of what to make of us. I could feel the adrenaline start to kick in as we got closer to the building. I felt anticipation, fear, awkwardness, and excitement all at the same time and was reminded of the time we had taken over the movie theater in North Carolina. This was just like that, only on another level. I could tell that others were feeling it too as we all started to walk and roll faster toward our target.

Because the front entrance to the RTD building wasn't accessible, we headed instead to a separate entrance on the left-hand side of the building. Wade had gone ahead of us to open the door and ensure that we could roll in smoothly and quickly before anyone realized what was going on. We entered the lobby, and a few RTD employees and visitors began to scatter as we quickly filled the place up. The lobby of the RTD building was a large and spacious atrium with high ceilings, surrounded by balconies from each floor that allowed you to look down into the lobby. The security guards, who, up until now, had been sitting quietly behind their desk up, were now on full alert as they surveyed this ragtag crowd that was facing them.

Wade walked to the front of the crowd and waited until he was sure members of the press were present, then started speaking about how RTD had reneged on its promise to provide accessible public transportation and how that violated our civil rights. He called for the director to meet with us and discuss a resolution. As he spoke, employees and visitors from the floors above gathered along the balconies and watched the proceedings, while members of the press asked some questions and took pictures.

The press conference was very brief. When it was over, we headed to the elevators to go up to the third floor director's office; however, as we neared the doors, we noticed signs on both elevators that read "out of order." We knew full well that the elevators had been in fine working order when we had arrived and realized that the RTD leadership, anticipating trouble, were trying to prevent us from going upstairs.

That's when things got crazy. About twelve of our group members immediately rolled or ran over to the doors. Half of them went outside, where they blocked the entrance and exit to the parking garage. The rest resolutely planted themselves in front of the doors, preventing anyone from getting in or out. Several other members spread out around the lobby, claiming the space and chanting "we will ride" at the top of their lungs. Meanwhile, three of us who were in wheelchairs began heading as fast as we could toward the stairwells with Wade and Barry in hot pursuit. As soon as we reached them, those of us in wheelchairs turned around so that our backs were to the stairwell, while the other two began working to pull us up the stairs. Our intent was to get upstairs by any means necessary or to at least block the stairs. All of this had been carefully planned last night, and within three short minutes, we had shut the place down.

Barry and I started up the stairs first, followed by Wade and a guy named Stephan. We were about halfway up the first set of stairs when Bob West, RTD's head of security, came running down the stairs and tried to block us from continuing upstairs. He yelled at us to turn around and leave, insisting that he wasn't going to let us obstruct the business of RTD. We yelled back at him, making it clear that weren't going to back down. Mr. West stood in the middle of the staircase, but Barry and Wade brushed past him. As they did, the security officer moved in to block them, and there was a bit of a scuffle. But after a few seconds, Mr. West must have started worrying about the liability because he stepped back and allowed us to get up to the first landing, halfway between the first and second floors. He and a few other RTD employees then stood in a line across the stairs above us to prevent us from passing.

It was at that point that I made a snap decision. Looking up at Barry and Wade, I said, "Alright. Go ahead and cuff me to the rail. I'm staying." Wade walked over with a set of handcuffs.

"You sure about this?" he asked.

"You bet," I answered. "Take my wallet and keys and leave me my license." Wade reached into my pockets and collected the items, making sure to tuck my ID back into my pocket. He then clasped one end of the cuffs around my right wrist and the other end around the stairwell rail. I heard the click and felt the permanency of my decision. I was committed to seeing this through to the end, whatever that looked like. But I was glad to see I wasn't alone; Stephan was also chained to the landing rail, while another woman who'd been blocked from getting up the stairs was cuffed to the railing on the first floor.

As Wade and Barry walked away to check on the other protestors, I looked up and saw a group of RTD employees and visitors gathered in the doorway and staring down at Stephan and me. Seeing their stares and hearing their whispers caused something deep within me to become unleashed. Twelve years of being treated differently and denied access and opportunities solely because of my disability started pouring forth in an intense explosion of rage and energy. It was a feeling I'd never experienced before, but I understood it intrinsically. It was the feeling of having my heart ripped out of me after the RTD board voted against our proposal. It was the frustration of seeing a simple solution—to make accessible transportation available for everyone—made complicated and political. It was the sheer lunacy of how we turn our differences into oppression and discrimination. It was the anger from seeing how we make life harder for people with the greatest needs. It was all of that finally reaching the surface and finding a voice and an outlet.

"What are you looking at?" I yelled. "I'm not paying for you to stare at me! Get back to work and make those buses accessible! We're not going anywhere until you do!" I continued to alternate between yelling and chanting, as my anger ebbed and flowed.

After about thirty minutes, the police arrived. We continued to chant and block access to the building, even as the officers moved among us and tried to intimidate us into backing down. Tiring of this, police captain Bill Brannan ordered our group to leave the building and threatened to arrest anyone who insisted on staying. Eventually, some of the group members did leave, but Stephan and I both stayed put not only because of the handcuffs, but also because, at least for me, I wanted to see this through. I was determined to make a statement for the rights of people with disabilities. A police officer finally came by and began to take my name and other information. As he did, a photographer from the Denver Post took my picture. The officer then arrested me, charging me with obstructing a government operation and obstructing a public passageway, then escorted me out of the building. By then, Wade and all the others had left and were waiting for me around the corner, ready to talk about next steps.

When I arrived home that night, Susan asked how my day had been.

"Fine," was the only answer I could muster. I was physically and emotionally exhausted and wanted only to go to sleep.

The next morning, Susan went to the airport to meet Karen, her former roommate who had just flown in from Charlotte. From there, the two headed out toward the mountains to go skiing for a couple of days. Around noon, they stopped at a McDonald's to use the restroom and grab some lunch. Susan came out of the bathroom to find Karen staring at a copy of *The Denver Post* that was lying on a nearby table. Looking up at Susan, she asked, "Hey, did Mark get arrested?"

"No!" exclaimed Susan, laughing at the absurdity of the question.

With an amused smile, Karen handed the paper to Susan and said, "Well, there he is on the front page of the Metro section."

My first arrest, and the photo Susan and Karen saw in The Denver Post

Chapter 28

In-Laws

The takeover of the RTD headquarters set off a series of actions around Denver as we continued to pressure RTD to meet with us and reverse their decision about the express buses. Following the example of the Gang of Nineteen, we blocked buses, sat at bus stops with signs, and disrupted RTD board meetings. Throughout, we made it clear that we were doing this—and would continue to do this—until they agreed to make every bus accessible.

In the midst of this campaign, in the summer of 1982, Susan and I decided to get in the van and head southeast for two weeks to reconnect with loved ones we hadn't seen since the wedding. We stopped first in Charlotte to see my family and our friends, then headed to Atlanta to see Peg and Tim. From there, we drove to Sarasota, Florida to spend some time with Susan's parents. We hadn't seen them since the wedding. While I sensed they were doing their best to accept me into the family, I knew the relationship was still somewhat tenuous. I was hopeful that spending some quality time with them on their turf would help the relationship. Still, I was nervous.

Susan's family, like mine, loved being near water. Thus, it was not surprising that Sally and Tom lived in a beautiful beach house that Tom had built on the Gulf Coast. After spending time in landlocked Colorado, Susan and

I were both thrilled to get to spend time soaking up the sun and playing in the surf. The day after we arrived, Susan, an expert sailor who'd spent many summers working on and racing sailboats, wanted to show off her skills. She suggested we go out on her parent's Sunfish. I'd been around enough boats to know that a Sunfish was small. Even though this one was a two-seater, it was still called a personal-sized watercraft for a reason. I didn't see the need for both of us to be on it. But when I suggested she go by herself, she said, "I want you to come with me. It'll be fun!" Something in the way she said it told me it was important to her that I go along. I got the sense that she needed to show her parents that I could still do many of the things that she could. I agreed to go.

Susan and her dad worked together to get the boat ready, while Sally and I watched and chatted. When the boat was ready, Tom started to head toward me, but Susan moved quickly to get ahead of him. She handed me a life jacket, which Tom helped to strap on, then she reached down, picked me up, and set me down in the hull of the boat. If Tom was surprised by this, he didn't say anything. Instead, he helped to push the boat off the beach and called out, "Have fun, you two," as the water began to carry us away. Susan positioned the boat so that we were headed down wind and the sail was full, and within a few minutes, we had crossed the waves and reached calmer waters. While she confidently steered the boat, I sat back, feeling the wind on my face and watching her deftly manage the ship.

At one point, Susan decided to turn up wind, which meant that she needed to shift her weight and the beam to the other side of the boat.

"I'm going to need to adjust the sail. You're going to have to duck so that the beam doesn't hit you in the head, okay?" I wasn't really sure how well this was going to work, and I asked her to make the move slowly. As I ducked, she guided the beam smoothly over my head. "Great job!" she cried, and I returned her smile. Throughout the journey, she had to do this a couple of more times, and we gradually developed a nice rhythm. It was great to get to share this experience with Susan, to see her in her element.

We'd been out in the open water for about an hour when I asked Susan to head back in. Reluctantly, she agreed. Once we got in near the shore, Susan had to pull the rudder up so that it wouldn't hit the sand and tumble us over. Doing this, however, required her to reach over me while still steering the boat from the back, and as she did this, a wave hit us, causing the boat to tumble over. We both fell into the water, with the sail landing on top of me. It was light enough that it didn't hurt, but her parents, who'd been watching from shore, freaked out when they couldn't see me and started running toward us. I could hear them shouting to Susan and splashing through the water as they ran toward us. Susan, on the other hand, was completely calm as she ambled through the knee-deep water and pulled the sail off of me just as her parents reached us. As the mast raised up, I looked up to see Tom and Sally staring down at me.

"Hey!" I said, smiling. They both started laughing.

Susan and I going sailing

After that, Tom and Sally both seemed to relax a little more. I think they recognized that Susan was not going to have to give up the activities that were important to her just because she was married to me. We could continue to do the things we both loved as long as there was acceptance, flexibility, and humor in the mix. That was the power of our relationship.

But just as my relationship with my in-laws began to relax, the tension with RTD increased.

CHAPTER 29

ADAPT

While Wade, I, and the other advocates kept the pressure on RTD, local politics began to shift in our favor. Since its inception in 1965, members of the RTD board had been legislatively appointed; however, local citizens were becoming increasingly frustrated with the board's lack of accountability and began calling for an elected board. When the legislature agreed, it ignited a flurry of people filing for candidacy. A record fifty-nine candidates came out of the woodwork and began campaigning for the fifteen positions, creating the board's most competitive race in history. Seeing this as a great opportunity, Wade began a campaign of his own to get me to run for the board. He thought that with my clean-cut, conservative look and affable personality, I could get elected and represent the needs of people with disabilities.

This was not the first time someone pressured me to run for public office nor would it be the last. Back in Charlotte, I'd been asked to run for a city-council position, and since then, I've been asked to run for various state offices. Fortunately, or unfortunately, depending upon your perspective and political leanings, holding public office has never interested me. A lot of people see it as the only way to create change. I don't. The public-policy process is only one piece of the puzzle to change society for the better. I don't need a public office to develop relationships and change attitudes. Plus, I'm a little too selfish to run for office. I have a mile-long list of things that I think need to be addressed. If I was elected, I'd want to work on all of them, probably to the exclusion of some of the concerns of my constituents. Thus, I'm content to work with legislators, raising issues, educating, and, when necessary, putting pressure on them to do the right thing.

That being said, I did agree to run for the RTD board position for my district. I don't know if I couldn't say no to Wade or if I really saw an opportunity to improve public transportation from the perspective of someone with a disability. Either way, I agreed to run for public office for the first and only time.

Since you had to be a resident of Denver for at least a year before running for public office, I filed my candidacy paperwork exactly one year and one day after moving to the city. That was the easy part. I had no idea how to run a campaign and had very little money to support one. I was running against four other people in District K, where I lived. I was pretty sure they knew a lot more about this kind of thing than I. Still, I gave it my best shot. Some of my neighbors came over one day and helped me create campaign signs. They were hand-painted on leftover pieces of plywood, a far cry from the slick, professionally designed banners that were touted by my opponents. Since I couldn't afford a mass-mail campaign, my friends and I hung out in parking lots, handing out leaflets. And while many of my fellow candidates were annoyed by the flurry of surveys sent to us by the press and various organizations, I filled out as many as I could, taking advantage of the free exposure.

One of my homemade campaign signs

Mine was a grassroots campaign in more ways than one. Surprisingly, people seemed to respond to it. Even with my homemade signs, I was starting to gather some solid support, and not just from my friends and neighbors. *The Denver Post* actually endorsed me, while *The Rocky Mountain News* called me a viable candidate, even if it expressed concern that I was focused on only one issue. But on the off chance that I didn't win my district, we also spent a lot of time talking with the other candidates about their position on making the all buses accessible. As we did, we were pleasantly surprised to find more candidates who supported the issue than were against it. It looked like either way, we were in good shape.

On November 9, 1982, Susan, Wade, and I, along with many of our friends, went to the polls to cast our ballots, hopeful yet realistic. When the results were announced at the end of the night, I had come in second in my district, behind a guy with rail experience. Not bad for my first and only run for office.

Two months later, the newly elected board met for the first time and decided that their first order of business—their first! —was to vote on whether to reverse the decision of the appointed board and require that all newly purchased buses, including express buses, be made accessible for people in wheelchairs. Clearly, our protests, campaigns, and discussions had a significant impact on the public's attitudes and opinions about people with disabilities. As the members cast their votes, we heard many more "ayes" than "nays," and in the end, the new RTD board voted overwhelmingly in our favor. From that point on, every single bus that rolled through the streets of Denver would have a lift on it, whether it was a fixed-route bus or an express one. People with disabilities now had the same access to public transportation that everyone else did, for good. We had won.

As the first accessible express buses began to roll into Denver, Wade started getting calls from disability-rights advocates around the country. Word about our victory had spread throughout the disability community, and people wanted to know how we'd gotten RTD to agree to make all buses accessible. A few cities, such as San Francisco and Seattle, made public transportation accessible. In most cities, however, this was not the case. Many other groups had tried and failed to get accessible public transportation where they lived. Like us, they had started by writing letters, asking for meetings, testifying at hearings, and lobbying elected officials. And like us, they had been stalled, ignored, ridiculed, disparaged, treated like children, and ultimately told "no." And in the end, people with disabilities were still left sitting on the sidewalks while inaccessible buses rolled quickly by.

Wade explained that after "playing nicely" didn't work, we had "bumped it up" and started using civil disobedience—or direct action—as a way of forcing public leaders to take us seriously and address the issue. That was the one thing that had worked for us and the advocates in San Francisco. It was the common thread connecting us with lifts on buses, both literally and figuratively. It seemed that you needed to be willing to chain yourself to a bus or two in order to get what you needed. Hearing this, most of the advocates were frustrated enough to consider protesting and wanted to know more about how to go about it, though a few said, "No, thanks," and ended the conversation. Not everyone was ready to get in the opposition's face.

For the ones who were, however, we wanted to help. After hearing about the number of calls, Wade and I recognized that we had an opportunity to help our fellow advocates by providing civil-disobedience training, particularly as it related to campaigning for accessible transportation. We could develop the structure and content for training that could be replicated and shared throughout the country. But we also recognized that as a small, Denver-based group, we didn't have the exposure and network necessary to reach advocates in other states.

As luck would have it, Barry had gotten a grant for HAIL to host a conference on independent living (IL) called "Beyond Survival." Never before had IL advocates from around the country been together in the same place to network and share ideas. It was the perfect opportunity to meet with other advocates who were interested in learning about direct action. In addition, Wade and I agreed that the National Council on

Independent Living (NCIL), which was going to be present for the event, was in a prime position to offer training on civil disobedience—or "CD," as we called it—and organizing since they had the network and national reach. We could develop a training program and then hand it off to NCIL, which could then offer it as a service to its members. It seemed like a perfect plan, and we decided to take advantage of the NCIL Board's visit to Denver to propose it to them.

While IL advocates from across the country started pouring into Denver wearing the conference's butterfly logo T-shirt, Wade, I, and several others went to the local La Quinta Inn to meet with the NCIL Board of Directors, who had agreed to give us a spot on their agenda to make our proposal. Together, we did our best dog-and-pony show, explaining our idea and the need for a training program to help advocates push for accessible public transportation in their local areas. We offered to design the training, using our experience, and then give it to NCIL to promote and disseminate as a service for its members. The board members listened, asked a lot of questions, and were exceedingly complimentary of the things we had accomplished in Denver using direct action. When our presentation was over, however, the members didn't take any time to discuss whether to adopt our proposal. Instead, the chair politely explained that NCIL had already issued a position paper on the need for accessible public transportation, and they were waiting for a response before they did anything else. They thanked us for our time and then politely dismissed us. Clearly, they were still focused on playing nice.

We walked away from the meeting shaking our heads. We'd never even considered that NCIL's leadership wouldn't be interested in our proposal. It was obviously a win-win for everyone, and a great way to help people with disabilities across the country. We were both dumbfounded and disappointed. In a way, it was worse to be turned down by fellow disability advocates than by public officials. The advocates were supposed to get it. Dejected, we went back to the Atlantis office to figure out our next step. Not surprisingly, Wade had already begun to consider what to do next.

"I think we're going to have to do this ourselves," he said, as we gathered around his desk.

"Do what?" I asked.

"Teach people to organize and demonstrate. I think we're going to have to form our own group to get out there and do CD stuff and continue to fight for accessible transportation. We can invite folks to join us, and in the process, they can learn the techniques and strategies and share it with others, like a kind of on-the-job training, so to speak."

"Are we going to have to set up another nonprofit to get this started?" asked Babs.

"Nah. I don't think it needs to be that formal. What's most important is getting a group together that's willing to do the work and train others. And all of that can be done as a project of Atlantis."

Clearly, Wade had been thinking ahead of us for a while now.

"What do you want to call the group?" I asked.

"I don't know. What do you guys think?" said Wade. We began to throw out a number of ideas as Bob Conrad sat quietly in the corner with his eyes closed, clearly working through something in his head. Then he opened his eyes and held out his hand for us to stop talking.

"How about 'Americans Disabled for Accessible Public Transit,' or "ADAPT" for short?" he suggested. We looked around at each other, smiling and nodding our heads. Aside from the fact that the advocacy world didn't need another acronym, we liked it.

"Alright, now that we have a name, what kind of leadership structure should we have? How's this thing going to work?" asked Babs.

"I don't think we need one particular person to be the leader," I said. "I think this is a chance to develop a wide range of people to be leaders and then they'll be empowered enough to go and help other groups do what we do. I've seen what happens when people depend on one person," I said, thinking of my days as "Mr. Handicapped Charlotte."

"I agree," added Wade. "We can do this as a group. We'll work together to make the decisions."

The group appeared to be comfortable with this idea and moved on to discussing what, exactly, ADAPT was going to do. As the new name implied, we agreed that we would be strictly about fighting for accessible public transportation. There were a million other injustices that affected people with disabilities. We knew we needed to stay focused in order to be effective, and we were already off to a good start with this one. Since we had already addressed the need locally, we decided it was time to go national with our campaign. That meant going from a local target, which had been RTD, to a national one, which could mean only one group: the American Public Transportation Association (APTA). Since its inception in 1882, APTA had represented the interests of public-transit authorities across the country. It was APTA who had sued Secretary Lewis and gotten Reagan to create the local option. It was APTA who had a strong lobbying arm that continued to influence the US Department of Transportation and its decisions. And it was with the support of APTA that transit leaders at the local level were voting against making all of their buses accessible. If the world of transportation was going to change in our favor, we were going to have to start with them.

As we sat in Wade's office discussing all of this, Molly, one of my colleagues who had recently begun to date Wade, started making some phone calls to research where APTA's next national convention was going to be.

"Oh, wow, you guys!" she said, putting down the phone. "You're not going to believe this!"

"What?" asked Wade.

"APTA's getting ready for their annual convention this October and Secretary of Transportation Elizabeth Dole will be there. Guess where it's going to be?"

"Where?"

"Here in Denver!"

ADAPT, it seemed, was going to get to take on APTA right in our own backyard.

APTA

The day before the APTA conference began, about twenty people from across the country flew into Denver, ready to participate in the first official ADAPT action. These were all people who had called us previously to ask how we had successfully gotten accessible transportation in Denver. After forming ADAPT, we had called them back and invited them to come and be part of an actual action so that they could see for themselves how it works. Almost all of them had quickly taken us up on our invitation, especially since the Atlantis Community provided some funds to help cover their travel and lodging expenses.

Wade greeted the new ADAPT members at the airport and wasted no time in putting them to work. "I want some of y'all to take these signs that we've made and form a picket line on the sidewalk. You'll be the welcoming committee for the APTA members as they arrive!" he said, smiling mischievously. He then took the remaining folks and drove them to APTA's hotel—the Hilton—where they joined Atlantis members who were staging a similar greeting party for APTA members. Our guests, who included Barbara Toomer from Utah, were totally game and seemed happy to be getting involved so quickly.

After a few hours of picketing we gathered everyone from the airport and hotel and took them to this really funky Jewish synagogue that Wade had rented. There, we gathered for a potluck meal before beginning our first official ADAPT training. We started by reviewing our demands for APTA. Primarily, we wanted APTA to sign a resolution calling for lifts on all new buses. We also wanted APTA to go on record that they wanted the Section 504 rules to be returned to their original, pristine condition. No more local option.

After reviewing our demands, we described our efforts to dialogue with APTA prior to this conference. We explained that we had shared our demands with the APTA leadership in hopes that we could discuss them during the conference. Not surprisingly, the leaders had neither agreed to our demands nor offered to sit and discuss them during their time in Denver. However, after reviewing our demands and recalling the history of Wade and the Gang of Nineteen, it had not taken the APTA folks long to connect the dots and foresee the potential for our disrupting their conference in Denver. Thus, in their wisdom, they attempted to negotiate with us to minimize the degree of disruption. In a series of phone calls and letters, we agreed to dial down some of our protest activities. In exchange, APTA gave us twenty minutes to lead a plenary session for its members during the conference. We spent a lot of time trying to decide the best use of our time on stage, knowing that it was a rare opportunity to explain our case. After much discussion, we agreed to perform a skit, thinking that would keep the audience's attention and be a positive and effective way to express our point of view.

In addition to our negotiations with APTA, as part of our intelligence gathering we had tracked down an advance list of the conference's keynote speakers and were surprised and delighted to learned that Atlanta mayor Andrew Young was planning to speak during the conference. Given his involvement with the civil-rights movement, we thought he might support our efforts and tried to arrange a meeting with him, though we were unable to track him down. We also made attempts to contact Department of Transportation Secretary Dole but weren't successful.

Although we had agreed to decrease our civil-disobedience actions, we had not agreed to stop them entirely. Thus, we spent the remainder of the training talking about different kinds of direct-action activities. We covered blocking buses, taking over buildings, and other tactics. We assigned roles and responsibilities according to each person's gifts, personality, and abilities. Finally, we addressed the biggest question on people's minds: what to do if you get arrested. We wanted them to know what to expect and how to handle themselves in the event they were arrested, not to make it easier for the police but out of concern for the ADAPT members. This wasn't something to be approached lightly, and we wanted every person present to understand that. As he had before, Wade emphasized that we didn't expect or insist that people get arrested, particularly if they weren't up for it. Every person had something to offer ADAPT, but not everyone was up for being arrested. Still, most people in the room seemed resolute in their commitment to civil disobedience, even if it meant getting arrested. They understood that this was part of the process of creating change and taking back some power for ourselves. Ghandi and Dr. King had proven that.

When the training was over, our out-of-town visitors were paired with members of Atlantis and went home with them for the night. The Atlantis members were a motley crew who came from a variety of backgrounds and lived in a variety of settings throughout the city. Most lived at or near poverty level, which meant that some of our guests ended up in some pretty poor neighborhoods. The next morning, we had to counsel a few of the visitors who had been somewhat traumatized by the experience, but we felt it was an important part of the ADAPT experience. It built solidarity, gave credibility to the Atlantis members, and certainly underscored the need to advocate with the most marginalized people in our society.

We arrived the first morning of the convention and surrounded the Hilton, positioning ourselves about ten feet apart from each other so that people could still walk between us. Bundled up in our coats and hats, we wore buttons that read "We will ride" and "ADAPT," held signs that read "Accessible Transportation Now," and had multi-colored balloons tied to the backs of our chairs. We were there to make a statement in whatever way we could. As the convention began inside, most of us sat outside and chanted without ceasing, while several others went inside and did their best to track down Secretary Dole, who managed to avoid us with the help of her security team. The press—including *The Washington Post, USA Today*, and *The McNeil-Lehrer News Hour*—took note of our protests and included us in their stories. Although it was cold, we stayed the entire day, a clear sign that we were committed. The second day was just as cold, but we showed up and again surrounded the building.

On Wednesday, the day of our session, we arrived early and rode the freight elevators to the floor where the convention was being held. Upon entering the room, we saw a large crowd; during the negotiations, we had insisted that the meeting room be full before we would begin. We wouldn't tolerate token attendance. We made our way through the room and up to the stage, as Wade and several other people carried our one large prop, a cardboard bus. As soon as they had it set up, we were ready to go.

From the very beginning, we had agreed to present the issue of accessible transportation as a civil-rights issue. As such, several of our nondisabled members pretended to be sitting on the bus. At one stop, more nondisabled people got on the bus, including one who was pretending to be Rosa Parks, the woman who made buses a civil-rights issue for African-Americans in 1955. The person who was playing Rosa then reenacted the events of 1955. When that part was finished, the bus continued to its next stop, where I, in my wheelchair, was waiting. When the bus stopped, I made a point of asking the driver if it had a lift. He loudly stated, "No." I then turned to the audience and said, "Rosa Parks wanted to be able to sit in the front of the bus. I just want to get on."

When the skit was over, ADAPT members who had been sitting in the audience began softly chanting, "We will ride! We will ride," gradually gaining confidence and momentum until their voices were the only sound in the vast room. The rest of us on stage joined in. Looking over the crowd, we noticed that some of the APTA members were starting to chant as well. At first, it was just a couple, then, slowly, a few more. I looked around at my colleagues on the stage, who had noticed it too. It wasn't a lot of APTA members, but it was some—enough to know that, gradually, we were starting to get their attention.

As we were leaving the convention center, already satisfied with the results of the day, Mayor Young followed us out and offered to talk with us. We went across the street to a local park. There, we talked with him about the similarities between the civil-rights movement and our fight for the rights of people with disabilities, as well as the need for accessible transportation. He seemed interested in understanding our needs and asked questions about how he and others could help. He was so nice that someone started to apologize for disrupting this convention where he was speaking. Mayor Young quickly interrupted him and shook his head saying, "You gotta do what you gotta do."

After the conference was over and the newest members of ADAPT had returned to their home cities, several of us met in Wade's living room to process ADAPT's first national-level action. Overall, we were pleased with a lot of things. We were thrilled to have committed advocates from across the country fly in and get involved as easily and as well as they did. And we were excited about the impact we made. From the press attention, to the formal presentation, to the follow-up meetings, we could see that the action had been effective in establishing ADAPT as a representative voice for people with disabilities.

But it hadn't been effective enough. We hadn't gotten APTA to agree to any of our demands, and we agreed that our work was not done until that happened. We also knew that to get their agreement, we were going to have to stay on the heels of APTA and shadow their every move. This would mean showing up at every one of their conventions, no matter where in the country they met. Looking up their schedule, we learned that the next one was scheduled for Washington, DC, in October, 1984. On our journey toward nationwide accessible transportation, our next stop was the nation's capitol. Before that, however, I would need to take time for some important developments at home.

CHAPTER 31

LINDSEY

When I was injured, I had a lot of questions my body and sex. I wasn't alone. Once I started working as a counselor in Charlotte, I heard many people with spinal-cord injuries give voice to their questions. How will my injury affect my sex life? Can I still have children? It was enough that a colleague, Wilma Asreal, and I developed a three-day intensive class on sex for newly-injured patients. The class was designed to answer many questions and help them understand that paralysis leaves plenty of room for a robust sex life, particularly if you're willing to be creative.

As for having kids, the answer to that question is certainly "yes," with some qualifications. It all depends on whether the injury to the spinal cord was "complete" or not. For people who have a complete injury, in which there's a clean break to the cord, it might be necessary to pursue any one of the many reproductive technology options available, such as in vitro fertilization or egg donor, or else adopt one of the many, many children in the world who need loving families. However, if a person's injury is "incomplete" and some feeling and/or function can still be transmitted through the cord, then it is possible for that person to produce a child by traditional means, in other words, via good old-fashioned sexual intercourse. It's not a given, but it's a possibility.

At the point that Susan and I began to get serious in our relationship, we had had the usual conversations about kids. We both wanted to have a child, and we both understood there was a good chance that I wouldn't be able to father a child on my own. I knew I had an incomplete injury. I still winced at the memory of being wheeled down to the X-ray lab, weights hanging from my head, in pain. Yet an incomplete injury wasn't a guarantee of anything. A few weeks before our wedding, I went to my urologist, Dr. Asreal, and had some testing done to check my sperm count and get a sense of what my chances were of producing a child naturally.

On the day of our wedding, Susan was gathered with Peg and her bridesmaids in the church narthex, waiting for the ceremony to begin. Dr. Asrael, arriving late, saw Susan and walked quickly over to her.

"Susan, you're so beautiful!" he gushed before leaning over and whispering something in her ear. He then turned and entered the sanctuary to find a seat. After he was gone, Peg looked over to see Susan smiling, a single, delicate tear flowing down her cheek.

"What's wrong?" she asked.

Wiping away the tear, Susan shook her head and said, "Nothing's wrong. In fact, Dr. Asrael just gave us one of the best wedding presents. We're going to be able to have babies!"

About a year after our move to Denver, Susan and I decided it was time to test Dr. Asrael's prediction. By then, many of our friends were starting to have children, and as we visited them and held their newborns, we realized that we wanted in on the joy, fulfillment, lifestyle change, and sleep deprivation. Susan went to see her gynecologist, who checked her out and said she was healthy and ready to have children. But then Susan hesitated, explaining that I, with my injury, might not be able to produce a child.

"Just try it!" said her doctor. "You won't know until you try."

"Fair enough," we thought, and so we "tried." And sure enough, Susan got pregnant on the first go round. After noticing some changes in her body, and feeling, as she describes it, "a connection," Susan went back to her doctor and got confirmation that she was, indeed, pregnant. At her first opportunity, Susan called me at work.

"Hey!" she said.

"Hey!"

"Guess what? I'm pregnant!"

I laughed and said, "Wow! That was fast! You must be a real Fertile Myrtle!"

In the early hours of June 28, 1984, little Lindsey Nicole greeted the world. Two days later, we took her home from the hospital. From the very beginning, Susan insisted on bottle-feeding Lindsey; she wanted me to be as involved as she was in Lindsey's care. That meant that we took turns getting up for the midnight feedings. Well, I should say, either way, Susan had to get up and pick Lindsey up out of her crib; if we had forced Lindsey to wait for me to get up, transfer into my chair, then wheel into her room before feeding or tending to her, we'd owe a lot of money to a therapist today. Instead, Susan would bring Lindsey to me with a bottle, climb into bed, and go back to sleep while I listened to my daughter quietly suck from her bottle. Many nights, Lindsey and I would both fall asleep after her feeding. I enjoyed the coziness of having the three of us together.

Lindsey and I in Colorado

For the first few weeks, we had the steady stream of grandparents, aunts, and uncles from both sides flying in to meet Lindsey and help with her care. After that, however, Susan and I agreed that we needed some more permanent help. While I did as much as I could, I still had my limits. The one thing I didn't do was change diapers since my lack of dexterity would have made that process both messy and comical. Conveniently, one of my attendants had a daughter who wanted to become an attendant as well and needed some experience. We invited her to move into the bedroom down in our basement and serve as a type of live-in caregiver for Lindsey and a part-time attendant for me. This was an enormous help for us once Susan returned to work, and it made me feel a little better about leaving my wife and newborn for a week when it was time to head to Washington, DC, for our next confrontation with APTA.

NOTHING ABOUT US WITHOUT US

After the success of ADAPT's first action against APTA in Denver, Atlantis began receiving more calls from advocates wanting to know about direct action. Seeing a great opportunity, Wade applied for and received a grant from the Campaign for Human Development. The grant paid for advocates from across the United States to meet us in DC to participate in training, which we called the "Access Institute," as well as the action against APTA. This new training was designed to expand on the model we had created for the Denver action, giving us much more time to review the history of the disability and other civil-rights movements, the particulars of direct action work, and the methods for fighting for accessible transportation, both nationally and on the local level. It would also allow the participants plenty of time to try out their direct action skills during the APTA action and then come back and talk about their experiences with the group. Hopefully, all of this would enable and empower the trainees to take these skills and this knowledge and use them as necessary, including addressing issues in their own communities.

The grant also allowed us to invite Shel Trapp, one of Wade's mentors, to lead the training. Shel was a former Methodist minister and well-known community activist and organizer from Chicago. As the cofounder of National People's Action, he traveled extensively across the country training grassroots organizations to organize and address the injustices in their communities. We were thrilled when he readily agreed to help us. Wade was happy because he really didn't want to be leading everything. Wade knew that Shel would have a lot of wisdom to share with the group.

Community activists and organizers are typically a passionate bunch. They are generally people who are on the fringes of society either because of their economic status, race, belief system, sexual orientation, or, in our case, disability. They are the ones who have experienced firsthand the discrimination and alienation that comes with being different in some respect. Shel, given his experience, had worked with a wide variety of groups and people from all walks of life. That's why we were shocked when he arrived in DC, took one look at our group, and declared, "It'll never happen," when told we were going to take on public transportation at the national level. Apparently, even Shel doubted the ability of people with disabilities to affect meaningful change.

Despite his doubts, Shel approached the training with great energy, fully committed to teaching people how to tap into their own power. A short, bald man, Shel cussed a lot and liked his cocktails. Bob Kafka (who, with his partner, Stephanie Thomas, was coming to his first ADAPT action and would become close friends of mine), described him as a "scary, fire-hydrant-built man." But he was also very emotional and brought a great deal of intensity and humor to the training sessions. Participants in the training ate it up. Having come from a wide variety of states—including Virginia, Utah, Arkansas, California, New York, and Texas—they were ready to soak up as much knowledge and experience as possible. I think it helped that the Institute was held at New York Avenue Presbyterian Church, chosen because it was the church that Abraham Lincoln and his family had attended. The symbolism and connection to a leader who had stood up for the rights of others enhanced the tone of the training.

We wasted no time in giving the trainees their first taste of direct action. On the first morning, Shel led a session titled "Power, Issues, Strategies," which set the perfect tone for our time in DC. That afternoon, Wade and I and several ADAPT members had arranged to meet with Ralph Stanley, director of the Urban Mass Transit Association, to ask the association to issue a policy supporting lifts on all new buses. While we were glad that Mr. Stanley was willing to meet with us, we were aware enough to know that he would not agree to our demands. We strategized with Shel about the best way to handle the meeting. Shel coached us not only on how to handle the meeting, but also on where to hold it.

"Are you planning on holding the meeting here in the church?" Shel asked Wade.

"That's what I was thinking," he replied.

"Don't do it," Shel insisted. "You invite these bigwig bureaucrats to meet with you in a little old classroom in a church, and the power stays with them." He watched us, making sure his point was getting across. "You've got to keep the power if you're going to get anywhere with them!"

We looked at each other. "Well, where do you suggest we have the meeting then?" I asked.

He made a point of looking around the room at all of us before saying, "This is a meeting about transportation, isn't it? So have the meeting in the middle of the street!"

We stared at each other with grins on our faces. The idea seemed crazy and obvious all at the same time. We understood immediately that it was the perfect move for a group that was all about civil disobedience. Ralph Stanley expected us to play by the rules. Boy, were we going to surprise him.

Sure enough, when Mr. Stanley and his entourage stepped out of their black limousine, they saw a table with chairs sitting in the middle of New York Avenue, a major four-lane thoroughfare at the time. Wade and Mike both approached Mr. Stanley to greet him and invited him and his people to join us at the table. With Shel's coaching, we had staged it so that ADAPT members sat on one side of the table, while Mr. Stanley and his folks sat on the other. They all looked distinctly uncomfortable, glancing around at the drivers and pedestrians who watched as they took their seats in the middle of the street. It didn't help that drivers were honking their horns and staring at us as they were forced to slow down and drive around us. We had to raise our voices to ensure that we were heard, yet we were clear that Ralph had heard us before the meeting had even begun. Shel was right; we held the power.

While several ADAPT members handled the meeting, Wade and Shel led the training participants out to the street in front of the church where they began to surround Mr. Stanley's limousine. When the meeting was over, Mr. Stanley, who had indeed refused to support our request, stood up and turned to walk toward the waiting car. As he did, he was greeted with shouts of "We will ride! We will ride!" from the raucous group that surrounded his car. He turned back to look at Wade, then shook his head and walked away. The rest of us took our places around the car and joined in the chant. I took the time to look around at the trainees, who looked both nervous and excited. I recognized that look, that sense of beginning to recognize one's own power. It was a great way to end the first day and to begin the Institute. When the police arrived, we backed away, allowing Mr. Stanley to get in his car. It was too early in the process to get arrested. There would be plenty of time for that part of the training.

Shel knew that blocking buses was one of ADAPT's signature actions. I could tell that he was even a little curious to see a demonstration. Again, we strategized with him and decided that while we could take over any bus, we were in DC. Why not stop a bus right in front of the White House? We gathered outside the Hotel Harrington, where we were staying, and rolled or marched the half dozen blocks down to Pennsylvania Avenue. Once we had all arrived, we waited patiently for the first bus to pull up, then quickly swarmed around it before the bus driver knew what was happening. The driver did what he could to get us to move out of the way, though he seemed to understand that it was pointless. He was in for a long day. Within minutes, police officers arrived and moved from person to person trying to figure out who was in charge. Eventually, they headed over to Wade, who was standing with Shel along the sidewalk. Wade made it clear that we weren't going anywhere anytime soon. The officers turned to talk among themselves and decide what to do. In any other case, they would have immediately arrested the protestors. But they didn't have any experience arresting people with disabilities and weren't sure what to do. Meanwhile, word of our action had clearly spread, as members of the media began to arrive with cameras in tow. We made the front page of the paper the next day.

Inspired by their first bus takeover, the training participants were hungry for more. When the APTA members arrived in the city the next day, trainees were more than ready to use newfound skills and power to greet them. We conducted our usual actions that were meant to interrupt the convention and inconvenience the APTA representatives. One of our most creative actions occurred on the second day of the APTA convention, when we blocked a bus full of APTA spouses who were off for a day of sightseeing. We thought it was important that they understood our position, particularly how it felt to be unable to get where you need to go.

These were some of the most memorable moments of ADAPT's first time in our nation's capitol, but there were other important moments that were subtle but no less critical. These included the ways in which ADAPT gained both confidence and identity as a group. Having followed APTA to a second convention site, and having delivered a highly successful training, we were really establishing ourselves as a key leader in the fight for accessible transportation. It was gratifying that the training participants were leaving with a sense of empowerment. They could take the fight for accessible transportation to their own communities, to their friends, and to their families.

One of the most poignant memories of our time in DC involved Shel, the esteemed community organizer who had so confidently declared that we would never have any impact on the transportation industry. Throughout the week, he watched us. He observed us as we daringly held a meeting with a high-level official in the middle of a busy street. He saw how we blocked buses and shut down Pennsylvania Avenue, in full view of the president's home, without reserve. He stared as we bravely tussled with police, even to the point of arrest. And he saw how some of the APTA members whispered words of encouragement as they passed us. Throughout all of this, he repeatedly took his own questions and thoughts to Wade, who served as both counselor and confessor to Shel, carefully helping him to navigate through his own prejudices and attitudes about disabilities. And when, on the last day of our action, Shel cried as he watched our demonstration against APTA, I knew that, of all of us, he had learned the most these past two weeks. We'd made a difference because we were doing the work for ourselves. "Nothing about us without us," was the common refrain. We were owning our own power and would continue to do so until we reached critical mass, finally tipping the scales in our favor. Yet, even as we were learning to claim our own power, my dad was having to surrender to a higher power.

Chapter 33

Surrender

On February 14, 1986, my dad walked into a treatment center for alcohol and drug addiction and asked to speak with a counselor. A year and a half earlier, he'd been watching television when he saw a commercial that described the center's services.

"I've got to go there," he thought to himself as he quietly sipped on some scotch, one of many drinks he'd had that day. A few weeks later, he drove slowly by the center, staring into the windows and trying to imagine himself inside. He didn't stop. "I really need to go in," he said, still trying to convince himself before continuing on his way. This went on for over a year until he finally decided to give himself and his family the ultimate Valentine's Day gift. He bravely walked through the facility's doors, fueled, in part, by the drink he'd had just before going there.

By this time, Dad was keeping a galvanized tub in his home office full of iced-down beer and Four Roses Bourbon, with plenty more in the trunk of his car, his briefcase, and the shed out back. He drank morning, noon, and night. Although he had fifteen salesmen who reported to him and was busy traveling to colleges in five different states to recruit new ones, he was drinking a fifth of scotch a day and finding that it wasn't enough. He kept waiting for someone to call him out, to notice that his hands shook continuously to the point that he couldn't hold a cup still. No one did, except for one twelve-year-old boy.

One Sunday morning, after a particularly hard night of drinking, Dad had showed up to teach his seventh-grade Sunday school class. As he began the lesson, one of the students eyed him intently. Eventually, he sidled up to Dad during a break.

"Boy, Mr. Johnson, you must have really laid one on last night," the boy said.

"Why do you say that?" my dad asked, feigning ignorance.

"Because you look and smell like my dad does on Sunday mornings," the boy replied. Dad was shocked to think that anyone had noticed his drinking and horrified to think that his shining image as the likable dad, successful company man, and chief church volunteer might be tarnished. But the boy just smiled and never said anything else. For the child, it was status quo to have inebriated adults in his life. Meanwhile, Dad decided that the best way to remedy the situation was not to stop drinking, but to stop teaching Sunday school.

Walking into the center, he was terrified that once he explained the extent of his drinking, the staff would lock him away in an "insane asylum." He went in anyway, knowing he had nothing to lose. He was tired of the binges, the secrecy, the lies, the desperation, and the pain. When he sat down with the counselor and began to describe his drinking, the stories poured out of him in a rush of words that he couldn't stop. He began to feel some relief that he could finally talk openly about this long-held secret. The man listened to him talk, then offered some treatment options.

"Do you want to do an outpatient program? You'd be coming in for both group meetings and private sessions. It takes longer, but you could still live at home and go to work."

"No, sir. I'm a traveling salesman. I'm usually out of town during the week. I wouldn't be able to come to a lot of those meetings. Plus..."

"Yes?" asked the counselor.

"Plus, I don't think an outpatient program will be enough for me. I've been doing this for most of my life, and I'm up to a fifth a day. I think I need more than that right now."

"Well, we have an inpatient program. You'd be living here for twenty-eight days straight. You'd have to put your job on hold and prepare your family. It's more intense, but it does sound like that's what you need. Can you do it?"

"Yes," said Dad, without hesitation.

"Okay. Then you'll need to show up here next Friday, and we'll get you checked in."

"Sounds good."

Dad went home and had a drink, then explained to my mom that he was planning to check himself into rehab for alcoholism within the next week. Mom was relieved. She was fed up with living with a drunk. She was tired of the lies, the smell on his breath, the arguments, and the fear that one day, he would hurt himself or someone else. But she was also a little scared, not knowing if rehab would do the trick.

The next day, Dad went into his boss's office.

"Gus, I'm drinking too much, and I'm tired of it. I've decided to check myself into a treatment center for a month and try to get clean. I'm going to need some time off."

"C'mon, Bill, you're kidding! You can't be drinking that much or you wouldn't be able to keep a job or be as successful as you are," said Gus. "And I know you don't drink more than I do. I've been out with you many times, and you never once had more to drink than I did."

"That's because I don't drink much when I'm with people. But alone, I'm drinking all the time. Gus, I'm drinking more than a fifth of scotch a day! And my hands won't stop shaking…" he said, holding up his hands for Gus to see. "I need to get some help, or I will end up in a ditch somewhere. There's times when I don't even remember driving home."

Gus readily agreed to give my dad the time off.

The night before he checked himself in, Dad decided to have one last binge. Better that than throw away all the beer and liquor he had stashed away, he reasoned. He invited a coworker over and together, they sat in his home office and drank the night away. The next morning, Dad picked up his suitcase and rode with Mom to the treatment center where they said their good-byes.

During his first private session that day, the counselor asked Dad what his priorities were in life. "Religion," said Dad. "Religion has always played a big role in my life. And family. I love my family."

"Well, Bill, here you will have to give all that up for now. Right now, your priority is getting sober. Once you're clean, then you can focus on the other things that matter to you."

And so, for twenty-eight days, Dad endured the grueling process of getting sober after more than forty-five years of drinking. For the first four days, he shook and cried and shouted as his body slowly rid itself of the alcohol under the close supervision of the treatment center staff. They often had to give him various injections in his "skinny rear" to facilitate the withdrawal process. Later, he would think this was funny, given that he often joked about the Johnson family trait of having "no ass at all." After the withdrawal process, Dad's body slowly began to recover, and he was able to participate in therapy, group meetings, and family therapy sessions with Mom.

At the end of his treatment, Mom picked up Dad and drove him home.

"Betty," he said, turning to her, "I'm an alcoholic, and I'll always be an alcoholic because there is no cure." Once he got settled, he sat and wrote a letter to his children, explaining the same thing to us. He also apologized for the ways in which his drinking had hurt us and committed to staying clean and sober. The letter arrived in our mailbox in Denver, and Susan and I sat together reading it in stunned silence. When I called Jody and Oogie, they expressed the same sense of shock. We had never known our dad was an alcoholic. Obviously, we were just kids, but even as we got older, I don't know if we simply missed the signs or were in complete denial. It's hard to say. Knowing that he was a heavy drinker did explain all the times when he'd come home from work and fall asleep in his recliner. We had always thought that the life of a traveling salesman must be pretty wearisome. And it did explain some of those times when he'd gotten angry at us and lost control. Perhaps, deep down, we had known but hadn't wanted to admit that our dad was a drunk.

BACK TO THE SOUTH

Dad's letter arrived just as we were packing up boxes and preparing to move to Atlanta. Since having Lindsey, Susan and I felt it didn't make sense for us to live in Colorado when our family members were all concentrated on the southern end of the east coast. While we both loved our jobs and living in Colorado, we didn't like the fact that Lindsey was not growing up close to her grandparents, aunts and uncles, and cousins. It was expensive to call or visit people on the east coast. We'd started keeping an eye on job opportunities in the region. Originally, it looked like we were bound for Richmond, Virginia. I had been offered a great job as the director of a statewide coalition of disability groups, so Susan began sending out her resume and was soon offered a job working with people with brain injuries. On the surface, it looked like her dream job, one that would allow her to really grow in her career. However, after she spent some time really looking into the job, it became clear that it wasn't going to be a good fit for her, and we kept looking. Finally, Susan landed a good job in Atlanta.

"Are you up for moving to Atlanta?" she asked me.

"I think so. Do you really want to go even though I haven't found a job yet?" I asked.

"Yeah. It's a good job, we'd be close to my sister and right in between all of our other family members. And I'm sure you'll have no problem getting a job there."

"Well, here's the thing," I said, trying to put into words the thoughts that had been in my head for the past few weeks. "I'm at the point where I don't want to take just any job. I left a great job in Charlotte to move to Denver. Now I'm leaving another great job to head back south. And I was ready to take this other great job in Richmond, but that wasn't going to work out as well for you. I'd like to be able to take a year to create the ideal job for me, one that's a mix of all the elements of the best jobs I've had so far. That would give me plenty of time to get to know the area, and talk to people, and see what the needs are," I paused. "Can you handle that?"

She studied me for a minute. "Absolutely. We've got enough money in the bank to keep us going on one salary for a while. I think you should take some time to figure out what you want to do."

"Then let's do it," I said.

The next day, I went to Atlantis to talk to Wade. He knew we were trying to relocate to the south, and I wanted him to know we'd made a final decision.

"Hey, man!" he said.

"Hey!"

"What's up?"

"Well, we've decided to move to Atlanta," I said.

"Cool! The heart of the civil-rights movement! That's great! Did you already land a job there?"

"No. Susan has, but I haven't. Actually, Susan and I talked last night, and she's agreed to give me a year to come up with the perfect job. I told her I wasn't willing to take just any job. I want a job that's the best of all the jobs I've had so far: community education and activism. But first, I need some time to get a lay of the land and see what's going on in the disability world and then find that ideal job."

"That's great, Mark! That's perfect." He paused and thought for a minute. "Actually, you know what? Since you won't be working for anyone right away, why don't you work for Atlantis for a little while? We could pay you to organize in Atlanta and set up an ADAPT affiliate."

"Really?"

"Yeah! Atlanta has all this civil-rights history, but it doesn't have an ADAPT affiliate. I get the impression there's not much activism going on down there that's related to disability. You could help get it started."

"Great! That would really give me something to focus on while I'm out meeting people. It would certainly give me a foot in the door."

"Exactly! But know that it wouldn't pay much. We'd give you our standard rate, which is three hundred dollars a month."

"No problem," I said.

Soon after this, Susan and Lindsey flew to Atlanta where Susan set up our new apartment and started her job. I was staying back until our house sold, giving me plenty of time to meet with Wade and plan for my work in Atlanta. I was glad to have this opportunity to work for Wade and Atlantis, especially since it gave me a way to channel this passion and energy from working with Wade and ADAPT these past few years. They had fired me up, and I wanted to be able to take that passion and share it with other people with disabilities.

It made leaving Denver a little easier. It would be tough for me to leave Wade, Atlantis, HAIL, and my fellow ADAPTers. We had formed incredible bonds, both as friends and fellow advocates. Especially Wade. He had helped to free me of the "Mr. Handicapped" persona that I'd had in Charlotte and understand that, if real change was going to happen, it was going to have to be led and owned by a wide range of people of disabilities, not just one. It's hard for one person to create meaningful and lasting change; plus, it's exhausting. Just because I have a disability doesn't mean I can speak for everyone who has a disability. I'm well-educated and know where my next mortgage payment is coming from. I can't speak for the people who are impoverished or alienated from society, but I can encourage and support them to speak for themselves. More importantly,

Wade helped me tap into those feelings that lay far beneath the surface—of anger, sadness, and loss—and use them to identify injustices and infuse my efforts both to affect change and empower others. Through all of this, he'd been willing to let me set my own course, test out my own theories, and find my place in the community—the one that was the most comfortable, effective, and best-fitting. Now, I had the chance to do for others what he had done for me. I was grateful for my time in Denver and looked forward to the opportunities that lay ahead in the land of the civil-rights movement.

SECTION 4

Taking It Personally

"Social revolutions occur when people
who are defined as the problem
seize enough power to redefine the solution."

—Saul Alinsky

ATLANTA

My involvement in Atlanta's campaign for accessible transportation began something like this:

> July 25, 1986
>
> Dear Metropolitan Atlanta Rapid Transit Authority (MARTA) Board,
>
> I trust this introduction and informational packet finds you well.
>
> My name is Mark Johnson. I moved here from Colorado on July 8, 1986. I'm an experienced community organizer and advocate for the civil rights of persons with disabilities.
>
> In Denver, I was a rider of the Regional Transportation District's (RTD) accessible mainline bus service. You see, in Denver, RTD has been purchasing lift-equipped buses since 1978. As a result of this purchase policy, RTD's fleet—currently over 700 buses—will all have lifts.
>
> How important is this policy to me and other disabled riders? It means freedom of mobility and integration. It

means an end to oppression, separate, unequal, and different treatment. It means equal opportunity.

Atlantans like to talk about themselves in superlatives. They see Atlanta as the "greatest" city, their economy as the "most dynamic," their future as the "brightest." They refer to their airport as the "world's busiest," their attitude places them among the "most energetic major cities," their growth in jobs as "the nation's fastest." Their weather, of course, is "marvelous," quote taken from a recent advertisement.

Mayor Young has said, "We have a community that is well integrated, socially and racially."

Personally, I find these superlatives and statement a bit ironic. Atlanta still has a mainline bus service that denies me and other persons with disabilities access to the same buses our nondisabled peers ride.

I encourage you to read the enclosed materials, resolution, and recommendations.

Because the rail system is closely integrated with the MARTA bus network, it's imperative that mainline buses be lift equipped. MARTA must adopt a purchase policy like that of Denver, Seattle, Los Angeles, and other major cities in the US.

Sincerely,

Mark Johnson

I arrived in Georgia's capitol and hit the ground running. I was ready to meet people, find out what advocates in the south were doing to make public transportation accessible, and start an ADAPT affiliate in Georgia. Before leaving Colorado, I had contacted Mary Johnson, editor of *Disability Rag* magazine, and asked her to give me contact information for *Rag* subscribers from Georgia. The *Rag* was an independent, radical publication—really, it was the only publication—that covered the activity of the disability-rights movement in detail, including ADAPT's actions. It seemed like a good idea to meet with *Rag* subscribers. I was pretty sure they could help me connect to the disability community in Georgia. Mary agreed and sent me her list. I mailed a letter to everyone on it, introducing myself and asking to meet with them and learn what I could about the status of disability issues in Georgia. Though they didn't know me from Adam, a number of people responded and offered to meet. As soon as I settled into our rented duplex in July, 1986, I began meeting prospective colleagues in and around Atlanta.

During this period, I paid close attention to the issue of accessible transportation and confirmed that Atlanta did not have lifts on its buses. I didn't think there were since ADAPT had been keeping a close eye on what cities were making progress in this area. Still, I'd hoped that the home of Martin Luther King Jr. and the civil-rights movement would have begun to address this civil rights issue. I started looking to meet people who were either trying to improve access to public transportation or who were dependent on public transportation. These would be the people who might be interested in the idea of an ADAPT affiliate. As luck would have it, I learned of a group of people who fit both categories. The group was a part of a loose network called DIA, or Disability in Action, which had groups in cities throughout the country. DIA is still a grassroots organization of people with disabilities whose primary focus is fighting to end discrimination against people with disabilities. Atlanta's DIA group was small—a good meeting involved about seven or eight people—and was led by an African-American man named Calvin Peterson in his tiny, one-bedroom apartment in one of Atlanta's housing projects.

In meeting with Calvin and DIA, I learned that they had been trying to work with MARTA, Atlanta's public transportation system, on the issue of accessible transportation for about a year. MARTA was another one of those systems that was using Local Option as an excuse to get out of putting lifts on their new buses. But in an attempt to placate people with disabilities, MARTA was in the process of developing a plan to serve people with disabilities and had invited us to attend the meetings and serve on its "Elderly and Handicapped Advisory Committee," which would, in theory, "advise" MARTA on development of the plan. However, given that the Advisory Committee had been in place in 1975 and the city's transit system was still inaccessible, I didn't have the sense it held influence over the agency and its policies. Indeed, DIA had been attending these meetings, and the way that Calvin described it made it clear the committee members were merely window dressing. So far, MARTA officials had cited the same old reason for not putting lifts on all new buses. As Calvin talked, I recognized his frustration; it was the same frustration I'd felt in trying to negotiate with RTD in Denver—that same feeling of hitting your head against a wall, those same efforts to dismiss a group of disabled people. Calvin invited me to attend the August Advisory Committee meeting, which I agreed to do. Before attending, I used ADAPT letterhead to send the first of many letters to the MARTA Board. I wanted them to get to know ADAPT as soon as possible.

During the Advisory Committee meeting, the MARTA staff explained that they had been charged by the board to review the 504 regulations and develop an "accessibility plan" to present to the board. As a result, they wanted to create a 504-study committee to help with this process. It seemed like they were further diluting the process by creating another committee—a point that several people made—but in the end, the idea for a study committee was upheld. The MARTA staff proposed a time line for development of the plan, which called for final recommendations to be completed in February of 1987, a series of hearings in March and April to allow for public comment, and final approval by the MARTA Board in May 1987. I can't say I left the meeting with high hopes. It was clear the staff were just going through the motions, much as RTD had done. I knew I needed to continue to put pressure on the MARTA board until we saw evidence of actual progress.

I wasn't surprised when there was no response from the board to my first letter. They didn't know this Mark Johnson guy and figured they could ignore me. Five days after the Advisory Committee meeting, I sent another letter. This time, I received an immediate response from Theodore Williams, MARTA's Director of Service Planning & Scheduling, inviting me to serve as a representative of ADAPT on the study committee (Calvin had also been appointed as a representative of DIA). I'm sure the

MARTA folks thought that putting me on a committee would appease me. However, in my reply, I neither accepted nor rejected his invitation; I pressed MARTA for additional information on the purpose and meeting schedule of the study committee, making it clear that I and others had certain expectations about this process. I also asked the following:

- Has anyone ever given this group a presentation about mainline lift-equipped buses supported by paratransit systems? If not, why not?
- Does MARTA believe the needs of disabled and elderly are the same?
- ADAPT believes disabled people have the right to ride the same buses as their nondisabled peers. Has the staff or Board ever taken a position on this civil-rights issues? If not, why not?

I then asked for copies of various documents as well as data on MARTA's fleet. Hopefully, the letter made it clear that I was serious. It must have done the trick because within days, I received a response from Mr. Williams. He assured me that MARTA was in the process of compiling the information I had requested. In the meantime, they wanted to know more about ADAPT, including our history, by-laws, names of officers, and members. I was amused by his request. It wasn't just because ADAPT is not organization and therefore doesn't have by-laws and officers. I also knew such a request was highly irregular; MARTA didn't go around asking nonprofits and other community organizations to explain their structure. This was designed to intimidate me, which meant that MARTA was feeling the pressure from my persistent inquiries. It was the beginning of a dialogue that would continue over the next several months.

While MARTA began convening meetings of the study committee, I began talking with DIA about ADAPT and how we had gotten lifts on Denver's buses using constant pressure and direct action. Calvin and the other members were really interested to know how people with disabilities had done protests. As I detailed stories of ADAPT actions, I could see their minds at work, wondering whether it was time for direct action in Atlanta.

After one meeting, I stayed back to talk to Calvin and Bernard Baker, one of the other primary members of the group.

"I'm impressed with what y'all are trying to do with MARTA, and I see your frustration. And I'm not trying to replace DIA, but I wondered if y'all would be interested in forming an Atlanta affiliate of ADAPT and doing some direct action."

Calvin and Bernard looked at each other, then back at me. Calvin spoke first.

"I think it might be a good idea. We don't seem to be getting very far with our meetings and letters," he said.

"I agree. And I think it'd be good for us to learn more about how ADAPT works," added Bernard.

"Well," I said, "ADAPT's next national action is in Detroit. Why don't you come with me? ADAPT will help raise funds to cover your expenses, and you can see for yourself what we're all about, and even try your hand at direct action. APTA's having their fall conference there."

Without hesitating, they both said, "Great!"

When I told Wade that we not only had the makings of an ADAPT affiliate in Atlanta— which would be ADAPT's thirty-third affiliate— but also two people coming to the Detroit action, he was thrilled and immediately started making plans for our trip. Atlantis had funds available to support me, Calvin, and Bernard on the trip. But we wanted to do some fundraising too, thinking it would help build local awareness and support for our cause. We held a few small fundraisers and talked it up among our friends and associates. We also applied for, and received, six hundred dollars from the Funds for Southern Communities, a local foundation. Meanwhile, I sent letters to all of the *Rag* subscribers, letting them know we were putting together an Atlanta affiliate of ADAPT and sending three local advocates to the Detroit action. I encouraged them to send donations to support the action if they could. When the first check came in from a woman named Eleanor Smith, it was my turn to be thrilled. The Metropolitan Atlanta ADAPT affiliate had participants as well as supporters. We were off to a good start.

PHOENIX

ADAPT's action for Spring 1987 was planned for Phoenix, Arizona. After cutting their teeth on the Detroit action last fall, Bernard and Calvin were ready for more. Better still, they were working hard to recruit new converts and bring them with us. A few weeks before we headed out, they introduced me to an attractive, young black woman with cerebral palsy.

"Mark, this is Kate," said Calvin. "One of my folks for the Phoenix trip dropped out at the last minute, so I asked Kate to come with us instead."

Kate flashed a wide smile at me and waved her hand in greeting. "Hi."

"Hey, sister!" I replied.

Her smile instantly vanished. I could tell I had offended her, but I didn't really know how or what to say to make up for it.

"So, you're up for a little direct action in Phoenix, eh?" I offered, smiling as brightly as I could at her.

"Sure," she said. "Sounds like fun."

Phoenix, Arizona is the home to world-class hotels and resorts, fine dining, exhilarating adventure, breath-taking golf courses, trendy shopping, modern nightlife and enriching culture. In 1987, it was also home to a transit system that had a fleet of more than three hundred buses, only thirty-six of which were accessible, and no plans to become 100 percent accessible. This made it a fitting host to APTA's spring convention and ADAPT's eighth official action. It would prove also to be one of our more memorable actions, especially for me.

On the first day, we formed our usual "welcoming" gauntlet for the APTA members and their spouses who were arriving at Sky Harbor Airport. There's nothing like walking through a long line of about eighty to one hundred people with disabilities, all of whom are chanting things at you, to make you feel welcome. They walked by us very quickly, many with their heads down. Calvin, Bernard, and Kate gave it everything they had as they chanted, grateful finally to have a release for their anger and frustration after so many ineffectual MARTA meetings.

Because ADAPT always does its homework, we knew APTA's itinerary by heart. That evening, the APTA members were scheduled to have dinner at Rustlers Rooste, fifteen miles outside the city. The restaurant sits high on a butte which, according to legend, was a favorite hideout for cattle rustlers in the days of the Wild West. This was probably because the location provided an excellent 360-degree view of the area, which, today, includes the sparkling lights of downtown Phoenix.

Unfortunately for the APTA people, we were already settled high on the hill and had an easy view of them as they made their way up to the restaurant, only to find that we had blocked the main road and entrance to the Rooste. Undaunted, they parked at the bottom of the hill and began hiking their way up the side of the hill. Because this dinner was scheduled to be a fancy affair, the men were dressed in their finest suits and the women in their nicest dresses and high heels. Tom Olin, ADAPT's long-time photographer, was participating in his first ADAPT action and got some great photographs of the men in their tuxes and the women holding their high heels as they trudged up the steep, rocky mountain path. Eventually, they made it to the top, a little dustier and more out of breath than they had anticipated.

As they sat eating their porterhouse steaks and fresh rattlesnake, we sang as loudly as we could and chanted “we will ride” at the top of our lungs. Some of the people with power wheelchairs had hooked up air horns to their chair batteries and would repeatedly blast them as long as they could, ensuring that the APTA members would hear us inside the restaurant. During all of this, we could see the police and restaurant managers talking and strategizing, knowing that we were fully prepared to block the members from leaving the restaurant. By the time the dinner ended around eleven o’ clock, they had set up barricades to keep us from blocking the exit. They had also gotten all of the APTA members organized and ready to leave. All at once, two vans came whizzing past us and up to the front of the restaurant, where the APTA folks quickly got on board.

In those few minutes, we began moving toward the barricade to try to block the vans, but as we did, several police officers began shoving us away, which instantly upped the level of intensity for both sides. We were all riled up and so were the cops. A few ADAPT members got past the barricade and raced up to sit in front of another van that had come for the next group of APTA people. One woman who was on a stretcher wheeled herself out in front of a van as it came barreling down the hill. She lay there, looking defiant and proud, as the cops lunged to grab her stretcher. We held our breath. The van finally came to a stop, and the police escorted her away. As they did, a few more ADAPTers were waiting in the wings to take her spot in the middle of the road. Once the police figured this out, more officers arrived to keep us at bay, and eventually, all of the APTA members were safely escorted to their cars without further interference. As we headed back to the hotel, I looked over at Kate. In the few days we had been together, it was clear that we were going to become very good friends. We’d had a chance to talk about our initial meeting, and Kate declared that my “sister” comment was “not cool.” I appreciated her frankness and had readily admitted to my mistake. Turns out I’m not immune to making assumptions and social blunders at times. But she was very forgiving and over time, we’d discovered that we shared a similar sense of humor and a passion for social justice. Now, as I watched her staring out of the window, I noted a look of complete satisfaction on her face. I recognized that look, the kind that comes from finally feeling like you're getting somewhere after taking numerous dead-end turns.

"She's hooked," I thought. "ADAPT's got itself a new convert." I smiled all the way back to my room.

When we arrived the next morning at the Hyatt—convention headquarters—it was obvious that the police had stayed up through the night preparing for a confrontation with us. There were more officers present than usual, more barricades, and off to the side, we could see a police pod had been brought in to hold anyone who might get arrested. To date, no other city had been as prepared to push back against us. Instead of intimidating us, it made us even more determined and more energized.

"We will ride!" we shouted defiantly as we rolled in to block the doors and prevent APTA members from getting in or out. Immediately, the police began pulling us away. Like the night before, as one person was pulled out of the way, another rolled in to take his or her place. Eventually, the police got fed up with this and began arresting people. Fifteen of us were arrested and placed in the waiting prison pod. It had been freshly painted, and the smell of paint surrounded us, adding to our sense of confinement.

As the officers worked to get us processed, they learned that Mike Auberger, Bob Varley, and I all had high-level spinal-cord injuries and would require certain medications, a particular type of mattress to sleep on, and an attendant to assist with our bowel programs. This was way out of their comfort zone and capacity. They shipped the three of us off to the prison infirmary and locked us in individual cells. Meanwhile, the rest of the advocates were sent to the main jail facility where they were allowed to stay grouped together by gender with the general population. The jail staff appointed "trustees," those inmates who had earned privileges as the result of good behavior, to serve as attendants for the advocates who needed help to do things like going to the bathroom. Once they heard our story, these inmates were impressed with the fact that we were not only questioning authority but also kicking butt. They did everything in their power to offer assistance and encouragement.

Although this was my sixth arrest, this was the first time any of us been separated or held in the infirmary. It would also be the first time that we were held for more than a day. Usually, we were released either the same day or the day after being arrested. Being confined in the infirmary was much harder than any of my other arrest experiences. Most jails operate on their own very weird time clock that is completely disconnected from reality: breakfast is at 5 a.m., lunch is at 11 a.m., and dinner is at 5 p.m. When you add the rigid medicalized schedule of a jail infirmary – where they're checking on you and forcing meds on you – then your whole sense of time starts to get really off kilter. On top of that, it was clear the infirmary staff had no idea how to care for people with spinal-cord injuries. I felt more than a little vulnerable. When you're dependent upon others to take care of you, you're biggest hope is that they know what they're doing. That was clearly not the case here.

It was also hard because we were alone with nothing to do and no one to talk to. I realize that the whole jail experience is not meant to be pleasurable, but I was used to being in a cell with fellow advocates, or at least with other inmates, so this was very different. I began to look forward to the daily visit from the library cart. It was the first time in my life I got excited about books, although it offered a limited supply of tattered novels and out-of-date magazines. Mike passed the time counting the holes in the ceiling tiles. In the beginning, I was a little freaked out by the isolation. It was hard to be alone—especially for an extrovert like me—every hour of every day. I'd roll up to my cell door and look down the hallway, but because of the way our cells were positioned, we couldn't see each other. Initially, we tried to talk to each other through the walls until the staff closed the doors to discourage this practice (were there solid doors or iron bars?). After that, we'd listen out for the whir, whir, whir of each other's wheelchairs to remind ourselves that we weren't in this alone.

The one bright spot during our detention were the visits from Wade. As an ordained Presbyterian minister, he was able to flash his credentials to the jail staff who allowed him to make daily clergy visits, unaware that he was also one of the leaders of ADAPT. Wade always came in with a grin on his face, fully appreciating the subterfuge, to bring us updates on the action and encourage us to stay strong.

"Wade, I don't know if I can do this," I said on my second full day in jail. "This is awful."

"I know, man. I know it's tough," he said, putting his hand on my shoulder. "But it would be good if you can hang in there. We've set up an entire phone bank at the hotel and ADAPTers are manning the phones as we speak trying to drum up support and get media attention. Plus, the local community is really starting to respond. Volunteers from the independent-living center, ministers, and leaders of some of the other progressive groups are coming and offering to help. They're even talking about setting up a vigil to show their support for you!"

I sat staring at the floor. "That's all great, but I don't know if I can hang in there. The loneliness is killing me. The nurses don't know what to do with me, and it doesn't look like we're getting out anytime soon. I'm starting to wonder if it's really worth it."

Wade looked at me, clearly concerned. "Mark, it's worth it. You've got to believe me that it is. Every day that you are in here, we're getting more and more media coverage. People are starting to really pay attention to what we're trying to do with transportation. We may even get national coverage, which would take the issue to a new level." He paused, watching me. "I promise we'll get you guys out soon."

I sighed. I really couldn't take much more of this, but I also couldn't say no to Wade.

"Okay. I'll stick with it. But I need you to call Susan and tell her what's going on."

"I will! You hang in there. I'll be back tomorrow to check on you. And just know that we're all praying for you," he said as he stood up to leave.

That afternoon, Wade called Susan to explain the situation and report that I wasn't going to be home on Thursday as expected. By now, she was used to me getting arrested, but she understood that this situation was a little different and started to get concerned. Plus, we were scheduled to leave for vacation on Friday, and she was worried that we were going to have to delay our plans. She called my mom in Charlotte, who agreed to be on standby in case she needed to come take care of Lindsey while Susan flew out to Phoenix.

While we lay in our cells, the folks on the outside continued their protest at the Hyatt, seizing any opportunity to make life difficult for the APTA attendees. They even disrupted a luncheon for the APTA spouses, which led to seventy-six people being arrested and then released, including Bernard and Kate. Another group of ADAPTers stood outside the jail on the other side of the razor-wire fence, chanting continuously for our freedom. Meanwhile, Wade and the volunteers kept the phone bank busy with calls to alert the media and put pressure on public officials. The media responded and began to get very interested in the action and to file stories about its progress. Gradually, these stories began to focus on the fact that fifteen people with disabilities were being jailed, including eight women. The mayor soon expressed public support for ADAPT while the police faced increasing pressure to release all or some of us from jail.

On Wednesday, one of the jailers approached the women and reported that everyone—both the men and the women—were being freed, but when Wade showed up with the van, only the women were released. It quickly became clear that the staff had lied to the women—knowing they wouldn't leave without the guys—because they were starting to face a lot of pressure for detaining women with disabilities. The public was used to men with disabilities being arrested. They'd seen plenty of Vietnam vets in their wheelchairs and on crutches protesting the war and getting arrested. But they weren't comfortable with the idea of detaining women with disabilities, especially ones who had been disabled all their lives, like my friend and colleague, Diane Coleman.

Undeterred, the women quickly returned to the hotel and joined the phone bank. By now, the advocates were starting to get really concerned about the three of us in the infirmary. They guessed that the staff didn't have the expertise to care for us and knew that inadequate care could lead to us developing potentially life-threatening conditions, such as dysreflexia, a problem that generally affects people with higher-level spinal-cord injuries. Dysreflexia is often caused by a back-up in the bladder or bowels and can lead to seizures, stroke, or even death. Diane and the others made sure to emphasize this point as they lobbied for our release. Two phones down from Diane, Wade was keeping my very worried wife up-to-date on our status.

On Thursday, a local minister and a member of the ACLU joined ADAPT in a press conference, during which they called for our release. The press conference was picked up by *Good Morning America* and other national outlets, which took the level of pressure on the mayor and police up by several notches. By then, Bob was starting to show signs of stress and illness in jail, so the police quickly released him. Meanwhile, many of the advocates were starting to leave town since the APTA convention was over. Wade and Diane and a number of others stayed to wait until the rest of us were released. Calvin, Bernard, and Kate maintained a constant vigil outside the prison infirmary, waiting for my release. Finally, on Friday morning, Wade walked in and announced that national interest in the story had, according to Wade, "brought the City of Phoenix to its knees," and we were being released immediately. We rolled out of the jail to the cheers of the people who had worked so hard for our release. We were exhausted but otherwise in good spirits, having just survived the longest detainment of our careers.

As we prepared to fly home, Bob Michaels, executive director of the local independent living center, praised ADAPT and the action saying that there had been more public discussion in five days about the need for accessible transportation than there had been in more than five years. The mayor of Phoenix had publicly stated his support for adding lifts to all new buses. (Indeed, just two months later, the City of Phoenix would adopt a policy to equip all of their public buses with lifts.) It was also gratifying that, throughout the week, both the transit officials and the media had begun to refer to us as professional protestors, which indicated, at least to us, that we had achieved some measure of respect and integrity for our position. Wade had been right; those monotonous days in jail had been worth it. People were starting to take us seriously.

WE WILL RIDE

Two weeks after we returned from Phoenix, we attended the next public hearing. By now, there had been many public hearings and study committee meetings. In that time, we had done everything we could to get MARTA to understand the need for accessible buses. We had surveyed the local disabled community, arranged for disabled MARTA users to testify at hearings, and shared our findings with the MARTA leadership.

When it became clear that they would not listen to us, we decided to introduce an alternative to MARTA's plan, one that we had written ourselves. The three-page, legal-sized document included myths and facts about MARTA's accessible services, a brief review of Section 504 regulations, and our plan, which called for lifts on all new buses. We recognized that the life span of a bus was generally ten to twelve years, which meant it would be awhile before every public bus had a lift. But we also understood this was the most plausible plan the board could accept. It wasn't realistic to insist that every bus be made accessible in one fell swoop. At every meeting and every hearing, we would distribute our plan to everyone in the room. Over time, the media had become interested in our efforts and begun to follow our progress. As they did, MARTA began to experience increasing pressure from the public to adopt our plan. Still, MARTA remained unmoved. We didn't have high hopes for this hearing.

After this, there would be only one more public hearing before the MARTA board met in May to adopt an accessibility plan. With the increasing pressure for MARTA to adopt a plan, there were more people and members of the media starting to come to the hearings. There were about one hundred people in the room. Even some members of the MARTA board were present, though they weren't required to be, making it clear they were paying attention to the issue. The air was thick with tension.

Over the course of more than an hour, more than twenty people testified that they were opposed to the two plans that were being presented by the staff. When they were done, I rolled up to the microphone and addressed David Chestnut, MARTA's Board Chair.

"Mr. Chairman, I'm Mark Johnson. I'm a quadriplegic and a member of ADAPT. I'm also a member of MARTA's study committee, and as you know, we have officially opposed both of the plans proposed by your employees. Plan A proposes that only half of the city's buses be equipped with lifts. That means that people with disabilities have to wait at a bus stop until they get lucky enough for a bus with a lift to stop and pick them up. That's unacceptable." I paused. "Plan B calls for extending MARTA's L-van services and paying for taxis and such when the L-vans aren't available. That's also unacceptable, particularly when the L-vans require a reservation—which means that people with disabilities have to plan way in advance, and that visitors from out of town can't use them at all—and they are usually late. People can't keep jobs or go to school and have a social life when they don't know when their ride is going to show up."

I turned and looked at the many people with disabilities who were sitting in the audience, then turned back to the microphone.

"We do not accept either of these options. We have presented MARTA with an alternative plan that calls for a lift on every new bus. That is the only acceptable option."

"And we've considered your alternative plan, Mr. Johnson, but we don't know that we can approve it at this time," said Mr. Chestnut.

"Then we will take our fight to the streets."

"I don't see how that will help things, Mr. Johnson. Our board doesn't react to threats."

"I'm telling you, we have tried for months now to explain the need for a fully accessible system, but it doesn't look like we've made a lot of progress. So we can do it in the suites or we can do it in the streets. You decide." I turned and rolled to the back of the room as my fellow advocates clapped and cheered.

The next day, *The Atlanta Constitution* ran an article titled, "MARTA faces 'street' action, activist for disabled warns." In it, they listed me as a "professional activist" who was "no stranger to civil disobedience," then talked about my arrest in Phoenix earlier that month. MARTA was on notice that what ADAPT could do in other cities, it could easily do on their turf as well.

The last hearing was held at the end of April, and we arrived to a room full of people. Media coverage of the previous hearing and our threat of direct action had ignited the public's interest in MARTA's planning process. There were reporters, people with disabilities, and members of the general public everywhere, giving the room a vibrant energy. We were all curious to see which plan the MARTA staff would recommend to the board. As soon as the meeting was called to order, everyone got quiet, listening intently as they reviewed the minutes and other items on the agenda. Finally, the chairman turned his attention to the audience.

"As many of you know, we've been working for a while to develop a plan to provide public transportation services to people with disabilities, and while we've worked very hard to gather input from the disabled themselves, it seems our plan doesn't go far enough. And you also know, a group called ADAPT has recently issued an alternative plan that calls for MARTA to install lifts on every new bus until the fleet is one hundred percent accessible." He paused, looking out at us. "This alternative plan has been reviewed by staff, and we have decided to include it in our final report to the Board."

Bernard and I looked at each and smiled. Now we were getting somewhere. Sure enough, the staff forwarded our plan to a committee of the MARTA board, which also reviewed it and voted to recommend approval of the plan by the full board at their May meeting. Still, ADAPT and DIA began planning "We Will Ride" day, calling people together for a march and rally that would immediately precede the board meeting on May 26, 1987. In the off chance that the board did not approve our plan, we wanted to be able to show the strength of our support and our potential for further direct action. However, by the day of the meeting, we were assured our plan would pass. As a result, "We Will Ride" day was about celebration rather than confrontation.

Following the rally, we filed into the MARTA headquarters as the Chairman called the meeting to order. After reviewing the minutes and several other matters of business, he finally reviewed the staff and committee's report and recommendations to adopt our plan. Another board member made a motion to approve the committee's recommendation, which was seconded.

"All those in favor, signify by saying 'aye'," said the chairman. Slowly, every member did.

"Any opposed?" The room was quiet.

"Then the motion carries."

Immediately, the crowd in the room went crazy, clapping, whooping, and hollering. No one could believe it. With a plan, constant pressure, and the threat of civil disobedience, MARTA had taken us seriously enough to consider our plan and agree that it was viable, even necessary. From now on, people with disabilities in Atlanta would have access to public transportation.

POWER OF ONE

As Atlantans began to enjoy the benefits of accessible buses, I began spending more time at the Shepherd Center. Located just north of downtown Atlanta in the Buckhead area along "cardiac hill," well-known to Peachtree Road Race runners and wheelchair racers, the Center was founded in 1975. James Shepherd was on a backpacking trip around the world after graduating from the University of Georgia in 1973. While bodysurfing in Rio de Janeiro, Brazil, he sustained a spinal-cord injury. James spent the next five weeks in a Brazilian hospital, and when he was stable enough to travel, he returned to the States for rehabilitation. Unfortunately, they weren't any rehabilitation facilities in Atlanta that specialized in spinal-cord injuries. Six months after receiving treatment in a Colorado facility, James learned to walk with the use of a cane and a leg brace. After returning home, James and his parents, Harold and Alana— with the help of Dr. David Apple; Clark Harrison, a family friend and former DeKalb County commissioner; David Webb, a lawyer who had served as chairman of President Carter's White House Conference on Handicapped Individuals; and support from the community—founded the Center. Today, Shepherd is a nationally recognized, state-of-the-art facility with 152 beds, including a ten-bed intensive-care unit.

After getting settled in Atlanta, I began volunteering at the Center. Volunteering provided a nice blend of my experience and interests. It was a good way to return to my roots and my work at Carolina Rehabilitation Hospital with people who had recently been injured. I was reminded of the vulnerability and searching that characterizes that point in people's lives. It was satisfying to provide some sense of hope as a peer. It also tied in nicely with my current work because I could offer a channel for frustration when people encountered the usual attitudinal and physical barriers. Sure, not everyone was interested in getting involved in advocacy, but some individuals were. In fact, in May of 1987, Shepherd's Therapeutic Recreation Department brought a bus-full of patients to a rally, the victory celebration to put lifts on new MARTA buses.

Around the same time, Shepherd Center was applying for a Model Systems grant, which would enable them to conduct research and continue to expand the Center's services and reach. It was an ambitious move for this young center because the grant required that the Center offer a broad continuum of services for people with spinal-cord injuries in addition to conducting research. But it was worth the effort because it would really help put the Center on the map in terms of spinal-cord injury rehabilitation in the country. The staff worked diligently to prepare for the grant, evaluating their services, and identifying any gaps. When the Center received word that it was being awarded the grant—and thus the coveted designation as a "Model Systems Center" —the staff celebrated and then quickly got to work. The timing appeared to be just right for Shepherd and me. I got a call about interviewing for an advocacy position.

Sitting across from Lesley Hudson, who had been working for Shepherd since its inception, she conducted the interview. She started by saying, "This is a new position, as you may you know. You'll have a lot of flexibility in how you set it up."

"Perfect! I kind of did something similar in Charlotte, although I'd like to develop it even more here."

"It sounds like you've got some ideas for the position."

"Definitely. I think it should be about educating people about disability, whether it's the people who have been injured, their loved ones, the broader community, or legislators. We've got to address the attitudes and the ways those attitudes prevent access. And I think one way to do that is to make sure that advocacy is embedded into Shepherd's mission and culture."

"Well, you've got a great resume, you come highly recommended, and James Shepherd is aware of your work in the disability community. And, quite frankly, based on all that, you're the only person I was planning on interviewing for the job."

"Thanks."

"Yep. James says there are not many people like you, and we'd be lucky to have you."

"Wow."

"That means you've definitely got the job," she said.

"Great!"

"One thing you need to know: it is part time, you'll get a paycheck every two weeks, and I'll check in on you periodically. Otherwise, you're on your own. Just do what needs to be done."

Developing the Center's Advocacy Program was an evolutionary process. I knew that I had to start with the Center's mission. I was only one guy, and I recognized that I couldn't cover all the advocacy issues for everybody. If this was going to work, I needed all of Shepherd's employees to understand what advocacy was about and how it connected to the hospital's mission. I needed advocacy to be a part of the culture. For that to happen, everyone needed to understand how they could integrate advocacy into the work they do, enabling me to coordinate and work on some of the groups in the community. Still, it took a while before the staff stopped sending any and every advocacy issue to me.

"Hey, Mark," one of outpatient therapists said. "I've got a guy who can't access programs at his local recreation center. Can you call him and help him work it out?"

"Actually, let me give you this handout that explains his rights and talks about Section 504. Give it to him and encourage him to call the rec center and set up a meeting to discuss the access issues. If he runs into any problems, then he can call me," I'd say.

I'd do the same for the many requests, whether it was parking, housing, airline, or other issues. As many times as nondisabled people parked in handicapped spots, I could stay busy doing nothing but handling those complaints. Same with voter registration; eventually, I gave the Center's library a stack of voter registration forms and a list of contacts so that they could be a resource for people.

The push back worked. Gradually, the staff began to understand how they themselves could support people to be self-advocates. This was not only empowering for the patients but also for the staff. You could see it in their eyes and the way they went about their jobs.

It was awhile before I could really appreciate the depth of the opportunity I'd been given to develop Shepherd's Advocacy Program and culture. Initially, I didn't realize how much the Shepherd Center and I were meant for each other. When James was injured, his parents focused on getting him stabilized and ready to come home, but they were always thinking ahead to their next step. They wanted a place for people in the southeast to get rehab, so they built it. They wanted patients to have opportunities for recreation and other pursuits, so they created them. Not once did they consider that people's injuries should stop them from living life to the fullest. Not once did they accept the social attitudes that said James and other people with disabilities should go to a home or an institution and live quietly behind closed doors. His injury was just a blip on their radar screen as they pressed forward with their goals and dreams. It was this philosophy that infused the work of the Shepherd Center, where the walls, today, are lined with photographs and stories of former patients who left the Center and continued to pursue their own dreams. And it was this philosophy that supported the vision for my position. The Shepherds recognized that I could help to raise awareness and address the attitudes in the community that prevented people with disabilities from achieving their dreams, the ones that kept them behind closed doors.

To their credit, the Shepherds also understood the value of my work with ADAPT and allowed me to go to actions throughout the year, though I tried to be mindful about how I represented the Center, especially with any local ADAPT actions. I didn't want to jeopardize any relationships the Center had with donors and elected officials. The Shepherds were good sports on the multiple occasions when I got arrested. In fact, over time it became a habit for my coworkers to come up to me with amused expressions and say, "Alright, Mark, which bus will you be chaining yourself to today?" Even as Alana Shepherd would give tours to potential donors and other VIPs, she'd inevitably introduce me as "Mark, the guy who chains himself to buses." It was always said with a mixture of amusement, pride, and admiration. I think this is because Ms. Shepherd—like the rest of her family—is a natural advocate.

When Atlanta won its bid to host the 1996 Olympic Games, there were no plans for it to host the Paralympic Games as well. The two events were still considered to be separate and certainly not equal. But after a group of disability advocates presented a formal request to the Atlanta Committee for the Olympic Games to host both sporting events—and were turned down—Ms. Shepherd got involved. Given that Atlanta was home to the civil-rights movement and the Shepherd Center, she would not let this city miss the opportunity to host the world's premier athletic event for people with disabilities. She got the Shepherd Center's board to agree to lead the bid effort, committed office space and employee time to prepare the formal bid, and led the effort to raise millions of dollars and generate sponsorships. In the end, not only did Atlanta host the Olympic and Paralympic Games, but the International Olympic Committee declared that from that point forward, any city wanting to host the Olympics had to agree to host the Paralympics as well. This has led to increased media coverage, sponsorships, and public support for this world-class event. Thanks to Ms. Shepherd—and many others— the world now sees images of powerful, skilled, and highly trained athletes with disabilities. There is no question this is changing our culture.

Lindsey running with the Paralympic Torch

In 1994, the Shepherd Center's leadership added another advocate in the form of Gary Ulicny, who was hired to be its new president and chief executive officer. Gary and I had met at a rally in 1981, establishing an immediate connection that had lasted over the years. I was excited to hear he was joining our team. On his first morning at the Center, I rolled over to this office to welcome him and was startled and humbled when he told me one of the reasons he had taken the job was because he was impressed that Shepherd had hired me. I hadn't expected that, but it was great to hear of his support for my work in the advocacy program. Over time, Gary and I developed a mutually beneficial partnership. Where I could serve as his Jiminy Cricket, he could give additional focus to and help generate support internally for my work. This was really useful, given that, from my point of view, every situation presents an opportunity to get organized. I could use a little refocusing now and again. To this day, Gary and I meet every other Wednesday to check in with each other.

In particular, Gary supported my involvement in public policy issues. Given the Center's visibility and credibility, he understood our potential influence on legislative issues, especially those that affected people with disabilities. While we were involved in many initiatives, the one that brought us a great deal of satisfaction centered on the creation of Georgia's Independent Care Waiver Program (ICWP). In 1989, a man named Larry McAfee petitioned the court for the right to die. Four years earlier, he had been severely injured in a motorcycle accident, leaving him paralyzed from the neck down and needing a ventilator to breathe. Following rehab at Shepherd Center, Larry lived in his own apartment with the help of twenty-four-hour attendant care. But when his private insurance funds ran out, he was forced to rely on public funds. Since Medicaid wouldn't pay for support to keep Larry in his own home, this thirty-three-year-old former sportsman was going to have to move to a nursing home. But Georgia's nursing homes refused to take him, since Georgia's Medicaid system paid the same rate to nursing homes, whether the person was aging and needing part-time nursing care or dependent on a ventilator and requiring around-the-clock support. Larry thus became a human pinball, bounced between out-of-state nursing homes and Georgia Grady Hospital until he lost the will to live.

The disability community immediately launched into action since Right-to-Die cases are personal for us; too many people think it is preferable to be dead rather than have a disability. We recognized that Larry wasn't asking to die because of his disability; he was tired of how the state was treating him. Thus, we focused our attention on the problem: the state's Medicaid program. If people with disabilities—particularly those with low incomes—were going to have a chance at a quality of life, they needed to be able to choose where they lived. But this would be possible only if Medicaid changed its policies and redirected its funding from nursing facilities to attendant services provided in the home. What was lucky was that the Centers for Medicare & Medicaid Services (CMS) in Washington allowed states the option to apply for a "waiver" of federal regulations, allowing the state to divert the funds to independent living. What was unlucky was that we were dealing with a lack of elected leadership in Georgia and a state that had a history of not thinking outside the box. Many other states had long since diverted money away from institutions to home- and community-based services. We made requests. We offered research that proved it was cheaper to support people in their own homes rather than in institutions. We argued. We protested. Yes, Georgia's Department of Medical Assistance remained unconvinced of the need for a waiver. This went on for almost two years.

At the same time, a woman named Jenny Lynn Langley, a soft-spoken woman in her early twenties, was admitted to the Shepherd Center. Jenny had been through rehab twice. Her second injury left her more dependent on support. Eventually, the family couldn't afford the costs of her care, and Jenny was dropped off at Piedmont. Jenny was confronted with limited options like Larry's. Over the period of a month, Jenny and I met several times; she eventual volunteered to be the face of the campaign to create the ICWP. The Shepherd Center provided funding for a pilot project that would give the state the proof it needed that home- and community-based services were cost-effective. Pat Puckett, one of my colleagues and friends, designed the model. By the end of the pilot project, we had proof that it was cheaper and better to support someone with a disability—even a significant disability like a high spinal-cord injury—at home rather than in a hospital or nursing facility. A year later, the state approved the Independent Care Waiver Program, which would provide waiver services for a limited number of Georgians with disabilities. Although it is still plagued by politics, the Program continues to provide support to people to this day.

Today, the Shepherd Center is a highly regarded rehabilitation hospital. Indeed, for over ten years, it has been consistently ranked as one of the best rehabilitation hospitals in the nation by *U.S. News & World Report*. In addition to serving people with spinal-cord injuries it also offers some of the highest quality rehab services for people with brain injuries (I'm a bit biased here since Susan directs Shepherd's Brain Injury Program). It also serves people with multiple sclerosis and other neuromuscular disorders.

But in my mind, what makes the Center such a great place is its fundamental commitment to advocacy. Sure, I just celebrated twenty-seven years with Shepherd's Advocacy Program, but that's not what I'm talking about. It's more than that. From its founders, to its leadership, to its staff members and volunteers, to its patients and families, everyone works together. The Center has become a place to learn to take it personally. As a result, when a new employee arrives at the Center, instead of saying, "Welcome to the Shepherd Center," I say, "Welcome to the movement."

Chapter 39

Let's Get Together

Taking a break from my work at the Shepherd Center, I sat across from Eleanor Smith. I could tell she was uncomfortable. We'd been sitting for a half hour at a corner table at Eat Your Vegetables restaurant, a funky little vegetarian restaurant in the heart of Atlanta's equally funky Little Five Points district, chatting about the MARTA victory and ADAPT's latest action. All the while she had seemed uneasy, shifting in her seat, choosing her words carefully. This was very different from the personable, confident Eleanor I'd met three weeks ago at the MARTA board meeting where we had celebrated our victory. Finally, she paused and thought for a moment, then turned to me, clearly having made some decision in her head.

"Mark, you should know something."

"Okay," I said, not knowing where this was going.

"I'm a lesbian, and I'm not used to hanging out with men. I've put a lot of energy into the women's movement, and I've chosen to work with women. You're really the first man that I've taken seriously in a long time." She took a deep breath, then relaxed, clearly relieved to have this out in the open. The whole time, she watched to see how I would respond.

"Okay," I said. I really wasn't sure how to respond. "Thanks? I mean, thanks for telling me." I paused, not sure where to go next. "If it helps,

I haven't been around many lesbians before either." I smiled, trying to lighten up the mood.

Eleanor smiled and laughed, "Then we should make good company!" We both laughed.

From there, the conversation flowed more easily as we got to know each other and talked about disability issues in Georgia. In talking with her, it was easy to see how intelligent she was and how deeply she thought about the issues that resonated with her. We both had ideas and found that we made good sounding boards for each other. After talking for two hours, we agreed to meet again at her house to continue the discussion and continue to develop these ideas. But as we prepared to leave, she stopped me.

"Mark, I want you to know that I've been waiting for a while for someone to come and take charge of the disability movement around here. There are a lot of pockets of people doing good things in Atlanta and around Georgia, but so far, it's all been disconnected. I've been reading the *Rag* and seeing what people are accomplishing in Denver and Seattle and San Francisco, and I kept thinking, we need that here in Georgia! And I really feel like you're starting to do some of that. I mean, advocates had been trying for years to get MARTA to get lifts, but just ten months after you introduced ADAPT, MARTA adopted a plan to make its services accessible. That's amazing."

"Thanks," I said. "But it's not only me. Bernard and Calvin and the others were the ones who were willing to try direct action. That made all the difference."

"Yes, but they only did that once they understood that they had a right to accessible transportation. Once you understand that you have rights, you're willing to fight for them. That's what's changed everything," she said, then smiled and rolled out the door.

The August evening was milder than usual, less humid. We decided to hang out on the front porch of Eleanor's home near Grant Park, an eclectic neighborhood that included the Atlanta Zoo and Cyclorama, a somewhat cheesy, revolving Civil War diorama that was an Atlanta institution. Following our lunch meeting, we'd been meeting here almost every week for two months, slowly developing our own think tank of sorts as we swapped ideas and made plans. What had started with Eleanor and me now included a few other people, including Elaine Kolb, a musician and activist, and sometimes Eleanor's partner, Barbara. Together, we'd talk late into the night, getting drunk on the possibilities that seemed endless and vast. We called our group "Let's Get Together," underscoring our optimistic efforts to develop ideas that would bring people from all walks of life together. Our discussions had started focused on transportation issues, since that was ADAPT's focus and what had brought us together, but over time, our conversations led down new paths.

As we were meeting one night in September, Eleanor said, "You know, Habitat for Humanity just finished some new houses not far from here, and last night, Barbara and I drove over to see them."

"Yeah, I heard about them. I bet they're nice houses," said Elaine.

"They are…" Eleanor paused. "But you know what I kept thinking? I kept saying to myself, 'These are all brand new homes, and they all could have been built to be accessible.' It would've been easy to do."

"But I'm sure they've got budget restraints. Maybe that's why they don't," replied Susan.

"But that's the thing," said Eleanor. "I'm not talking about major modifications. All you would need is one entrance with no steps and doors wide enough to fit a wheelchair. That would be it. That wouldn't cost that much money on new construction. What costs a lot is adding ramps and widening doors after houses are already built."

"They probably don't have a lot of clients with disabilities," Elaine offered.

"I know. But why not make houses accessible for everyone so that if you have friend who has a disability, that person could come visit? Or if your grandmother uses a walker, she could come visit."

"Or if you're daughter breaks her leg climbing trees, she doesn't have to climb steps with her crutches," I added.

"Exactly!" said Eleanor. "It would benefit everyone! That's why I wish every home had a no-step entrance."

I looked at her. "A lift on every new bus..."

"...a zero-step entrance on every new home," she finished. She flashed a big smile. "Wouldn't that be something!"

"Sounds like a good plan," I said.

"Do you think ADAPT would support it?" she asked.

"They don't need to. ADAPT's focus is transportation right now. But that doesn't mean you can't work on something else. Pick your passion!"

"Well," she said, "every new house accessible is my passion."

"Then go for it," said Elaine.

And she did. Soon, Eleanor was researching the costs of incorporating basic access features in homes under construction, talking to builders, and looking for other advocates who were focused on housing. During our meetings, she'd update us on her research and throw out various ideas for us to brainstorm. It was during one of these meetings, as she and I bantered back and forth, that we came up with the name.

"You know, to kick this off, maybe we should do a statewide project that people will see," I paused. "Maybe we could get all the 7-Eleven stores to change to a zero-step entrance, since right now they all have a step leading into the store." I shook my head. "We need some kind of concrete change."

Eleanor laughed. "No pun intended," she said, referring to the fact that concrete would have to be poured to create the zero-step entrance.

I looked at her and she looked at me. We were thinking the same thing. In unison, we said, "Concrete Change!"

"I like it," I said.

"So do I," smiled Eleanor.

And Concrete Change was born. Immediately, Eleanor went to work on her campaign for basic access. Her first victory would come in 1990, when the Atlanta chapter of Habitat for Humanity began to incorporate the accessibility features, eventually building more than one thousand houses with basic access. With that, Concrete Change became a national, and later, international, source on basic access, creating houses that were, as Eleanor dubbed them, "visitable." Indeed, according to one source, Eleanor is now the leading expert in North America on "visitability." Because of Eleanor, children with disabilities today have the hope of visiting their friends.

As to community, Eleanor would also go on to help form East Lake Commons, a cohousing community in Decatur, Georgia, where she now lives. As the development was being planned, Eleanor shared the visitability concept with her fellow community members, who agreed that all the homes would have wide interior doors and one entrance without steps. As a result, Eleanor and her partner, Barbara, live in an intergenerational community where their neighbors can rest assured that if they break a leg, or return home from surgery, or grow older, they will have access to their homes. And, Eleanor, for the first time, can go next door.

Over time, Let's Get Together would be involved in the creation of a number of organizations and efforts, many of which are still in existence today, including:

- Georgia ADAPT
- Concrete Change
- Life Worthy of Life, now Not Dead Yet
- The Disability Action Center (now disAbility Link)
- and Self-Advocacy Networks around the state of Georgia

When people who share a common worldview, a commitment to direct action, a shared style of working, a sense of humor, and a history of shared action and mutual support, the possibilities of what can be achieved are endless.

BELIEVING IN A HIGHER POWER

While I continued to support Eleanor and Concrete Change, my dad was starting a new chapter in his life, one that had taken root on that Valentine's Day when he'd decided to get sober. After returning from treatment, he'd struggled to navigate life without the aid of alcohol. It wasn't easy to say the least. Without the drug's effects, he was forced to learn how to face his feelings, most of which were only slightly familiar to him and held a lot of pain and fear.

He and Mom had to figure out how to relate to each other without the presence of alcohol in the mix. Neither of them was really sure how to do this. In the beginning, none of us—not even them—were sure if their marriage would survive. They argued a lot, with Dad trying to blame Mom for his drinking. Fortunately, she always had a clever retort: "If I had that much power over you, I wouldn't have wasted my time on alcohol. I'd have made you earn a million dollars!" That always shut him up, at least for a while. It's a long, hard process when you have to take responsibility for the havoc you've wreaked on your own life and that of others. Eventually, he resorted to drawing a line through the middle of the house, literally. For months, they lived on their separate sides of the house, not sharing meals together or speaking, even when they encountered each other in the hallway or on the stairs. To protect herself, and to give Dad some much-needed space and time to himself, Mom started taking trips, rekindling that wanderlust that had been such a part of her childhood. She also spent a lot more time volunteering, finding solace in helping her church and community. In the end, it would take my parents almost seven years to regain some sense of balance in their marriage.

Still, while things weren't going well for Dad at home, after a year, he was beginning to see the benefits of sobriety in other areas of his life. He realized that his body felt better than it had in a long time, that he was able to engage fully in conversations with people, and that his life was no longer ruled by secrets and deception. He was starting to understand that he didn't have to control everyone or everything. Instead, he could relax and focus solely on himself. He was learning to "let go and let God." Indeed, for the first time, Dad was able to have an honest relationship with the God who, he now realized, had never left his side. Whether he was happy or angry or sad, Dad finally understood that he could bring that to God and the church, knowing that he would be accepted just as he was.

Grateful, Dad wanted to give back and share the gifts he had received in sobriety. When Jody, who is an accountant, reviewed Dad's finances and announced that he was at a good point for retirement, Dad knew exactly what to do. With the blessings of the treatment center staff who knew him well by now, he set up an office within the center and began volunteering his time, helping other alcoholics through the process of reaching—and maintaining—sobriety. Every day, without fail, he went to twelve-step meetings, helped facilitate family interventions, visited people in treatment, or spoke at conventions. He was a man on a mission, dedicated to helping anyone who needed to see that life without alcohol was not only possible, but preferable. It was a message that he wished his two uncles and his father—all of whom had been alcoholics—had heard, and he didn't want anyone else to miss out on it.

Over time, Dad became a fixture in his local twelve-step program, serving as fellow addict, mentor, and sage. As time went on, the members set up a special chair in the corner that is known as "Bill's chair," where, to this day, Dad holds court at daily meetings. But Dad's presence isn't limited to the walls of the treatment center or the twelve-step meeting room. With his love of people and his easy humor, he has developed strong bonds with people in the community, sharing his gratitude and message of hope with anyone who needs it as he also builds networks to support people in recovery. Even the local Starbucks is in on it. Early each morning, the staff loads Dad up with boxes of baked goods that didn't sell the previous day, which he then takes to the twelve-step meeting. Now, instead of handing out Double Bubble and Nik-L-Nips, he's sharing day-old Cranberry Bliss Bars and chocolate chip muffins. You'd be surprised how delicious they can taste to someone who is hungry on many levels.

Before he died, if you had talked to my dad, he would have told you with great clarity and conviction that he was still, and always would be, an alcoholic. He knew all too well that alcoholism is a disease that can never be cured. He had to work every day to stay sober. It was his reality. At the same time, he wanted everyone to know that recovery is possible and offers abundant reward. He dreamed of standing on top of the highest mountain and shouting to the world, "I'm Bill Johnson, and I'm a grateful, recovering alcoholic!" It was his message of love.

CIVIL RIGHTS

As my dad sought to share his message with the world, ADAPT continued its campaign against APTA. By 1989, our fight for accessible transportation had reached a fever pitch. There were ADAPT affiliates in most major cities, leading more and more cities to vote to provide accessible public transportation. Besides Denver, San Francisco, and Seattle, now the list of accessible cities included Austin, Portland, New York City, and Washington, DC. Meanwhile, at the national level, ADAPT actions against APTA were drawing hundreds of people each time, and word was spreading that more and more APTA members were in favor of the resolution to require lifts on all buses, even though the APTA leadership continued to block it. We were getting closer to our goal, though our biggest hurdles remained ahead of us.

Since ADAPT's inception, there had been a lot of debate within the disability community about whether it was more effective to use civil disobedience or the court system to make your point. Many people preferred filing lawsuits, in part because it was civilized and followed protocol. It was a way of playing it safe. But, as Wade often pointed out, lawsuits could be drawn-out political affairs that ended badly, depending upon one's perspective. Civil disobedience, on the other hand, got attention and gave momentum to agendas, primarily because it got people to feel something. Wade was always emphasizing the importance of emotional change. Sure, the two could work together, though it always frustrated me when lawsuits were won after an ADAPT action. It felt like people who weren't willing to risk their freedom were willing to ride the coattails of those of us who were.

By this point, however, it was clear that ADAPT needed to do both in order to make that final push for accessible transportation, so it filed suit against the Department of Transportation. The suit alleged that the Department of Transportation's (DOT) "local option" policy was unconstitutional since it prevented millions of people with disabilities from having access to public transportation. It also argued that the DOT's policy that transit systems didn't need to spend more than three percent of their budget on disability access was arbitrary. On February 13, 1989, the U.S. Court of Appeals agreed with us by declaring that the local option policy was unjust and by requiring all new buses purchased with federal funds to have lifts. It also declared the three percent cap as "arbitrary and capricious." Undeterred, APTA and the DOT asked the Court to reconsider, particularly since only three of the eleven justices had been present for the February decision. The Court agreed to rehear the case on May 15 in Philadelphia, Pennsylvania.

Immediately, we began planning to go to Philadelphia. At the same time, we started to issue a flood of press releases and flyers that cried, "Where is George?" We were targeting President George Bush, newly in office, not only because he had the power to intervene but also because when he accepted his party's nomination for president he had said, "I'm going to do whatever it takes to make sure the disabled are included in the mainstream. For too long they've been left out, but they are not going to be left out anymore." When asked to specify what initiatives he would support he said, "Improve transportation and work place accessibility for existing facilities and insist on accessibility for all new construction." Clearly, he believed that supporting the civil rights of Americans with disabilities was part of his envisioned "kinder, gentler nation," and we wanted to see proof of that.

Without much advance notice of the hearing, more than one hundred ADAPT members traveled to Philadelphia to show our support for what we believed to be a civil-rights case. To emphasize that fact, we met with Attorney General Thornburg on Friday and explained how critical it was to have accessible public transportation. He seemed to hear what we were saying, which was encouraging. The next day, we made a show of trying to get on inaccessible buses—with some of our members crawling up the steps—while others blocked buses and chanted. On Sunday, we marched from Independence Hall to the Liberty Bell to the march of a beating drum while wearing white wigs and patriotic clothing. I wore a powdered wig and one of those triangular-shaped hats. At the front, members carried a flag that had been designed by Diane Coleman, Babs Johnson, and Lori Eastwood, and sewn together in Babs' kitchen. It was reminiscent of a colonial flag, but the stars formed the shape of the international access sign (the form of a person in a wheelchair that is found on handicapped parking places, etc). We gathered around the Bell in a circle while I read the Declaration of Independence for Disabled People that had been adopted by the United Nations in 1975. We had planned to stage a vigil all night long in front of the Bell, but the Liberty Bell Center security guards weren't having that and ultimately had to remove us forcibly from the building. Instead, we spent the night in front of the courthouse singing, telling stories, cooking hot dogs, and talking with the media.

When the court went into session, we were tired but excited. Tim Cook, ADAPT's attorney, argued the case well, but we wouldn't know the outcome of the case for several months. When the Court finally issued its ruling in July 1989, the decision was split. Eight of the judges ruled in favor of ADAPT, while the other four did not. As a result, the Court sent the case back to the lower court, which asked the Department to rewrite the regulations again. It wasn't the victory we had hoped for. We were going to have to take our fight back to the streets.

By the time ADAPT gathered in Atlanta that fall, the stakes were high. Still angry about the outcome of the court case in May, we believed that APTA and the Department were being allowed to continue to stall progress. At the same time, the Americans with Disabilities Act (ADA), a new piece of legislation that was being hailed as the Civil Rights Act for people with disabilities, was steadily gaining momentum in Washington. Advocates were buzzing about its potential, particularly since it included language about accessible public transportation being required throughout the country. If it became the law of the land, our battle would be won. We could tell we were closer than ever to victory and were prepared to do whatever it took to win. I had never seen ADAPTers so hungry for a fight.

Given the potential passage of the ADA, we had decided to spend more time and effort pressuring the feds—and ultimately President Bush. It wasn't that we were letting APTA—which was also here in Atlanta for their fall convention—off the hook. But if it was true that the ADA was going to address public transportation, we understood that it made more sense to focus our efforts on that rather than on pestering APTA. Plus, we recognized the potential for a big problem: local authorities trying to buy inaccessible buses in the "eleventh hour" before the ADA was passed. We needed to make sure that didn't happen. Thus, in the midst of a particularly cold, wet, nasty day, we made the long slow march to the Richard B. Russell Federal Building.

Now, it should be said that a march, in the world of ADAPT, is not a march in the strictest sense of the word. Obviously, many of us are in wheelchairs and cannot actually march, nor are any of the nondisabled ADAPT members actually marching. Instead, we slowly, methodically, make our way single-file through the city streets in whatever manner we can: rolling, limping, or walking along. We have people in chairs, people with canes, and people with service animals. There are people with developmental disabilities, people with physical disabilities, people with intellectual disabilities, and people with psychiatric disabilities. There are also attendants and nondisabled people who support our cause. At times, we pause if someone is having an issue with their wheelchair or to wait for everyone to roll around a pothole or negotiate other barriers. We go, we pause, we go again, always keeping to our mantra: "Single file. Keep it tight."

While it may not be readily apparent, there is a measure of sophistication to the way in which we prepare for and manage these actions. Because the success of an action is dependent, in part, upon the element of surprise, we cannot publicize our destination, not even to our members. This is primarily because in our early years, APTA would send "spies"—people who would sidle up to one of us in a hotel or on a street corner and casually ask, "So, where're y'all going?" With some pride, a member would explain that we were planning to stage a protest at the capitol or in the federal building. Sure enough, there would be an army of police officers or barriers waiting to greet us. Since then, we have kept our plans under wraps, disclosing them only on a "need to know" basis.

This works because we have "day leaders" and "color leaders." The day leaders are a select few experienced ADAPT members who have met to strategize and plan the action. They know the destination, the route, the target individual or audience, and the demands. During an action, they have the authority to call the shots and negotiate with the police. On the night before an action, the day leaders tell the color leaders where and what time to have their groups meet the next morning. That's it. The color leaders are then responsible for assembling their teams (which are, not surprisingly, organized by color) at the given time and place. They must also check with their members to find out who's willing to get arrested; those who are willing must then fill out a form detailing their particular needs (in terms of attendant care, bedding, medications, diet, etc.), which is then given to our attorneys to keep on hand in case of arrest. Once the march begins, the teams follow the color leaders, unaware of our destination until we actually arrive.

We make quite the spectacle. As we make our way through town, passersby stop to watch this deliberate movement of people with and without disabilities marching together. At first glance, some people may think we look awkward, even pitiable. They may speed up to create distance between us and them. But for those who take the time to stop and watch, you can watch their faces as they realize that, indeed, this group is powerful, righteous, determined, strong, and dignified. They cheer us on or honk their horns in support. Many become emotional. We are challenging the images and messages they've been fed all their lives about people with disabilities.

While we are marching, we are also blowing horns and chanting, led by certain ADAPT members who have great lung capacity and conviction.

One leader will begin by chanting, "We will ride!" and everyone joins in unison. When that stops, another person may begin with a call-and-response type of chant.

"What do we want?" shouts the leader.

"Lifts on buses!"

"When do we want 'em?"

"Now!" we respond, before repeating the rhythmic pattern.

As soon as we reached the building, we charged the doors at full speed, chanting, "We will ride!" But the feds had clearly anticipated our visit because the security guards had already blocked many of the entryways. However, at least twenty of our members managed to get in, then busied themselves with finding and opening doors to let the rest of us in. Within an hour, there were two hundred of us—including Eleanor, Bernard, Kate, and me—in the building, blocking all exits and chanting at the top of our lungs.

We were able to maintain control of the building for several hours until the police began to cart us out into the pouring rain. Soon, however, the day leaders got word that President Bush had called in and ordered the police to leave us alone and let us stay in the building overnight. Federal staff members brought in army blankets for us as we slept on the cold marble floors. Around 3 a.m., waiters and bartenders who had gotten off work brought in doughnuts and coffee for us. It was a great show of support and a sign that public opinion was changing in our favor.

The next day, amid national news coverage, a helicopter brought in a White House staff member and Mass Transit officials to negotiate with us. While most of the ADAPT members held their spots in the building, I and several others met in the basement with the President's representatives. By the end of the meeting, we had hammered out an agreement that the Bush Administration would do everything in its power to pass the ADA and would not approve any "eleventh hour" requests for inaccessible buses. We also agreed to another meeting with the president's representative in two weeks. The fact that the president was paying such close attention to us was an excellent sign, and we knew it. What we didn't anticipate was that the world was watching too, as news of our meeting was broadcast as far away as London and Belfast. Additionally, the DOT Secretary went over to the APTA convention and emphasized his and the president's commitment to passing the ADA, putting APTA on notice that any attempts to block it would not be tolerated.

As the White House official went back to his helicopter, we called all the ADAPT members out of the building to update them on the outcome of the meeting. Unfortunately, the news wasn't well-received by many of our members. It wasn't that they weren't pleased with the agreement, but they knew that it was ADAPT protocol to insist that the targeted individuals—in this case, the president's aid or the UMTA official—be the ones to report on the outcome of the meeting to the group. It was a way of promoting accountability and ensuring that our opposition took ownership of whatever had been decided. We were also used to a more democratic process where everyone was involved in making the decisions. Unfortunately, in this case, we had had very little time to negotiate and make key decisions, which prevented us from being able to run things by the group. Though there weren't any long-term effects from all this, we did learn a valuable lesson, and, to this day, we ensure that we are never put in the position of having to make on-the-spot critical decisions.

For a while, it appeared the ADA would make a relatively smooth journey toward passage, but by the early part of 1990, it started to experience some turbulence. Not surprisingly, many businesses opposed passage of the bill because they were worried about Title I of the proposed Act, which addressed employment of people with disabilities. They seemed to be hung up on the costs of having to provide accommodations for them, and by March, the bill was stalled in the House.

We had come too far and risked so much to let the ADA die; as soon as we could, ADAPT showed up in Washington to make one last push for the bill. On the morning of March 12, we marched to the Capitol to gather at the steps for a rally. Everyone was wearing shirts or buttons reading "ADA: America wins" or "Pass the ADA now" or holding signs that said, "Access is a civil right" and "We shall overcome." On the speaker's platform, there was a large banner that featured Martin Luther King Jr.'s quote, "Injustice anywhere is a threat to justice everywhere." Justin Dart, one of the greatest disability advocates of our time and chairman of the President's Committee on Employment of People with Disabilities, was on hand to speak, as were Wade, I, and several others. When it was my turn, I made my usual effort to pump up the crowd and get them ready for action.

When the rally was over, we started chanting, "What do we want? ADA! When do we want it? Now!" That was the cue. At that moment, more than seventy-five of our members dropped to the ground or were helped by others out of their wheelchairs. Then, slowly, steadily and—for some—painfully, they began climbing the steps on the west side of the Capitol, heading in the direction of the House. They used whatever they could to raise themselves up step by step: their arms, their shoulders, their elbows, or even their chins. They struggled, took breaks, then continued on, determined to illustrate the obstacles that people with disabilities face daily in our country. There were children, adults, and seniors. There were people who were paralyzed, people with cerebral palsy, people with polio, and people with other types of disabilities. As the rest of us shouted encouragement amid our chanting, a few of the nondisabled members shadowed the people who were crawling, ready to provide aid if necessary, though few needed it as they were determined they were to make it to the top. While some tourists and others who had business at the Capitol stepped over and around the protestors as they made their way up, most of them stopped and did not move, impressed by this display of determination and dignity. At the same time, members of the media followed the protestors up the steps, carefully documenting the scene, including a now-famous and powerful photo of Shaila Jackson scooting up backward, one step at a time, and one of little Jennifer, a very young girl with cerebral palsy who defiantly pulled herself to the top. When she reached the top step, her mother was there to greet her with a proud hug, as the remaining crawlers made their way up amid cheers from us, the bystanders, and even the media. It was one of the most profound and memorable moments in the seven-year history of ADAPT actions.

Representing ADAPT, I testified on the transportation provisions included in the ADA during a Congressional committee hearing in 1989

The next day, a small group of ADAPT members met in the Capitol rotunda doing their best to look like casual tourists. Gradually, however, more and more of us showed up until we filled the room. Gathering in a circle, we began chanting as loudly as we could. At the same time, someone began passing around a long length of chain, which we used to chain our wheelchairs together. By then, Capitol police had surrounded us and were attempting to get us to quiet down and untether ourselves. But we were here for one purpose. Very quickly, members of Congress, including House Speaker Tom Foley, Steny Hoyer, and Tony Coelho came running out of chambers to assure us that the ADA would be passed. That was, indeed, what we wanted, though we continued to chant as loudly as possible to be sure our point had been made. One hundred and four of us were arrested in the rotunda that day. ADAPT would not go away until the ADA was passed and people with disabilities were treated fairly in our country.

On July 26, 1990, President Bush signed the Americans with Disabilities Act into law. On the podium with the president was Justin Dart Evan J. Kemp Jr. I and many of my fellow ADAPT members were on hand to witness one of the greatest moments of the history of the disability movement—the world's first comprehensive civil-rights law for people with disabilities being signed into law. The ADA prohibits discrimination against people with disabilities when it comes to employment, public and private entities, communications, etc. But from ADAPT's perspective, the best part is that the ADA requires lifts on all new buses as well as trains and hotel and motel shuttles. Finally, public transportation was accessible to people with disabilities. It was everything for which Wade, the Gang of Nineteen, ADAPT, and other advocates had fought so hard. And more.

Wade had been right. Change wasn't going to happen until the powers-that-be experienced the issue at an emotional level. We could reason, debate, and argue all we wanted to, but nothing was going to change until people felt something. And that wasn't going to happen until we addressed the attitudes that lay hidden beneath the layers of compromises, platitudes, and pats on the head. But ADAPT had done the unthinkable. We had taken "the least of these" as they say—the people with disabilities, including those with significant disabilities—and we had defied social convention and expectation. We had stopped playing nice and stopped being polite. Instead, we stood up for ourselves, acted fiercely, stood firm, broke rules, and displayed tremendous courage and conviction. And finally, people had noticed. Finally, they had felt something. They had felt the pain, the anger, and the injustice. And they had been moved to do the right thing.

Sitting on the White House lawn for the ADA signing ceremony

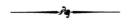

ADAPT could have justifiably disbanded after the ADA was passed. Accessible transportation was the law of the land. We had accomplished our goal. But our work wasn't done, and we knew it. There were still many barriers that people with disabilities faced, too many basic rights that were denied us. Plus, we had witnessed firsthand the power of a narrow focus, deep determination, and the willingness to take risks when it mattered. Why stop now?

Our next move was obvious. We had fought a great fight for accessible transportation, and the ADA had underscored our rights as Americans. Still, there were many of our disabled brothers and sisters who could never enjoy those hard-won rights because they were locked away in nursing facilities, state hospitals, and other institutions. This was the case even for people under the age of sixty-five—including kids and young adults like Larry McAfee and Jenny Lynn Langley. It was a simple case of inertia and greed. The majority of Medicaid funding for long-term care currently goes to nursing facilities. The problem is that if anyone needs public funding for their care—whether they are disabled or elderly—the assumption is that they will go into a nursing facility whether they want to or not. Most of the people I know and love would much prefer to live at home rather than in an institution. Like the Gang of Nineteen, many of our ADAPT members had themselves been institutionalized at one point or time and had yearned for the freedom and independence of life in their own homes.

Thus, not long after President Bush signed the ADA into law, ADAPT decided to change its focus from transportation to removing the institutional bias. To reflect this, we also changed our name to Americans Disabled for Attendant Programs Today (still ADAPT). This also meant that we had a new target; instead of APTA, we would have to focus on the American Health Care Association (AHCA), the trade group for the nursing homes industry that promoted our nation's bias toward institutions. Our mission was to get them to support a funding shift from nursing homes to home care, which would not only be the right thing to do, but would also be more cost-effective. All the research was proving that nursing-home care was more expensive than care in one's home.

Unfortunately, the fight for community-based living has not gone as well as our fight for accessible public transportation. As of 2015, the majority of Medicaid funding continues to go to the nursing home industry. The fight goes on...

Chapter 42

Tragedy

On July 26, 1992—the second anniversary of the signing of the ADA—the City of Denver installed a plaque at the corner of Colfax and Broadway. With its bronze lettering, the plaque honored the original Gang of Nineteen for their act of civil disobedience—those two hot July days fourteen years earlier when the Gang members held city buses hostage, sparking the events that would lead to the formation of ADAPT and the fight for accessible transportation in Denver and across the country. Wade asked that his name not be included on the plaque. As always, he wanted the focus to be on people with disabilities, the issues, and the movement. At the end of the day, he had had a choice in where he lived and what transportation he used. He knew the members of the Gang of Nineteen had not.

We Will Ride!
On July 5 and 6, 1978,
This intersection was the site of the first
demonstration for wheelchair accessible
public transportation.

Nineteen members of the
Atlantis Community chanting "We Will Ride"

blocked buses with their wheelchairs,
staying in the streets all night.

Twelve years later, the
Americans with Disabilities Act was passed
by the United States Congress and signed
by the president on July 26, 1990, ordering
all public buses be wheelchair accessible.

The Gang of Nineteen
Linda Chism-Andre
Renate Rabe-Conrad
Willy Cornelison
Mary Ann Sisneros
Carolyn Finnell
George Roberts
Mel Conrardy
Bobby Simpson
Debbie Tracy
Jeannie Joyce
Kerry Schott
Jim Lundvall
Lori Heezen
Glenn Kopp
Bob Conrad
Larry Ruiz
Cindy Dunn
Paul Bray
Terri Fowler

Placed by the City and County of Denver, July 26, 1992

Wade with his wife, Molly, and two of their children, Lincoln and Caitlin, sitting beside the plaque

In February of 1993, I was sitting in my office reviewing plans for ADAPT's spring action in Washington, DC. President Clinton had recently been sworn into office, and the First Lady was pledging to support sweeping changes in health care. ADAPT members understood this was a great opportunity to try to increase funding for attendant care and get people out of nursing homes, and we were doing all that we could to get the attention of the right people in Washington. I was looking forward to this action. I had missed the last one and was ready to reconnect with my fellow advocates.

The phone rang, and I picked it up. On the line were Bob and Stephanie, my close friends and fellow ADAPT members from Texas. Lately, we had been working together to prepare for the action, but as soon as I heard Bob's voice, I understood this was not a routine business call.

"Mark, something's happened," he said.

I took a deep breath. "What?" I asked.

"Wade's dead."

The air left my body. "What?" I asked again.

"Wade is dead. And so is his son, Lincoln."

This was not possible. Wade and his family were vacationing in Mexico. Wade hadn't had time off in fourteen years, but at Christmas, he had surprised Molly, Heather, Lincoln, and Caitlin with a two-week vacation to Todos Santos, Mexico, a small, coastal town whose name meant "All Saints." They were finally going to get to spend some quality time together. They were finally going to take a break from the constant pressures of their work at Atlantis. Wade had been so excited, sharing details of their plans every time I had talked to him.

"How? What happened?" I asked.

"Yesterday, they were at the beach. They had been getting ready to fly back home, but Wade wanted to take one last trip to the beach before they went to the airport. Lincoln was playing in the water when he got caught in the undertow. Wade swam out to rescue him but got caught up in it as well. They both drowned."

There was no way to process this information. It was all a jumble of words. I took another deep breath and asked, "And Molly, and Caitlin, and Heather?"

"They were back on the beach when it happened," said Stephanie. "Molly witnessed the whole thing."

"Oh no."

"Yeah."

After a long pause I asked, "How's Molly?

She sighed. "She's hanging in there, but it's rough. She is very, very traumatized."

"I can imagine. Is there any information about a funeral?"

"Not yet," said Stephanie. "We're keeping in touch with Babs. We'll let you know when we hear something. Meanwhile, some of us have been talking about doing something at the spring action when we're all together in DC."

"Makes sense," I said.

On a windy day in May, we gathered at the steps of the Lincoln Memorial where we had originally planned to hold a rally. Instead, several hundred ADAPT members gathered to pay tribute to our cofounder and his son, whose full name was Lincoln Memorial Blank. Most of us were familiar with Lincoln. He had grown up going to ADAPT actions. Wade would often carry Lincoln around as he coordinated the actions. There were even a few occasions when he had to arrange for childcare before he got arrested. But with our large ADAPT family, people were always available to look after Lincoln until his father was released.

During the memorial service, a number of people spoke, including Bob Kafka, Justin Dart, Even Kemp, Mike Auberger, and Stephanie Thomas. Colorado Representative Pat Shroeder was also on hand to speak. She was the one who, in the midst of that first action at Colfax and Broadway in 1978, had brought coffee and doughnuts to Wade and the others, a powerful message of support from a public official and the beginning of a longstanding friendship between Wade and Pat. Other public officials, including President Clinton, Representative Major Owen, and Senator Tom Harkin sent staff members to speak on their behalf in praise of Wade. Afterward, Elaine Kolb and Johnny Crescendo sang a song they had written about Wade.

After the memorial service, we marched to the White House and lined up along the fence that faced the grand front entrance. Reaching through the fence, we planted small crosses with the names of people who had died in nursing homes. In the following days, we protested at the national headquarters of the nursing-home lobby and in the Capitol. A good number of us were arrested. We got great media coverage from local and national media, including CNN and ABC's *World News Tonight*.

The days were punctuated with thoughts of Wade. His presence was palpable. He had always been integral to these actions. Many times, I found myself looking for him, expecting to turn around and be able to share an observation or talk through a strategy. That's what made his absence all the more gut-wrenching, the knowledge that he would have been here with us. We all felt it and often reached out to each other to reminisce, share funny stories, and cry together.

But I also found myself watching the action and thinking that now the critics of ADAPT would have to face the fallacies in their arguments. Over the years, many people had criticized Wade, alleging that he manipulated and controlled us. They accused Wade of thinking for us and calling the shots. They claimed he was using us for his own agenda. They made it sound like we were his puppets, acting only when he pulled the strings. A lot of this came because Wade was nondisabled, but also because people weren't comfortable with ADAPT's tactics. The sad thing was that we heard these condemnations from within the disability community as much as from without. For the most part, Wade stayed silent, not wanting to engage his critics, although he did make one attempt to address the criticisms in a letter he wrote to the *Disability Rag*:

> There is a class struggle going on in the disability movement. Could it be that those citizens with disabilities who have—jobs, vans and earned income—are being threatened by an organized group of have-nots on fixed incomes who are fed up with being locked out of the system?
>
> ADAPT has gone to San Antonio, Cincinnati and Detroit, all cities with inaccessible buses, and found the local disabled leaders are more concerned about tactics or image than their right to ride the bus. Do their leaders speak for the thousands of people who use wheelchairs for mobility? Most of them are not even willing to inform others of our planned actions. 'If I can't get my way, I won't play,' summarizes their position. They fail to realize the life-and-death feelings that ADAPT's core members feel about their rights. The jails in Detroit, Cincinnati, Washington, DC and Los Angeles held citizens with disabilities from all across the country. Where was the National Council on Independent Living? The Paralyzed Veterans of America? The Muscular Dystrophy Association?

The National Easter Seal Society? And the others? They were expressing dismay at our tactics, or pouting because they weren't consulted, or hiding out of fear for their jobs.

That's too bad! We are on a roll and it's too late to stop now. Either you are for us or against us. Not much more can be said than that. We Will Ride!

I apologize for being able-bodied—but that could always change, couldn't it?

Wade Blank

Denver

I had always thought the allegations against were Wade were offensive and shortsighted. Offensive because they gave the rest of us in ADAPT very little—if any—credit. They gave voice to the very attitudes that we were fighting against—the attitudes that said we were poor, helpless, "crippled" people who needed someone to speak for us and tell us what to do. Shortsighted because they came from people who didn't know Wade. Anyone who knew him understood that he was merely the man who had inspired us, who had lovingly and methodically mentored us, helping us to find our own voices. Wade was the guy who had prodded us to look inward to find the source of our own power and then given us the tools to channel that power and effect change by our own hands and in our own way. He was the one who taught us to take it personally.

BE THE CHANGE

I learned to take things personally when my access to decent transportation was denied. But while I continue to work today with ADAPT to campaign for community-based living, I know that my odds of ending up in an institution are low. One of the things that separates me from Larry McAfee, Jenny Lynn Langley, and other people with disabilities who are at serious risk of being placed in a nursing home is access to resources. It may be crass, but it's true. With their high-level injuries, Larry and Jenny Lynn required round-the-clock support and attendant services. That was enough to drain Larry's private insurance funds and Jenny's personal and family resources. When Larry and Jenny could no longer afford to pay the costs of services, they had to rely on Medicaid with its institutional bias.

I wouldn't say that I'm lucky and they're not, because luck doesn't have anything to do with it. We should be willing to help pay for attendant services in the home for people who can't afford it. It should never be a matter of the luck of the draw. Unfortunately, in our society, it is. I happen to have a good job and am married to a woman who has a good job, which means that I'm able to pay for attendants and know that my risk of being institutionalized is minimal. Since the time when I moved out of my parents' house in 1980, I've had a number of attendants, all of whom, for the most part, were all good people who provide valuable services. But no one has been with me longer than Carol.

Growing up in Jamaica, a neighborhood of the Queens borough in New York City, Carol established herself as a passionate advocate at the early age of four when her teacher not only made fun of a boy who had polio, but refused to allow him to go to recess because he could not keep up with the other children. Incensed by the teacher's cruelty, Carol confronted her, arguing that it wasn't fair to exclude him from recess because of his lack of mobility.

"It's doesn't matter," replied the teacher.

Carol kicked her in the leg and said, "Now your leg hurts too, but it doesn't matter." Although Carol was punished for her act of rebellion, it did not deter her. She was firm in her conviction that she had done the right thing. Indeed, Carol continued to reach out to help people in spite of her parents' objections. In the second grade, Carol learned that one of her classmates—as well as the girl's seven siblings—had lice and were hungry. Impulsively, Carol invited all eight of the children to come home with her, where she let them take baths and then sent them home with bags of her own family's clothes and food. For that, she received a spanking.

When Carol was fourteen, she met a boy in her neighborhood who had autism. Fascinated, she began spending time with him to the point that the boy's mother asked Carol to babysit him and his brother when she was out. There were times when Carol also accompanied the boy to school and assisted him in the classroom. This garnered the attention of the school's social worker, who was so impressed with Carol's talent for caring for the boy that she offered to help train Carol to become an attendant when she turned sixteen. Two years later, Carol took the social worker up on her offer and began attending training classes in the evenings after school, eventually receiving certification and a license to be a home-health worker.

When I met Carol in 1993, she was a single mother working as an attendant for a home-health agency. I had just lost one of my attendants due to a change in her life and called Carol's agency to ask if they could send someone to my house until I could make other arrangements. The following week, a woman in her early 40s with a thick New York accent showed up at my door and introduced herself as Carol Reidy. She assisted me with my personal care routines for a couple of weeks, and we worked well together. I asked her if she'd be interested in serving as my primary attendant. It just so happened that she was in the process of leaving the agency to do private duty work for another person and wanted an additional client. I had no idea that, more than twenty years later, Carol would still be assisting me. Not only that, she would end up being one of my closest friends.

I recognize that not everyone bonds with their attendant the way that Carol and I have bonded. Indeed, there are many people with disabilities who maintain strict boundaries with the person who assists them. For them, it's strictly a business arrangement, and they'd like to keep it that way. The attendant is there to do a job and nothing more. It's clean and neat, over and out. But I've never been known for having good boundaries. Plus, having an attendant is an intimate thing. Not only does that person see you naked on a regular basis, but he or she is helping you with personal things. You can try to keep something like that cut, dry, and impersonal, but it's hard to do. You must really trust your attendant. Once you do, you can't help but form a relationship.

What's trickier, though, is the relationship your attendant does or doesn't have with your family members. I mean, think about it. The attendant is coming into your home on a regular basis and getting really up close and personal, so to speak. In addition to helping me with my personal care, Carol accompanies me on trips and sometimes sleeps at our house on the nights when Susan is out of town. At times, she does our laundry or tries to help keep Susan organized. With all that going on, you have to hope that everyone involved is secure with themselves; otherwise it could easily get ugly.

Fortunately, the relationship between Carol and my family has been very good. Susan's always been comfortable having an attendant around, which makes me think that it's probably easier for spouses to handle having an attendant among the family when disability has always been a part of the equation. Susan knew that marrying me involved an attendant, unless, of course, she wanted to be my attendant all the time, and neither of us wanted that. That's truly crossing boundaries. I'm guessing the attendant relationship is much more of a challenge for someone who is newly disabled, and the spouse has to adjust to this extra person. Plus, Carol makes it easy to have near. She is helpful and involved when she needs to be but also has a knack for recognizing when she needs to blend into the background or even head outside for a while.

Lindsey liked Carol once she understood that Carol was going to be around on a long-term basis. When she was little, there'd been too many times when she'd bonded with an attendant, only to have that person leave after a short while. Soon after Carol began working for me, Lindsey came out to the garage where Carol was smoking and sat on the steps.

"Miss Carol, are you going to school?" she asked.

"Nope."

"Are you going to be a nurse?"

"No." Carol looked at her, wondering where this was going.

"Then why are you doing this?"

"What?"

"Why are you taking care of my dad?"

"Because I like taking care of people," answered Carol.

Lindsey eyed her for a moment, considering this response. Then she got to the point of her inquisition. "Well, are you going to be leaving my dad?" She stared defiantly at Carol.

"No, honey. I need the money too much."

"Good answer, Carol!" I called from the hallway, where I'd been listening to the conversation.

From then on, Lindsey felt safe enough to bond with Carol.

With her knack for helping people and the haughty bravado that comes from being raised on the streets of New York City, Carol is a powerful advocate. That's why it didn't require a rocket scientist to figure out that she would be a great addition to ADAPT. After she spent an evening grousing about the challenges that attendants face—the low pay, the lack of benefits, the abuse that sometimes comes from an angry client—I told her about ADAPT and invited her to the Lansing, Michigan, action that was scheduled for the fall of 1995. Curious, she agreed to go. But I warned her to be prepared. "An ADAPT action is not like anything else you've experienced. It can wreak havoc on you emotionally and physically. Just know you'll need about a week to recover." I could tell she didn't believe me.

One of our targets for this trip was Michigan Governor John Engler, a rising star among Republicans who would end up being seriously considered for the running mate position with Republican presidential nominee Bob Dole in 1996. Given his increasing influence and friendship with Speaker of the House Newt Gingrich, we wanted him to help convince Newt to sponsor legislation that would redirect Medicaid funding toward home and community-based services. Prior to our arrival, ADAPT sent the governor several requests for a meeting, all of which went unanswered or denied. Anticipating this, the Michigan members of ADAPT went on a reconnaissance mission to figure out where the Governor lived. After scoping out his neighborhood and mapping out a strategy, we decided to pay him a visit.

On a Tuesday morning that will long be remembered in ADAPT history for its snow, sleet, and frigid temperatures, several hundred of us assembled in a park that bordered the neighborhood and was out of view of the governor's mansion. There, we huddled together, covering ourselves with black trash bags and duct tape to try to brace ourselves against the arctic blast that had come in unexpectedly, and for which we were ill prepared. As we did, we relayed information about the day's plans to the color teams, determined who was up for being arrested and who wasn't, and tried to figure out how to get onto the governor's property, which was protected by a massive iron gate. Once we were ready we lined up—those of us willing to risk arrest in front, while the others were in the back—and began to make our way through the woods to avoid drawing attention to ourselves until we had safely reached the neighborhood. But, as you can imagine, trying to navigate hundreds of wheelchairs over uneven terrain is no small feat. We'd brought portable ramps to help us, though it was still a very bumpy ride.

Upon emerging from the woods, we took to the streets where we were able to pick up the pace. By the time we neared the mansion, we were coming along at a pretty good clip. As luck would have it, the gates began to open to allow a car from within the compound to exit. Realizing this was our ticket in, we rolled and ran as fast as we could, swarming around the oncoming car and forcing it to come to a stop. The two security guards began shouting and running out of their stand, but they were quickly overwhelmed by the size of our crowd. Eventually, they were able to close the gate, but by then, more than a hundred people were sitting on the governor's front lawn and with me on the front porch, knocking on his door.

In the meantime, Carol was standing outside the gate along with the rest of our group and the attendants. During any ADAPT action, we ask the attendants and other nondisabled people to stay in the back. There are a number of reasons for this. Most importantly, we think it's really important for the folks with disabilities—the ones who are directly impacted by the issue at hand—to be front and center in any action. They should be the ones leading the action, creating the demands, negotiating, and getting arrested. But we particularly don't want the attendants to get arrested. We need them to stay far away from the person they attend to, primarily because we don't want to make it easy for the police to arrest us. As ADAPT was getting started we realized that most municipalities have no idea what to do when they arrest someone with a disability. They don't understand the access issues, and they especially don't understand the kind of attendant services that need to be provided. While this is another reflection of how our society doesn't understand the needs of people with disabilities, ADAPT doesn't feel the need to assist the police with this particular issue. If they want to arrest us, great, but they need to learn what that involves. In the meantime, we're certainly not going to make it easy for them by handing over our attendants as well. That goes for service animals too. We've been known to corral all the animals during an action to prevent the officers from knowing which animal belongs to a particular person. The other reason we ask our attendants to stay back is purely practical. Many times, we aren't released from police custody until sometime in the middle of the night. We need to know there will be enough attendants on hand who have had a chance to get some rest so they can help us all get to bed when we finally arrive back at the hotel.

Soon after we arrived, a number of police came. In addition, some low-level governor's staff members also showed up and made efforts to get us to leave. When we explained that we weren't leaving until we met with the governor, they said he was unavailable. This was unacceptable, so we waited, vowing to stay for as long as necessary until we got our meeting. Now with any ADAPT action, down time—a lot of it—comes with the territory. We take over a building and wait to see if our demands will be met, which can take a few hours or all day (or even multiple days). As a result, we get used to biding our time, hanging out, chanting, and otherwise trying to keep everyone's spirits up. What was hard about this action, however, was that our group was separated by the gate, and it was difficult to relay information back and forth. Carol especially was having a hard time with this. With her go-getter personality, she was used to being in the middle of the action; plus, she was very focused on being my attendant and wanted to be close by in case I needed anything. As time passed, she got increasingly stressed, worrying that we didn't have any food. This was only her second action, and she still didn't understand that we ate large breakfasts and arranged for lunch from McDonald's to be delivered during our actions since we knew our days could be very long. It didn't help that the other people around her were starting to wonder about our well-being and what was going on, even worrying about the diabetics in the group.

As a result, Carol took matters into her own hands. With the help of another attendant named AJ, she pleaded with the police officers who had arrived to allow them to bring food in to us, but they refused. Eventually, Carol began to cry and threatened to climb the fence to come to our rescue. The officers assured her that if she climbed the fence, she'd be taken to jail. Carol looked at AJ, pausing to consider their options, but it wasn't long before that determined spirit that had enabled four-year-old Carol to kick her teacher in the leg took over. Soon, the two of them were gathering packets of sugar and crackers from other members, stuffing them into their pockets, then climbing over the fence. But as soon as their feet hit the ground on the other side of the fence, the officers arrested them.

"Hey, Mark," I heard someone yell. "Isn't that your attendant?"

I looked across the lawn to see Carol and AJ being led away in handcuffs. "Oh, yeah, it sure is," I laughed. "Wonder what prompted that."

While the two women sat in the back of the police car, the radio crackled with a message from the governor insisting that all of the protestors inside the gates be arrested. Knowing that Carol and AJ were attendants, the officer turned to Carol and said, "Sounds like we'll be taking everyone in. What are you going to need to take care of everybody while they're in jail?"

Carol started shaking her head vigorously. "No way. You arrested me. I'm now under the state's custody, and I'm off the clock. I'm not taking care of anyone."

The officer looked at AJ, who said, "You heard what she said."

"Then what if we let you guys go?"

"We're still not taking care of them," insisted Carol. "You arrested them, so they're your responsibility. You figure out how to take care of them." Frustrated, the officer started the car and headed for the local jail.

By late afternoon, the commitment of locals meeting with top-level aides ended our standoff, and we headed back to the hotel. When we arrived, we were met by Carol and AJ, who had been released.

"Wow, so you got to visit the jail, huh?" I said. "What happened?"

"We were trying to bring food in to you," said Carol.

"Really? Why?"

She slapped her hand on her thigh in exasperation. "Because you guys didn't have any food, and we were afraid you were going to get hungry!"

"We were fine," I said. "But what made you think you could get away with that?"

"I wasn't thinking about that! I'm your attendant! I was worried about you!"

I laughed. "I get it. Well, if it's any consolation, your rebellious act helped. The police started to worry that the crowd on the outside was going to start coming over the fence in droves and they'd have to arrest everybody."

"How is that a good thing?"

"It finally got things moving, which was great because I was freezing!"

With great flair, she put her hands on her hips. "So what you're saying is that you were using me to end the standoff?"

"No," I said. "No one asked you to do that. I'm saying that you had good timing, and things started to happen after you were arrested, which was a good thing."

But that didn't help. By then, Carol was convinced we had used her and spent the rest of the evening feeling bitter and resentful. I gave her space, knowing she needed some time to figure things out. Deep down, I wondered if she was embarrassed about having jumped the fence and was doing her best to cover that up. She didn't need to be. These actions can be emotional—especially when you're a newbie. It's an awesome thing to see hundreds of people with disabilities owning their power and using it to fight for their rights. It can be especially powerful for nondisabled people.

As we packed up to head back to Atlanta, I worried that Carol might not come back to another action. But in the end, my fears were unfounded. In our history together, Carol has rarely missed an action. She was just getting started.

Eventually, Shepherd Center hired Carol to assist me in the Advocacy Program. Over the years, we've had our moments, but we always figure out how to make it work. The bonus is that I've been able to watch Carol's sense of advocacy grow and mature.

Because she has such a good heart, in the beginning Carol was quick to take on everyone's problems and fix them, much in the way she did when she took in that family of eight kids in second grade. But in the same way that she learned that it wasn't healthy to give away her family's clothes and food, Carol began to figure out that she couldn't be the one to fix people and rescue them from their problems. She recognized that supporting people is really about giving them the tools necessary to fix their own problems. That's how they begin to understand that their power to change themselves and their world lies within them. It's the only way for them to stop being victims and start taking responsibility and being an advocate.

Granted, I've been preaching that message for a long time, which may have influenced her to a degree. There have been plenty of times when people have called into my office with gut-wrenching stories about their lives, clearly hoping that I, as the director of advocacy, can do something about it. When I ask them what they'd like to do about it, many of them respond with shock or anger, thinking that I'm being callous. But for the ones who don't hang up and who continue to talk with me, you can sense that they would love to have the power to control their own destiny if they had someone to push them in that direction. I know Carol has been a part of many of those conversations. However, I also sense that Carol has figured out the true meaning of advocacy through old fashioned firsthand experience. She's seen how helping can leave someone in a place of helplessness versus leaving them with a sense of their own power, and she prefers the latter for herself and those around her.

As a result, Carol has become passionate about two things: helping others to learn to, as Ghandi famously said, "be the change," to become their own best advocates; and addressing the needs of caregivers. Through all of her years of caring for people with disabilities, Carol has learned firsthand the difficulties of being a caregiver. Whether you're caring for a family member or you're a professional caregiver with a license and a paycheck, attending to the needs of people with disabilities and chronic issues is a tough job with few benefits. It is physically exhausting. Emotionally, it can be taxing. And let's not forget the financial piece and the fact that most family caregivers are not paid much. Nor do they have the funds available to hire someone else to help, leading to feelings of being trapped. But even for those "professional" attendants, the pay is abysmal. There is also little support or opportunities for raises.

In characteristic fashion, Carol decided to take matters into her own hands. She created an award for caregivers, which was appropriately named the Carol Jones SSS Award. The award was debuted at the 2009 ADAPT action in Atlanta. Wanting to create an award that had meaning for the people who received it, Carol approached the award process with a great deal of seriousness and professionalism. She reviewed the nominations carefully before taking the time to interview each candidate. She was looking for someone truly special. Her criteria included someone who had served as a caregiver for more than ten years but who didn't see it as just a job. She wanted evidence that the person truly loved the work he or she did. She also wanted someone who supported the rights of people with disabilities.

On the last night of the 2009 action, Carol presented the first award to Jan Jennings, who had been a Special Education teacher for more than eighteen years. Carol had received numerous letters of reference for Jan that described a woman who was passionate about her job and a staunch supporter of the rights of people with disabilities. One of them told how Jan had accompanied a young man with cerebral palsy on a trip to Las Vegas to fulfill his wish to have his first alcoholic drink in Sin City. Carol admired Jan's spirit and loved the sense of humor the two shared. She presented Jan with five hundred dollars (which came out of Carol's own pocket), a certificate, and a few gifts. Jan received a standing ovation, revealing the impact of Carol's award, which has become an ADAPT tradition. For days after, Carol was on the most incredible high. By acknowledging the hard work of attendants, she had found a way to advocate for her peers and, in turn, for herself.

The irony is not lost on me. I get it. I was in such a hurry to keep people from seeing me naked that I broke the first rule of swimming by diving headfirst into water that I hadn't first tested. And I got injured. Now, I have a woman who is not my wife not only seeing me naked on a regular basis, but also having to help me poop, bathe, get dressed, travel, etc. Life is funny that way.

One evening, after Carol had been with me about five years, I was sitting in my shower chair, sopping wet, joking with Carol about something. I don't remember what it was that we were joking about but I remember that she said something that was funny and characteristically Carol, full of her brassy confidence and earthy laugh.

"Man, Carol," I laughed. "If I'd had your personality, I'd be walking now."

She stopped and stared at me. "What do you mean?"

"I mean that you would never have worried about being naked. In fact, you would have just stood up and let everyone see you naked, and that would have been it.

"I still don't understand."

"I got injured because I went skinny-dipping with some of my friends, and I was scared for them to see me naked, so I dove into the water, hit the bottom, and got paralyzed."

She paused, and I realized she had never heard the story about how I was injured.

"You never would have been scared like that," I said.

"No," she agreed. "But if you hadn't been injured, you never would have met me."

Chapter 44

Acceptance

While ADAPT continued to confront the American Health Care Association around the country, I was at a time in my life when I couldn't participate in every ADAPT action. Nor did I need to. With each year, ADAPT was recruiting new members and developing new leadership. I had already started to take less of a leadership role. I thought it was important that others have the opportunity to nurture their leadership skills; plus, it was fun to wear a different hat and get to know and mentor the newbies. I never got tired of seeing the excitement and the adrenaline rush that comes from your first ADAPT action.

But the main reason that kept me from fully participating in the ADAPT actions in the '90s was Lindsey; I wanted to be around for her as much as possible.

Lindsey was five before she realized I was different from other dads. After seeing me in the yard with her one day, one of her friends walked up to her and said, "Your dad can't walk?" After processing this revelation in her five-year-old mind, Lindsey concluded that having a dad who used a wheelchair was cool. She started making a point of introducing me to her friends and even inviting them to ride on the back of my wheelchair.

One morning, we were sitting across from each other at the breakfast table. I was reading the newspaper while Lindsey munched on Frosted Flakes, eyeing me intently. I could tell something was up.

"Daddy?" she asked.

"Yes?"

"Will you come to school with me today?"

"Uh, why do you need me to go to school with you?"

She looked down at an errant flake that had fallen on the table, picked it up, and popped it in her mouth. Still chewing, she said, "I want you to come with me for show and tell."

"You want me to come see you do show and tell?" I asked.

With great exasperation, she said, "No, Daddy! I want you to be my show and tell!"

I laughed. "You do? Why?"

"Because I want my friends to meet you! And I want them to see your wheelchair and van. You could give them rides and stuff like you do for me."

Luckily, I didn't have any pressing appointments that day. I called in to work and explained that I was going to be late, then drove Lindsey to school. As we arrived, Lindsey's teacher made her way over to me, and I explained the situation. She laughed when she heard my daughter's plan and readily agreed to let me be the subject of Lindsey's presentation. I sat in the back of the classroom and waited until it was time for our turn. When it was, Lindsey walked confidently to the front of the classroom, where she proudly introduced me.

"This is my dad," she said. "He has a disability. He can't walk, so he uses a wheelchair to get around." I had purposely brought my power chair with me, knowing the kids would love it. They watched intently as I showed them how I used the joystick to go forward and backward.

"Oh!" they said. Playing to her audience, Lindsey jumped on the back of the wheelchair as I shuttled her around the classroom.

"My dad takes me for rides on his wheelchair," she exclaimed. Hands shot up as the kids begged for me to give them each a turn. In that moment, I was the cool dad.

After everyone had gotten a turn, and with the blessing of Lindsey's teacher, I invited the group to follow me out to the parking lot. There, I demonstrated how, with the push of a button, I could open the door and lower the lift on my van. They crowded around the lift and peered into the van.

"There's no seat by the steering wheel!" cried one boy.

"I know," I replied. "That's where I sit." I rolled onto the platform, raised the lift, and then moved into position in front of the steering wheel. Fifteen tiny heads peered curiously through the open door as I showed them how I locked my wheelchair into place; I had come a long way from the trough that Dad and Lloyd had dug out of my first van. Once I was in, the kids watched with great fascination as I showed them how I drove using the hand controls. Afterward, the teacher and I led the children back to their class. I asked her if the children were familiar with the song "The Wheels of the Bus."

"Of course," she said.

"Great!" Turning to the kids, I said, "Hey, y'all, can you sing the song with me?" And immediately, all there little voices started singing the familiar song. But as we got toward the end, I lifted up my hand to cue them to listen. "Okay, now we're going to add one more verse." And soon, the kids were singing, "the lift on the bus goes up and down, up and down, up and down..."

For days after, Lindsey was the cool kid in her class.

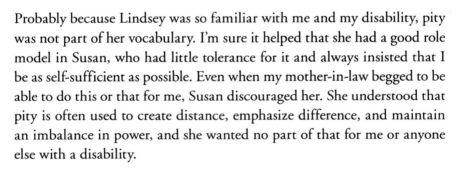

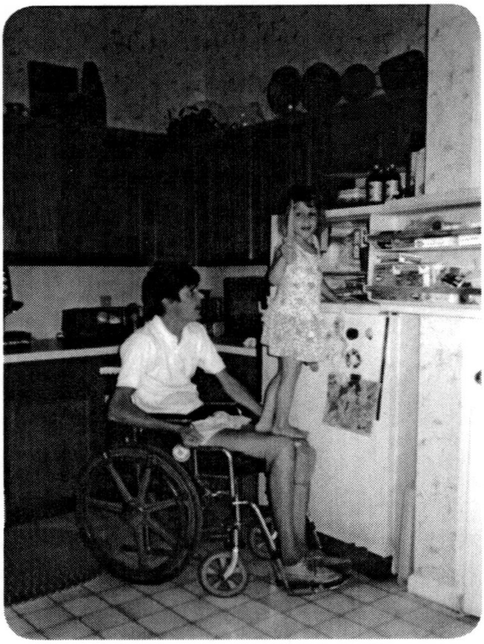

Lindsey standing on my lap to access the freezer

Probably because Lindsey was so familiar with me and my disability, pity was not part of her vocabulary. I'm sure it helped that she had a good role model in Susan, who had little tolerance for it and always insisted that I be as self-sufficient as possible. Even when my mother-in-law begged to be able to do this or that for me, Susan discouraged her. She understood that pity is often used to create distance, emphasize difference, and maintain an imbalance in power, and she wanted no part of that for me or anyone else with a disability.

One of my first opportunities to talk with Lindsey about the pity problem came when she was in kindergarten. In early March, she came home from school one day and handed me a piece of paper with green lettering and a smiling leprechaun on it. The happy-go-lucky Irishman was announcing the "Leprechaun Leap," a fundraiser for the Muscular Dystrophy Association and "Jerry's Kids." Also on the page was a picture of a child who was wearing leg braces. Like other "poster children," the child was looking straight at the camera and flashing a big smile. She was, in every way, just like Lindsey or her friends except for the braces. But what was most disturbing was the line that was printed in bold type above the child's head. It read, "Leap for those who can't leap for themselves!"

"Ugh," I thought. I hated this stuff. I immediately called the school administrator and arranged to meet with her the next day. Early the next morning, I dropped Lindsey off in her classroom before making my way to the front office. The administrator greeted me warmly.

"How can I help, Mr. Johnson?"

"Yesterday, Lindsey brought home this flyer," I said, holding up the green sheet of paper.

"Oh, yes! The Leprechaun Leap!"

"I wanted to talk with you about it. I know that it's a good cause and it's great to give the kids opportunities to help others, but I think it sends the wrong message."

"You do?"

"Yes. 'Leap for those who can't leap for themselves.'" I smiled. "It's catchy, but I think it promotes pity. It focuses on what children with disabilities can't do. It emphasizes that we need to do things for them. And the underlying message is, 'Thank God our children aren't like them.'"

"Hm," she said. "I don't know that I see that."

"It's subtle, but it's there. It's why people with disabilities protest the Jerry Lewis telethon. His whole message is about raising money for these poor, poor children. It's all about pity. And fear."

"But he raises a lot of money for them."

"Sure. But it's not worth it if it's also creating a sense of pity. That can do damage. People don't want to hang out with people they pity. And they don't want to see them. They want to keep their distance and be glad they're not like them. That's what leads to stereotypes and prejudices."

"Is there anything else?"

"One more thing. The flyer says, 'Leap for those who aren't as lucky.' I think it's important for people to know that disability has nothing to do with luck. I'm no more lucky or unlucky than the next person."

She looked intently at the flyer. Finally, she asked, "Are you saying we shouldn't help them?"

"No. But I'm hoping that maybe next year the school will do something different. In the meantime, I think it would be great if the school could find ways to build relationships between kids with disabilities and the nondisabled kids. Maybe create an event where they can get together and play or do something. We've got to find a way to teach the nondisabled kids that there's nothing wrong with being disabled and help them see what they have in common with kids with disabilities. If we can do that, we will be raising a generation that isn't afraid of people with disabilities and doesn't pity them. That would go a lot farther than simply raising money for them."

Lindsey didn't participate in the Leprechaun Leap. Instead, she raised money to support the Muscular Dystrophy Association's Family Foundation, which focused more on quality of life—rather than cure—issues. It allowed her to participate in a fundraiser but also set an example for more meaningful ways to support children with disabilities.

I am a tall person. You wouldn't know it because I am always in my wheelchair. I used to have a standing table, a piece of equipment that looked like one of those things in a fitness center where you balance your body weight on your forearms and raise your legs up and down to strengthen your abdominal muscles. It had a similar fitness function for me, helping maintain my bone density and reducing my spasticity. In the evenings, Susan would help me transfer from my chair to the stand, which actually started out in a sitting position. After strapping me in, she'd lift me up into a standing position. I'd stay there for an hour or more while I watched television or while I hung out with Susan and Lindsey.

I remember how Lindsey would stare up at me, amazed by this new vision of her father.

"You're so tall, Daddy!" she'd exclaim.

"It's really different, isn't it?"

She nodded. "What would happen if I took the straps off?"

"I would fall on the floor and probably land on you."

She giggled, then stopped and looked up at me. "Are you going to walk again, Daddy?"

"One day," I said, before adding, "but I don't know when."

She continued to stare at me, clearly pondering something internally. Finally, having reached some kind of conclusion, she clambered up the stand and gave me a hug and a kiss. Then she went off to bed.

Lindsey was a bright, active girl with a gift for gab, an inherent athleticism that she had come by honestly. She had Susan's enthusiasm and star power, which meant that she was perfect for the cheerleading squad. But she also loved sports and had a competitive streak a mile wide and was soon asking to sign up for softball. Since Susan and I both wanted to be involved in her life some way, we made a decision: Susan would coach her cheerleading squad, while I would coach her softball team. It seemed fitting since my dad had always dreamed of having a baseball career. While he never made it to "the majors," he was good enough to play for the Wilson Tobacconists, the North Carolina town's own semi-pro team which, back in 1941, had finished as one of the top one hundred teams in minor league baseball history. Throughout our childhood Dad was never far from a bat, a ball, and his well-oiled glove, and he spent years coaching each of the three of us through little league baseball.

Coaching Lindsey's softball team seemed like a great way to honor him and spend time with her. When the players showed up on that first day, I'm sure some of the girls on the team—and certainly their parents—were surprised to find that one of their coaches was a guy in a wheelchair. They weren't used to having someone in a wheelchair around the ballpark, much less in a coaching position. But that's okay; I could handle it. And so could Lindsey. For her, it was nothing new.

There was no question that Lindsey was growing up with a perspective on disability that was very different from the rest of society. For her, disability was a normal part of life. She was used to the attendants who came on a regular basis to help me with my personal care. Over time, she had grown to love Carol, who would take time to give her advice or listen to her day. As a little girl, she was fascinated by my hand controls and lift on my van and thought it was fun to ride up and down it. And she thought my wheelchair was cool. She loved to stand on the back of it and let me take her for rides and knew that she could crawl up on my lap after a long day of walking around at the park, or wherever we happened to be. She had learned that standing on my lap made it much easier to reach the popsicles in the freezer. And since we always had a spare wheelchair sitting around in the garage, she loved to invite her friends over to race wheelchairs or tie water-skiing ropes to the back and pull each other along. But hands down, the best thing about having a dad with a wheelchair was that you got to bypass the lines and go straight onto the rides at Disney World.

For Lindsey, these elements of my disability were part of our lives together, and they were no big deal. As a result, they weren't a big deal for her friends either. Whenever she introduced me to a new friend, there was inevitably a moment of confusion and discomfort as they realized I was disabled. I could see it in their eyes. But I would crack a joke or say something to make them feel at ease, and you could see them breathe a sigh of relief, as if to say, "Ah, it's gonna be okay." And from then on, it was simply a matter of getting to know each other as people, letting them figure out that it was okay to ask me questions about life with a disability, and to make jokes, and to laugh with me (and sometimes even at me). And helping them to understand that no pity was necessary; they didn't need to feel sorry for me, or uncomfortable, or, worse yet, afraid. I was just Lindsey's dad. Once they got to that point, that's when the real magic happened. That's when the true relationship began.

It was late on a Thursday afternoon when I left my office and headed to the ball field to meet Lindsey and the rest of the team for a game.

"Hey Dad!" Lindsey called out from the dugout when I arrived, where she was talking with some of her friends.

"Hey!" I yelled back.

"Do you need some help?" Jeff, my fellow coach, yelled out.

"I think I got it," I answered.

Lindsey, me, and her softball team

We had a great game and won it in the last inning. In my excitement, I rushed onto the field and flipped over. As soon as I hit the ground, I heard Jeff and some of the parents yelling and running toward me. Immediately, I felt several pairs of hands lifting me up while someone else righted my chair. Gingerly, they sat me down.

"Are you alright?" asked one the dads.

"I'm fine," I said, trying to brush the dirt off. It was then that I heard laughter and looked up to see Lindsey and two of her friends, Meredith and Lollie, laughing hysterically and looking at me.

"Dad, you're a mess!" shouted Lindsey, still laughing.

"Yes," I responded.

Still laughing, Lollie said, "Way to make an entrance, Mr. J."

We continued to laugh as I motioned for the girls to get off the field for the next game. As they did, I heard one of the newer players whisper to Meredith, "I can't believe you guys were laughing at him! That was awful how he fell."

"Nah," Meredith replied. "That's just Lindsey's dad."

"But he's in a wheelchair…"

"So? It's no big deal."

SECTION 5

Love

"I am not afraid of tomorrow, for I have
seen yesterday, and I love today."

—William Allen White,
on his seventieth birthday

CHAPTER 45

LET GO, LET GOD

The New Year is always a good time for me. I appreciate the quiet that comes after a busy Christmas season; plus, I love the feeling of a fresh start and a full year of opportunities ahead. But as we ushered in 2009, I realized I didn't have those same good feelings. It's not that anything bad was happening in my life; my family life was great. We had recently partnered with Peggy and Tim to purchase a lakefront home on the border of Georgia and South Carolina, where we spent many relaxing weeks with families and friends, far from our busy Atlanta lives. Susan was happy in her job, overseeing the expansion of the Shepherd Center's Brain Injury Unit and working with Home Depot founder Bernie Marcus to develop services for veterans with brain injuries. I count myself lucky to have shared life with an incredible woman who also has a passion for advocacy. Lindsey, meanwhile, had finished her master's degree in education, was an excellent teacher at Mimosa Elementary, a Title 1 school for at-risk and low-income students, and was adjusting to adulthood life.

Meanwhile, I was doing a lot of work in the community, particularly with the North Metro Miracle League, a baseball league and inclusive social program for kids with disabilities. I was working with the Interfaith Disability Network, which focused on helping faith communities become more inclusive and address the attitudes about disability—including pity—from a faith perspective. I continued to be busy and fulfilled by my work at Shepherd, which, in spite of the economy, was continuing to receive support from donors and expanding its buildings and programs. I was also working with President Obama's transition team to make sure the new president fulfilled his campaign promises to the disability community. ADAPT, having just celebrated its twenty-fifth anniversary, was continuing to push forward with its attendant services campaign, then in its nineteenth year. Although in 1997 we'd been able to get House Speaker Newt Gingrich to sponsor House Bill 2020—the Medicaid Community Attendant Services Act to redirect Medicaid spending from nursing facilities to home- and community-based services and end the institutional bias—it still wasn't the law of the land.

Behind all of this was a gnawing sense that something was off or missing. I didn't feel settled and secure the way I normally did. The more I pondered it and gave into the feeling, the more I got the sense that this wasn't so much about my job or my relationships. It was bigger than that. It seemed to be more about my relationship with God and whether I was doing everything I could to serve him. I felt it particularly during my morning devotion. Each day after getting dressed, I would sit and read the day's offering from *The Daily Word*, a little devotional book that I felt like God himself had handed me in 1996, via the hands of a complete stranger.

In the summer of 1996, Susan and I were on our way home from Florida, where we'd spent the past week visiting her parents and playing at the beach. As we drove, we passed a number of signs advertising orange and grapefruit stands and decided it was a good idea to pull off the highway and buy some. Pulling up to the nearest stand, Susan got out to make our purchase and borrowed my wallet since I was the only one who had cash on hand. In the process she inadvertently left my wallet at the stand, although we didn't realize it until we arrived home. By then we had no way of contacting the little roadside stand that was now over two hundred miles away. I went through the process of cancelling credit cards, getting a new driver's license, and buying a new wallet, and we moved on.

In November, I received a package in the mail from a name I didn't recognize. Upon opening its contents, I was amazed to see my wallet and even more amazed to see my cash, credit cards, and everything else still in it. With it was a note:

> Dear Mr. Johnson –
>
> A few months ago, I saw that you left your wallet at a fruit stand just off I-75. I ran after your van to try to give it back to you, but you didn't see me and pulled out of the parking lot. I tried to follow you but then saw that you were heading north while I was heading south, so I placed your wallet on the seat beside me, planning to mail it to you as soon as I got home. Unfortunately, the wallet slid under the seat, and by the time I got home, I had forgotten all about it. I didn't find it until this week when I was cleaning out my car. My apologies for the delay in getting this to you.
>
> I'm including a copy of *The Daily Word*. I hope you find it helpful.
>
> God bless you.

I picked up the small booklet and leafed through it to find a series of short devotions, one for each day of the month, written by a nondenominational organization called Unity. I turned to the meditation for the day and read it, surprised by how much I enjoyed it, especially given that I wasn't much into reading. The next day, I read another meditation, and the next day, another. By the end of the week, I had developed a routine of reading the day's meditation every morning after I was dressed and before I headed out to work. Over time, I realized that this time of devotion had become a fundamental part of my morning routine, setting the tone for the rest of the day. It helped me start each day with a greater sense that God is with me and is much more capable of handling the things that come at me each day. I was no longer going through the day alone. Even on those days when things didn't necessarily go well, the devotions gave me a sense of comfort and guidance.

Up until this point, I had never maintained a daily devotion practice. The last time I'd done anything similar on a regular basis was during that period after the Billy Graham crusade when I dutifully completed the workbook exercises that they had given us. My enthusiasm for that had lasted only so long, and afterward, I rarely cracked open a Bible or any other book for that matter. Yet, here I was, not only reading my devotion every day but actually looking forward to it, rarely missing a day. I think it helped that the devotions were short, enough to renew me and perhaps even giving me a bullet point or two to carry through the day. Eventually, I dialed the number listed on the inside cover of the booklet, ordered an annual subscription, and asked for a few additional sample copies, which I gave to Susan, Lindsey, Carol, and others.

Thirteen years later, I was continuing to use *The Daily Word* to start my day, only now, it felt different. The only word I could find to describe what I was feeling was restless. As I sat in the space of my quiet time with God, I wondered if I was serving God well enough. Was I was doing enough to glorify God?

"Lord, help me listen so that I'll know your will for me," I'd pray and then spend the day searching for signs, for clues that I was headed in the right direction.

The title of *The Daily Word* devotion for Friday, February 13, 2009, was "healing" and the lead sentence was, "Divine love heals and restores me. I am alive, alert and enthusiastic about life." I read the devotion as usual, then began the day. But as the morning progressed, I started to feel sick. I had abdominal spasms that were so intense I was ready to call 911. However, just as quickly, they subsided. Thinking it was a bad urinary tract infection, I self-medicated, trying to continue on with my day and ignore the symptoms as best I could. Eventually, things got bad enough that I called Susan and asked her to come home early. I then slept for a while, waking up long enough to eat a little dinner before going straight back to bed. Throughout the night, the nausea intensified, and by early Saturday morning, I was throwing up repeatedly.

"We're taking you to the emergency room," Susan declared. Good thing since a CAT scan revealed that my appendix had ruptured and that my body was growing more septic by the minute. My spinal-cord injury made it impossible for me to feel the intense pain that usually signals appendicitis. I spent the next three hours in emergency surgery. I would not recommend it as a way of celebrating Valentine's Day.

Two nights later, I was lying in my hospital bed when something very strange happened. I felt my bed start to shake. Pressing the call button, I asked the nurse to come to my room. When she arrived, I asked her if my bed was shaking.

"No, Mr. Johnson, it's not," she replied while looking quickly at the monitor to make sure my vital signs looked okay. Apparently they did because she turned and left. I went back to paying attention to the bed as it continued to vibrate lightly in a slow, rhythmic way. I should point out that I didn't feel any fear. Instead, I was alert, curious, and conscious enough to recognize that whatever was happening was unusual. I kept closing my eyes and finally let my body relax.

I began to see images in my mind. For the next hour, I watched as the number seven flashed repeatedly in my mind. As it did, I felt a profound sense of awe and peace. When it was over, I fell into a deep sleep, waking the next morning feeling refreshed and peaceful. Throughout the day, I went over the night's events in my mind, trying to process what had happened, though I didn't tell anyone about the experience. I wasn't ready to talk about it yet.

That night, a similar thing happened. This time, instead of the bed shaking, it felt like my body was plugged into an enormous cord with all this energy pulsating through and around me. It was invigorating; I felt completely alive. I should say that I was not on any pain meds—I didn't need them—so I couldn't chalk this up to any kind of substance-induced hallucinations or euphoria. My mind was completely clear. Still, after the preceding night's events, I knew better than to call the nurse. That's why I was shocked when she came rushing into my room.

"Mr. Johnson," she asked. "Are you okay?"

"Yes, why?"

"The monitor is showing that your heart rate has dropped significantly," she said while taking my blood pressure and looking me over. She checked the monitor to make sure it was working. Finding nothing out of place, she returned to the nurses' station across the hallway from my room.

I shut my eyes and relaxed again. This time I began to see a slideshow of images and faces. I saw Susan, Lindsey, and other people I loved. There were friends from various times in my life and people I had worked with in the past, including Wade and Justin. I saw scenes from my advocacy work, a collage of images from ADAPT actions, speeches I'd given, the Shepherd Center, and groups I'd worked with. Eventually the scenes began to change. Now I watched as dozens of pictures of people started flashing across my mind, only this time I didn't recognize any of them. They were from all races and ethnicities, every country around the world, representing all religions and with all levels of ability. All were equal. All had value, and all were coming together to celebrate. Faster and faster, the pictures started coming at me, forming a human kaleidoscope, until they started to come together to form one cohesive community. Watching them, I had this image of myself looking up, back arched, with this stream of positive energy flowing into my body. It was beautiful.

When the vision finally subsided, I was left with no real images, only a feeling. It was light and airy, yet powerful and deep, as it pulsated through me, infusing every fiber of my body. The only word I could attribute to this feeling was "love," pure, unaltered, unadulterated love. Not the love of a parent, or a spouse, or a friend, but the distinct and encompassing love of God. Agape.

The whole event lasted several hours. As soon as it ended, I called the nurse in. When she arrived, I asked her to hand me my laptop. I had come away from the vision with a powerful sense of purpose that I wanted to capture immediately. It was still the middle of the night —too early to call anyone—but at least I could write down what I'd just witnessed. After helping me sit up, the nurse set the computer on the bed table in front of me, checked my vital signs one more time, then left the room. With great energy and clarity, I wrote the following:

1) Tell your story.
2) Create ID cards for people with spinal-cord injuries that would summarize the dos and don'ts of their care in and recovery from emergencies like mine.
3) Establish a legacy project dedicated to building community.

It's probably not fair to boil such a profound religious experience into a three-step action plan. Can you capture a message from God—especially one that lasts a few hours—in a neat, three-point list? No way, but it's what I do. I boil things down into sound bites and bullet points. It keeps things simple—especially something as deep as this—and makes it easier to process, remember, and convey the message.

In the end, I realized the restlessness I'd been feeling at the new year had been fueled by doubt. I was not feeling as grounded as before and wondered whether I should keep doing what I was doing. Should I be doing something more? Now I had a sense that this vision was God's way of confirming the work I'd been doing, while also saying that now it was time for me to tell my story. Until now, I'd never really done that. But I'd spent my career advocating with and for people, and over time, my work had evolved and I had gotten smarter and more strategic about the way I went about it. Hopefully, telling my story at this point in my life would be beneficial to people. At the same time, I felt that the vision was adding a spiritual component to my work that I had previously not shared. I'm not one to witness to people—it's not my style—but through the book and the legacy project, I could find a way to share my faith more intentionally; I could share the message that God loves us and calls us to community just the way we are.

Around 6:30 a.m., I called Susan and told her about the vision. I have no idea what I actually said, but knowing that I was still full of this mountaintop-experience energy, I imagine I didn't make much sense. In fact, my intensity scared her a little. Still, she got that I had had some kind of religious experience and needed to process it. I asked her to call Max Vincent, who'd previously worked as a chaplain at Shepherd, and ask him to come see me. He did. As soon as he walked through the door, I started talking, trying my best to describe what I'd seen in a way that might make sense. He listened patiently in the way that clergy do. If he thought I'd lost my mind, he didn't show it. Then, he began to ask me questions.

"What do you think the number seven means?" he asked.

"I'm not sure."

"It's often used to symbolize spiritual perfection."

I laughed. "That's definitely not me!"

"That's not any of us," he said, smiling. "But hopefully it's something we're all working toward. Perhaps it's a message of hope. Maybe God's sending you a 'keep up the good work' message!"

I laughed again. "All I know is that the number seven shows up all over the book of Revelation, but that's such a scary, negative book. Everything in my vision was positive, so I didn't see the connection."

"It's true that Revelation has a lot of heavy stuff going on in it, but there's also some really wonderful scenes of the whole world coming together and praising God. It's like one giant world block party to raise the roof and glorify God."

"Really? Well, that fits with what I was seeing."

Finally, Max asked, "What do you think the purpose of the vision was?"

"I think it's calling me to tell my story."

"Well, you do that already in a lot of the talks you give, you know 'faith, family, friends.' Maybe it's about telling more of it, going deeper."

"Yeah. I think I need to write a book," I said, then paused. "And it needs to be about love and transformation."

TIME TO REFLECT

I had not heard from or seen Tommy in more than forty years when I finally decided to call him in 2009. My experience in the hospital had gotten me thinking about my spiritual journey over the years, including that night when he'd tried to heal me. I was curious to know how he was, whether he remembered that night, and especially, what impact it had on him and his faith. I always wondered how that event had affected his faith in God. He had been so fired up about his new relationship with the Lord, so sure of himself and the power of God's love. There'd been no question for him that God would heal me if we simply believed enough. Had he been left questioning the strength of his faith? Worse yet, did he leave my house wondering whether God really loved him? Or was it the flip side? Did he leave wondering about the strength of my faith?

My curiosity got the better of me, and I decided to call him. Since my parents had seen his relatives from time to time in Charlotte and had often sent updates about my life and work to Tommy over the years, they were able to help me track him down. After procrastinating, I picked up the phone and called him, a little nervous and unsure of what to expect.

Tommy answered the phone, and I immediately recognized his voice. He always had a way of speaking with intensity, in a rapid and earnest succession of words and thoughts. It was obvious that time had not slowed him down. We chatted for a good while, catching each other up on family and career. He was now living in Virginia and working as a salesman. He seemed fascinated to hear firsthand about my activism and the work I'd done on disability issues. The conversation was, for the most part, easy and comfortable.

When I brought up the night in question, it was clear that he had not forgotten that episode. In fact, I got the impression that it had affected him deeply and had stayed with him over the decades, as it had for me. I could tell that he welcomed the opportunity to talk about it.

"Do you remember much about when you tried to heal me?" I asked him.

"Oh, hey, I wasn't trying to heal you. Only the Lord can do that. I was merely praying for you and hoping that the Lord would work through me to heal you," he stressed. It looked like his faith was still intact.

"Got it," I said.

Together, we recounted the events of that night. It turns out we both remembered it in much the same way.

"One thing I've always wondered," I said, "is why did you try to help heal me? I mean, I didn't ask you to do that, so I've always wondered what made you do that."

"Well," he started, "after your accident, I was really frustrated and anxious. I couldn't believe this happened to my good buddy, and I didn't understand it. I kept asking God, 'Why did this happen to Mark?'"

"Did you think God did this to me? Did you think he caused the accident in some way?"

"Oh, no. No way. I knew that God didn't cause your injury. But I did believe he was going to heal you. I thought, you know, that you were so active and accomplished, God would surely want to heal you," he said.

"What did you think when God didn't heal me?" I waited, listening intently.

"I have to admit that I was really frustrated and even more disappointed. I believed God was going to heal you that night. When it didn't happen, I wasn't sure what to think. But it didn't take me long to get over it. I knew there was a reason for everything that God does. If He didn't heal you that night, it had to be for some reason. Obviously, I couldn't foresee all that you've accomplished in your career, but now I understand what God had in mind for you. He was using you to make a difference in people's lives. It's really exciting to hear about all the things you've accomplished," said Tommy.

"Thanks," I said.

"But Mark, I've got a question for you."

I laughed and said, "Okay." I had no idea what to expect.

"If you were to die today, go to heaven, and see God, and if he asked, 'Why should I let you into heaven?' what would you say?"

I paused, trying to find the best way to answer. I could feel the familiar zeal of Tommy's faith, that same eagerness and intensity that he'd brought to my room that night forty years ago, and I felt some pressure to come up with an answer.

"I'd probably say, 'Because I did my best,'" I said.

"I used to think the same thing, that that was the best answer and the best way to get to heaven," he said. "But now I know that it's really about making sure that we have a personal relationship with Jesus Christ and that the true answer to the question is, 'Because I love you.' That's why God would let you into heaven."

"Good point, Tommy."

We talked for a few more minutes before the conversation finally waned, and we said our good-byes.

I was grateful for the opportunity to reconnect with my childhood friend and hear he was doing well. It was a relief to hear his faith was not only intact but still going strong after all these years. It was also helpful to recount the night's events and know my memory had, for the most part, served me well. It provided some closure. I know that was good for both of us.

I've never begrudged Tommy his attempt to lay hands on me. I know it was prompted by a deep sense of love from a friend who wanted only the best for me. The interesting thing is, Tommy isn't the only person who has tried to heal me. When Lindsey was about three, Susan and I took her on vacation to Myrtle Beach, South Carolina. While Susan and Lindsey were playing in the water, I sat poolside watching them and enjoying the warm summer sun. Eventually, a woman approached me. Sitting next to me, she smiled and asked if she could pray for me. Like Tommy, I understood she was sincere in her offer and thought she was doing a good deed. She may even have thought she was doing the will of God. I smiled back at her and answered, "Sure, as long as you know that I'm happy." I could tell my response startled her. Her smile vanished immediately. She awkwardly stood up and walked away without saying anything else.

I think Tommy and the woman by the pool represent a lot of people in society, and I understand their motivation. Disability is frightening to many people. It generally comes from birth, injury, disease, illness, or aging, and it always means that some part of the body—whether the brain, legs, arms, eyesight, hearing, bodily functions, or a combination of parts—don't work the same way they do in people without disabilities. In a society that places a high value on ability and being independent, we don't want to think that it's possible that we, too, could lose that. I understand that, and yet I see, too, how pity and fear are promoted when people focus solely on the disability. That's what leads to segregation and paternalism.

Every now and then, I go back to that night in my bedroom and wonder why God didn't heal me. Like Tommy, I have no good answer for it. I don't think it's because God had some big "plan" for me or some "reason" to use my disability. I think that's another way of saying that God caused my injury or somehow wanted it to happen, and as I've said before, I don't believe that. I do believe, however, that God can use the tragedy in our lives for good purposes. He doesn't cause the bad stuff, but he can give us the grace and strength to recover, move on, and still seek to glorify him no matter what our situation.

Indeed, that's where Tommy and I agree. In the end, what matters most is whether we love God. You've probably noticed multiple references to

Valentine's Day in this book. That day took on great significance for both me and my dad. In both cases, it represented a time of healing for us; Dad found healing from an addiction that had ruled most of his life, while I recovered from a potentially life-threatening physical condition. In both cases, we experienced powerful, life-changing religious experiences that led us to the same place: love. I am fascinated by this coincidence. I am in awe.

The Daily Word devotion for February 14, 2009—the day of my surgery—read:

> Divine love is its own reward, for the more of this love we express, the more love we have to give. The more open we are to being loved, the more love we receive.
>
> Being love in expression, we are patient and kind, considerate and thoughtful. We communicate how much we care for others and how thankful we are that they are a part of our lives—not just on a special day but every day...
>
> 'By this everyone will know that you are my disciples, if you have love for one another.' John 13:35.

Our love for God is revealed in our love for each other. And that love is about acceptance, respect, and trust. But for some reason, this isn't easy. It doesn't come naturally to us.

I think that's partly because we struggle to love ourselves. It seems to be human nature to dislike some part, or even all, of ourselves. We get so caught up in criticizing or loathing our bodies or abilities. We become so focused on looking for reasons not to love ourselves. That's when the self-loathing kicks in. In the Gospel of Mark, Jesus says that the greatest commandment is to love God and to love our neighbors as ourselves. It's interesting, that last part. Clearly, Jesus understands that if we can't love ourselves and revel in our differences, there's no way we can love our neighbors and their differences. One naturally follows the other.

Thus, while I don't think God will give me a pop quiz when I show up in heaven, I do think Tommy's right. While I'm on earth, God wants me to spend my time loving him, others, and myself. If I can do that well, then

I will naturally and inevitably want to love my neighbor, who, like me, is created in God's image. And when you see the variations in skin color, body size, abilities, languages, beliefs, and senses of humor, you understand clearly that God's image is vast, and vibrant, and beautiful. Every bit of it is worthy of love.

I'm grateful to have so many people in my life who love me: my parents and brothers, Susan and Lindsey, family, Wade, Bernard, Kate, Eleanor, the Shepherds, Gary, Carol, other friends, and colleagues. They love me just as I am. They don't focus on changing me or my disability. Instead, they see me as whole with my abilities and passions, my quirks and my faults, allowing and enabling me to live my life authentically. Because of that, I was able to share that message of love with others even if, in some cases, that message took the form of civil disobedience and protest. When you see an injustice and those in power fail to hear your cries for remedy, sometimes you are compelled to "bump it up," even if that means a risk to yourself. That, in and of itself, is one of the most powerful acts of love. How much richer our world would be if we could all risk ourselves for others in the name of love.

Though he is far from perfect, my dad was a very wise man. In his love of clichés, he understands that those -isms—pithy quotes—are popular and overused for a reason: they are true. Dismiss them for being too trite, and you miss the power of the message.

Take what has become his—and my—favorite quote: "I am not afraid of tomorrow, for I have seen yesterday, and I love today." It is such a statement of hope. Sure, it's a great reminder about how pointless it is to continually rehash what's already happened. But it's also saying that regardless of how well yesterday went, we're still here today, and we can both learn from and continue to grow from the past. It's saying that we don't need to agonize over the future, especially if we can learn to live in the moment and be fully present now, no matter our circumstances. If we can do that, then our todays and tomorrows (and, therefore, our pasts) will be much richer and joyful. Each day, I pray, listen, do my best, and "let go, let God."

I do not fear tomorrow because I can look back and see how far we've come, both individually and collectively, in working to make this world a better place and becoming more accepting of difference. And I can see today that these efforts to continue to establish connections, overcome anger and hatred, and create community. I can see so many acts of love.

That's why I love today.

EPILOGUE

Hope

Since our house is located at the end of a cul-de-sac, the area in front of my driveway often contains a collection of balls, bikes, skateboards, other toys, and a park bench. These signal the fact that numerous children live on my street and all of them naturally gravitate toward the cul-de-sac, where there is plenty of space to play and no one has to worry about traffic. Both Susan and I are used to driving very slowly in and out of our driveway, being careful to look out for both kids and toys. As we arrive home in the evenings, we often encounter a game in need of fans or a fashion show in need of judges. We are always willing participants, happy to see the kids and the activity. They are signs of our community.

Three of the kids on our street belong to the Regan family, who live directly across the cul-de-sac from us. They include Kelly, Jaime, and Abby. They and their parents, Dave and Dottie (Dot), moved into the neighborhood almost ten years ago, and we have enjoyed getting to know them and watching the children grow up. Of the three children, the one I know the best is Jaime. It is possible that we connect because we are both the middle child in our respective families and thus are social and outgoing. Or perhaps we get along because we both love sports; Jaime loves soccer and lacrosse. I know we both love animals. Jaime's family has all the makings of an animal reserve with two cats, one guinea pig, one bunny, a turtle, snails, and a dog. Our dog, Missy, a cockapoo/chow mix, who died in 2011, was the neighborhood dog. Using her doggie door, she loved to wander around the cul-de-sac visiting the neighbors, particularly the Regans, who considered her their "other dog." Now they also welcome Ottie, my rambunctious, ball- and water-obsessed blue tick hound/black Lab mix granddog, who has a serious crush on the Regan's dog, Bella.

The Regan family: Kelly, Abby, Dave, Jaime, and Dottie

Jaime and I connected because she has developed a certain comfort level with me and my disability. The kids on the block all know me. They see me as I get in and out of my van or when I'm getting the mail. When I have the opportunity, I love to talk with whoever's congregated in the cul-de-sac, catching up on their school activities or giving them rides on the back of my power wheelchair (though most of them are too old for that now). For the most part, the kids seem to be fairly comfortable with my disability. Every now and then, one of them will ask me a question about my accident, my wheelchair, or my van. I'm always happy to answer. I want them to feel comfortable with me and know they can ask questions. But Jaime is the one who goes out of her way to wave to me as I drive past, calling out, "Hi, Mr. Mark!" And in doing so, the others seem more willing to follow suit. At such a young age, Jaime is already creating a culture of acceptance.

From what I know, Jaime's comfort level with me seems to be the byproduct of a number of factors. She is clearly an exceptional young girl. Her mother readily describes her as "an old soul" because she exhibits a maturity and wisdom that far exceed her age. But beyond that, she also has parents who have used their experiences to raise her to be both tolerant and accepting. I think it started with her great-grandfather—Dot's grandfather—who, by virtue of being a doctor, encouraged his children to ask questions and discuss issues and conditions that the rest of society considered taboo. This was passed on to Dot, who has, in turn, passed it on to her children. When Jaime was in kindergarten, her family was standing in line for a ride at Six Flags. Jaime spotted another girl standing next to her who was wearing a prosthetic leg that was painted a bright lime green (a kindred spirit who would certainly have appreciated my orange van and hospital bed). Jaime was fascinated and eventually turned to her mother and, within earshot of the other girl and her mother, whispered, "Why is her leg like that?" Dot paused for a moment, embarrassed that the girl and her mother had heard Jaime's question, until she realized that this was a great opportunity to teach her daughter about differences. She bent down to Jaime's level and explained, "Some people have parts of their bodies that are different from yours and mine, and that special green leg helps her to walk, and run, and play just like you." Jaime seemed to accept that because she immediately turned her attention to something else.

Since then, Dot and Dave have continued to encourage their children to ask questions, which makes a huge difference for them. It makes them feel safer, and safety breeds confidence and acceptance. After meeting and getting to know me, Jaime was curious about why I was in a wheelchair but didn't feel comfortable asking me about it. Instead, she turned to her mom, who understood that Jaime's question seemed to stem more from concern about my well-being than from any kind of discomfort with my disability. Dot did her best to explain the concept of a spinal-cord injury in first-grade terms, and after that, Jaime seemed even more interested in learning about my disability. One day, I was rolling out to check the mail and saw Jaime playing with her friends in the cul-de-sac.

"Hey, Jaime," I called out, waving to her.

"Hi, Mr. Mark," she called out, waving back. I noticed her wave immediately. She was not extending her hand in the usual way that people wave. Instead, she had extended her fist with her thumb sticking out, mimicking exactly the way that I wave.

"That's cool," I laughed. She simply smiled and went back to playing with her friends. To her, it was no big deal.

There is another factor to Jaime's story, one that I think is significant. Dot has an uncle who had a similar experience to mine. Her uncle was just four years old when Dot was born, so essentially they grew up together, living only a few houses apart. Dot has vivid memories of her uncle playing with his army men, riding bikes, and racing his Big Wheel as fast as he could through the neighborhood. He was playful, adventurous, and had an air about him that always reminded Dot of Jesse James. When he was sixteen years old, her uncle was riding in a Pinto with three other teen boys, one of whom was driving drunk. As the driver careened around a hairpin turn, he lost control of the car and crashed into a tree. Although he walked away unscathed, the three other boys, including Dot's uncle, were all paralyzed. It was Mother's Day.

As Dot explains it, after his injury, her uncle and his family had access to "the Cadillac of care," particularly in rehab. In other words, her uncle had a wealth of resources available to help him recover from the accident, adjust to his disability, and explore what it would take to continue to pursue his dreams. Unfortunately, Dot's uncle did what too many people with a new disability do: he gave up. He rejected the help and resources that were offered to him, he stopped trying, and, as Dot tells it, he just gave up. He is now over fifty years old. As Dot tells this story, it is clear that she misses the man who was once adventurous and ready for a challenge. It's also clear that she recognizes that her uncle has missed out on a great deal in life.

Although Jaime and her sisters have never met their great uncle, he is clearly very present in their lives in the way that Dot is helping to shape her children. By inviting their questions and encouraging acceptance, she is helping them to understand that disability is no big deal. She wants her children to understand that there is no shame in having a disability and, especially, that life does not end with a disability. In her mind, I am a "rock star," as she describes me, because I got married, had a child, and established a successful career after my injury. I don't in any way think these things qualify me for rock-star status (though if it gets me on stage with Cher, a longtime idol, I'll reconsider). They are aspects of an everyday, ordinary life. But I understand where Dot is coming from when she says this about me. I understand that she sees what I have and what I've accomplished; that from across the cul-de-sac, she sees Susan and me leading busy, rich lives, and she compares that to the life of her uncle. She sees what he's missing out on and what he's given up, and she doesn't want that for her kids. She wants them to live abundantly no matter what their level of ability. She wants them to have hope.

You can never have too much hope. On good days, it adds that pep in your step and gives energy to your plans and routine. On bad days it compels you to get out of bed and put one foot in front of the other, even when that feels like an impossible task. Of course, it really comes in handy in times of trauma, when you're filled with fear, doubt, and a lack of control. That's when you almost need an IV drip filled with hope to keep you alive and breathing.

Obviously, I'm speaking from experience. When you start the day going for an afternoon swim and end it with Crutchfield tongs on your head and no function from the neck down, well, you start to understand how essential hope is to keep you going. I saw how it helped me during those weeks in the iron lung, those exhausting sessions in rehab, and those first tough months at home adjusting to a life with disability. I found, too, that it was hope that helped me deal with the injustices I experienced and the barriers I encountered after my injury. I understood I was bigger than the social attitudes and assumptions behind these injustices and that I didn't have to sit and take them anymore. I had the confidence enough to know that I had the power to do something about them, and I did, believing that my voice—and the collective voices of my peers—counted. Hope, too, led me to find love, to father a child, and to do all the other things that are part of an ordinary life, but which were predicted to be off limits to me. And, in turn, it gave me a life that is as rich and mundane, as ordinary and extraordinary, as the guy next to me.

During my recovery from an emergency appendectomy, I received dozens of cards, gifts, e-mails, phone calls, and other well wishes from family, friends, and colleagues. I got an e-mail from my niece, Claire, that made me cry. It had a picture of a heart drawn in the sand with the inscription "get well soon" inside it. Underneath was written "*Get well soon!* Love, Claire."

While all of these displays of concern and affection were very special to me and every one of them touched my heart, there was one in particular that really stuck out. It was a card from Jaime, my young neighbor from across the street. The card is made up of a single piece of wide-ruled notebook paper. Across the top she had written "Get Well Soon, Mr. Mark." Underneath this, she used markers to draw a large red heart that surrounds a picture of me. The picture has all the characteristics of a young artist: I have a large head, very long eyelashes, full, red lips, and skinny arms. She used a yellow marker to color my skin, so I am very yellowish/orange, a detail that was probably very accurate at the time, given all the nastiness that was flowing through my body from my ruptured appendix. I'm wearing a green shirt with black stripes over blue pants, and am clearly sitting in my wheelchair, as you can tell by the little green wheels that stick out from the four sides of the otherwise purplish chair. In the picture, I am waving. My fist is raised in the air with my thumb sticking out to the side. It is a perfect rendering of the way I wave, to the last detail. She has captured me accurately, honestly, and respectfully.

In the bottom right corner, Jaime started to write "sincerely," but crossed it out and instead wrote "love, Jaime." When asked why, she reports because "love was easier to write." That's true on so many levels. Love is easier.

One of my greatest treasures: Jamie's get-well card

Following is one of the articles from my *Charlotte Observer* newspaper column (1978):

"For Handicapped, Invisible Barriers Remain"

by Mark Johnson, Guest Columnist

In recent years, a lot of attention has been addressed to the rights of handicapped people. Handicapped people are finally being recognized as valuable and equal members of society. The physical barriers are coming down slowly but surely. But what about invisible barriers that come in the form of attitudes? Consider the following.

Have you ever:

- had someone assume you don't work?
- been encouraged to live off of the taxpayer?
- been denied public housing, transportation, and/or education?
- been told your basic needs aren't the same as those of normal people?
- had someone assume you live in a nursing home or institution?
- had someone assume you aren't capable of thinking or feeling—especially caring or loving?
- been denied entrance to a public building?
- had someone assume you have no interest in or need for recreation?
- had someone tell you you're different?
- been told you're not realistic?
- been denied hope?
- been unable to get into a bathroom?
- felt helpless?
- been told you don't qualify for fair treatment?
- been told that fair treatment costs too much?
- felt like an eyesore or obstacle?
- been portrayed as "those" people?
- been talked about and not to, as though you could not hear or speak for yourself?

Yes, the list seems endless. Unfortunately, these kinds of attitudes promote feelings of worthlessness, self-pity, frustration, and costly dependence.

Personally, I feel we all lack awareness and true empathy. We learn our habits of thinking, but we can choose to become sensitive to and understanding of the needs of all individuals.

But we must realize we aren't going to change the past. No individual need feel guilty unless he or she chooses not to change. We can benefit from the past. Future frustrations can be prevented. All people's needs can be addressed. Negotiating and mutual understanding can take place.

So I hope you read this column several times and be honest with yourself about how you feel about other people. I hope you share this column with others and that they confront themselves. But most of all, I hope you "make contact" with a person who appears to be one of "those."

Note: Today, the preferred language is *people with disabilities*, rather than *handicapped*.

About the Authors

Mark Johnson is a nationally-known disability rights activist and community organizer. He currently serves as director of advocacy for the Shepherd Center in Atlanta, Georgia. He is the recipient of numerous awards, including the 2007 Henry B. Betts Award, the New Mobility Person of the Year in 2001, and the National Council on Independent Living Distinguished Service Award in 1990. He has a love of family, "sand and surf," classic rock, Cher, and the Food Network, especially "Diners, Drive-ins, and Dives." To learn more about Mark, visit: www.facebook.com/markleejohnson.

Kristen Vincent has always loved theology, social justice, and writing. Thus it was a dream come true for her to have the opportunity to blend these passions into a book with Mark. Still, in the six years it took Mark to publish this book, Kristen authored two award-winning books: *A Bead and a Prayer: A Beginner's Guide to Protestant Prayer Beads* (Upper Room Books, 2013) and *Another Bead, Another Prayer: Devotions for Use with Protestant Prayer Beads* (Upper Room Books, 2014). Kristen is also a freelance writer and blogger, business owner, coordinator for The ADA Legacy Project, wife, and mom. She loves dark chocolate and continues her lifelong quest to find the perfect chocolate mousse. To learn more about Kristen, visit www.prayerworksstudio.com.